EARTH CROSSER

By

Lewis MacLeod

This book has been published by its author

This work is a work of fiction. The details of characters
described herein are inventions of the author and not
intended to resemble actual persons, living or dead.

EARTH CROSSER copyright © 2016 by Devon B Nickerson

ISBN 1539000699

published in the United States of America

September 2016

Contents

BERT RECEIVES A MESSAGE FROM SPACE

Genius Software Engineer Bertram Koslosky, aged thirty-eight years, would probably have missed his once-in-a-lifetime opportunity to destroy the planet if he had not had a gob of vanilla doughnut icing stuck to his thumb.

How it happened was like this. Bert was currently employed at ProCon Enterprises. His office, if you could call it that, was located on the third floor of ProCon's sprawling new Corporate Headquarters in Hartford, Connecticut. Bert had been inherited by ProCon from his former employer. Bert excruciatingly missed his former employer, and his former home town, and more particularly his former rental residence, a comfortable location in Albuquerque, New Mexico, where over a period of almost fifteen years he had made himself quite at home in a very nice apartment with Southwestern style decor. In Albuquerque, Bert had served as a Genius Software Engineer for E-Duce Communications, a smallish Defense Contractor specializing in UHF transmitters and receivers for reliable orbital operations, satellite-to-satellite—*rocket science*, as Bert was fond of bragging. When E-Duce had been the victim of a hostile buyout by ProCon Enterprises, a rapidly-expanding international behemoth in Communications of all types, Bert had been given the option of relocating to ProCon's headquarters in Hartford, or of getting the boot, out into an ice-cold, difficult and uncaring job market. Bert had gritted his teeth and made the move.

When Bert relocated to Hartford, he discovered that all he could afford by way of living quarters was a mass production, stainless steel and plasterboard, one-bedroom, high rise apartment overlooking a sluggish brown river. Instead of a homey, timber and stucco office-hacienda set within a tranquil, wooded, rolling landscape of the light-industrial park E-duce had occupied in Albuquerque, ProCon World HQ was a stark concrete shaft of twenty stories, with narrow windows like Medieval arrow slit embrasures, whose glass reflected the grey glare of a smog-diminished sun. For landscaping, the ProCon Tower was set in a vast, level plain of parking lots, stretching to a far horizon, without so much as a green leaf or blade of grass.

As one entered the grounds of World HQ in Hartford, Connecticut, one's eyes would be irresistibly drawn to the company's corporate logo, which was a rendering of the Taoist "Yin/Yang" symbol, indicating the cosmic duality of ProCon Corporation's more-or-less ambivalent ethics on anything regarding money, power, or common decency:

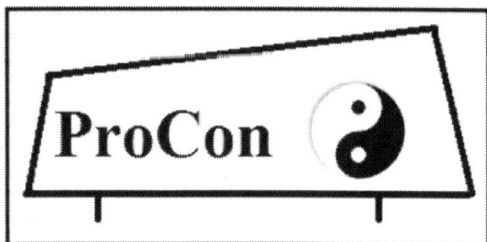

Just now, three years after that painful relocation, Bert was goofing off, tidying up his files. On commencing employment at ProCon, Bert had been assigned a minuscule workspace defined by a square of wobbly chest-high beige fabric partitions...and within that square Bert still resided, unpromoted and barely noticed, three years on. Bert's workspace was outfitted with an expensive albeit archaic 'tower' computer, with all the bells and whistles, which at one time had probably cost ProCon plenty. But

Bert's official computer also recorded every keystroke and touchpad click and audio input and eye blink and sneeze that Bert executed during his workday, and Bert didn't like that kind of snoopy spying very much. Bert *did* like his own customized, personally designed laptop, which he wasn't supposed to use at work, but did anyway. He had set his laptop up with a super-secret piece of monitor-spoofing software that he had written himself, which would build a nice, fake file of every keystroke and touchpad click, *et cetera*, that he made on *his laptop*, so long as he had the super-secret piece of monitoring software set to **work** mode. Except that the program would dole out the info about half as fast as Bert typed it in, allowing Bert to spend approximately half his work time working on stuff of his own choosing without being spied on, which is what he called **play** mode. Only Bert could switch this software between **work** and **play** at will, using a super-secret combination of three simultaneous key pushes. Oh…and also, the super-secret piece of software would wirelessly transmit all those **work** keystrokes *et cetera* to the unused piece-of-shit 'tower' computer, so that whoever was monitoring Bert's daily activities would *think* Bert was using his 'tower' computer for **work**, but would otherwise be none the wiser. And Bert was free to shut off the monitoring and go about whatever **play**ful part of his workday he felt like not being monitored during, inasmuch as all **work** and no **play** makes Bert a dull boy. Right now, Bert was *not* **work**ing.

This was because currently Bert had a very boring official job-related work task he was putting off, a task involving development of a subroutine to calculate the activity performance of a particular sub-sub-subcontractor, a subsidiary of X-Ploytt Industries, on Defense Contract Spec. FZ/AEP-9667d.fy2017 for the reconfigured microphasory adjustmentation of…blah-blah, yadda-yadda. One of his favored procrastination ploys was to tidy up his files. He had something like thirty-eight thousand files stored on the internal drive of his laptop. And he had something like 1.26 *million* files stored in any number of accounts belonging to him, Bertram Koslosky, in the name of one or another of his many whimsical electronic avatars, in the 'cloud' (wherever that might happen to be). But in fairness, this large number of 'cloud' files included such copious quantities of useless stuff as Bert's old forgotten e-mails (incoming and outgoing), his seldom-listened-to iTunes, his rarely-viewed pictures and video clips and image files, a small, select collection of mild, tasteful pornography, and a huge bunch of old, eminently discardable work-in-progress data he'd entirely forgotten he'd ever generated. So what he was doing right now was browsing through this enormous Virtual Attic of e-crap and throwing a great lot of it away. A file name would appear on the display and Bert would tap a zone on the *left* side of the laptop's touchpad to leave the file alone, or on the *right* side to delete the file from all possible future human perusal. Sort-of like a Nazi SS officer making gas chamber selections on the unloading dock at Birkenau: "*rechts...rechts...rechts...links... rechts....*"

Bert, also known to his close circle of intimates as 'B-Koz' or 'Aries' (a witty play on the last three letters of his last name and the last three letters of his first name, if it's bugging you...), had been down to the corporate cafeteria on his midmorning break, and had succumbed to the temptation of a big gooey old-fashioned chocolate doughnut with vanilla icing to go with his coffee. Because of his mild, innate slovenliness, Bert, in the munching of this doughnut, had accumulated a patina of icing on his right thumb, some of which had transferred itself onto his index finger. If he'd as much as stuck the offending digits in his mouth and sucked the frosting off, Planet Earth would never have come into peril, at least at *his* hands. But he didn't. So when a particular file came on screen for its fateful instant of consideration, Bert's finger slipped.

If you were to tap the MIDDLE of the touchpad, Bert's laptop would postpone the current file's live-or-die decision and attempt to display the *contents* of the file, if it wasn't a music file or something else nondisplayable. Because of the slippery vanilla-flavored icing on Bert's finger, displaying the next file's contents is exactly what happened.

"Huh?" cleverly spoke Bertram Koslosky, a.k.a Bertie-K, as a screenful of numbers appeared.

It must be understood that this Engineer, unprepossessing though his appearance may have been, was possessed of an astoundingly intelligent mind, if a somewhat offbeat and quirky one. Bert's eyes clicked in their sockets, rapidly assimilating the block of blue digits on the screen's black background. Within three—or perhaps as much as four—seconds, our boy had it figured what these numbers meant. In five more seconds, he had a hypothesis as to what he, and maybe a few talented compatriots, might accomplish with this data. In another jiffy, he had evolved a plan…a *bold* plan! In *exquisite* detail!

The figures were organized into thirteen blocks. Each block held 9 pairs of numeric values. The first value of each pair was a two-digit number—the lowest was 22 and the highest was 79. Most of each pair's second values were almost zero. The first through fourth values were something significantly greater than zero. The second pair in the list consisted of the value 26 followed by what was consistently the largest second value, averaging about 81. What was this mysterious data? If you cannot tell, Dear Reader, don't despair! Be patient and shortly all will be revealed!

Oh hell…it might be more comprehensible if one set of nine value pairs is displayed. Here goes:

22	3.1
26	81.2
27	1.9
28	9.6
31	0.1
32	<0.1
46	<0.1
78	<0.1
79	4.0

Do these numbers make any sense to you?

BERT SOLICITS SOME HELP

In order to continue misleading whoever might be spying on his every keystroke, Bert switched his proprietary snoop-spoofing program to **work** mode and actually doodled around with his godawful X-Ploytt Industries software-development assignment until lunchtime. Precisely at 12:00 noon, he clicked his laptop into its **sleep** mode (ProCon categorized **sleep** as a semi-legitimate kind of 'recess'…like, coffee-time or lunch or a potty-break) and hied himself on down to the cafeteria. He selected a tasty plateful of tuna glop on toast and a medium Dr. Pepper. He paid the somnolent cashier and headed for his customary table. Sure enough, his usual lunch buddy and confidant Malcolm MacDooley was already there, picking at a grilled cheese on rye while gazing wistfully at the back of a fluffily coiffed, bottley blond feminine head four tables over. The particular head, widely believed to be full of little more than low-pressure air, belonged to Jessica Violet Moonflower, Entry Lobby Receptionist and Telephone Message Mangler for the Developmental Engineering Division, and possessor of such a flagrantly counterfeit name one wonders how she managed to have passed the requisite security clearance when she'd been hired. Also, possessor of a fantastic set of boobies, possibly as counterfeit as her name.

Oh. Yeah. *That's* how she passed.

Malcolm MacDooley had spent his morning attempting to get himself motivated writing a technical instruction manual for the various methods of employment for a ProCon microprocessor chip no bigger than the dot over any letter 'i' in its own instruction manual. Instead of that destined-to-be-turgid document, Malcolm had written a poem, which he had tentatively titled,

A ProCon Enterprises M-17 Housecleaning Robot® with Infra-Red Vision Performs the Impossible

He'd written the poem in pencil, on paper, rather than using his computer, because, like Bertram, Malcolm was eternally wary of ProCon's desire to keep track of his every thought and movement. He didn't imagine that the spy cams which lined the ceiling in his work bay would have sufficient resolution to make out every letter of his scrawly handwriting. In this, our boy Malcolm was more-or-less mistaken. Here's what Dooley's poem looked like so far:

> The carpet appeared brilliant orange
>
> To its light sensors, working on low-range
>
> It tidily vacuumed up more grunge
>
> And would have been finished before lunch
>
> But its wheels got hooked on a floor flange
>
> And it could not go forward one more inch.

Who says there aren't any rhymes in English for the word ORANGE! mused Dooley smugly to himself.

"Hey Dooley!" Bert greeted his friend, interrupting his lyrical musings. He clanked down his steel cafeteria tray and rotated into a chair. "Dooley, do you like your job?"

An awkward question.   Almost nobody liked working at ProCon.   But, on the other hand, everybody steered clear of saying so out loud.   The gigantic international mega-corporation paid pretty well, and all ProCon sites offered big shiny office buildings very much of a type with Corporate Headquarters, and all of which were filled with little squalid fabric cubicles for geniuses and drones alike to toil in. Unless you were Middle Management, and then you got little squalid glass-and-plasterboard cubicles, possibly with a narrow, slitlike window, a door, and a guest chair, in which cubicle to pretend to work. Or unless you were Tiptop Management, and then you pretty much got an entire floor to loll about in, complete with a staff of sycophants and minions and underlings and subordinates and aides, and a salary equivalent to six hundred and eighty times what Bertram Koslosky, PhD., was pulling down.   We won't even talk about what sordid conditions ProCon's assembly line workers, loading dock attendants, and mailroom staff labored within.

"Not very much," replied Dooley to Bert's question, after very little consideration.

"What would it take to persuade you to quit?"

Jessica Moonflower crooking her little finger at me, just before doffing that clingy, knit sweater-dress along with whatever she's got on underneath it, Dooley contemplated lasciviously.   He dropped a half-eaten triangle of grilled cheese sandwich onto his plate, and considered Bert's question more seriously.

"Ahhh...a lot better pay if I had to do the same painful, tedious stuff they've got me doing these days. Actually, I'd take a fifty percent pay *cut* if I could find some halfway stimulating career to transition into!"

The problem is, Malcolm 'Mac' MacDooley had spent seven invigorating academic years at Yale University, where he'd acquired a Bachelor's Degree, followed by a

Master of Arts. In English Literature. This equipped him to do one of three things: (1) become a high school English teacher, presupposing he continued his higher education for two more years in order to obtain state licensure in Secondary Education; or (2) go on for anywhere from three to six more years of higher education to obtain a Doctorate in English Literature which would give him loftier credentials with which to do a marginally better job of Thing (1) or Thing (3); or (3) write. Mac MacDooley didn't like classrooms very much, and he didn't like adolescents *at all*, so he couldn't see himself (1) teaching. He had tapped out his parents' generosity as regards tuition and educational living expenses, and his finances were further gloomily colored by his having amassed $73,000 in personal college loans he was going to have to pay back someday, so he wasn't excited about pursuing more (2) education. (3) Writing isn't as hard as one might think, if you've got something to actually say or an entertaining story to tell. Getting something actually *published* once you've written it, now *that's* a *bitch*! Earning a living by way of writing is virtually impossible unless you are *already* a well known writer, or a renowned celebrity, or a widely known, notorious, infamous felon, like a serial murderer or a *really* crooked politician. So what did that leave Mac in the writing field for which, hopefully, someone would actually pay him a living wage? One answer was *technical* writing. Which is the most tedious, mind-numbing, soul-stealing, lackluster form of writing known to semi-literate humankind.

"Okay," Malcolm decided, his meditations concluded. "A lot of money, something exciting to accomplish, a chance to sometimes get out of that damned horse stall they make me sit in for eight hours every day…and…and no goddamn supervisor who is ignorant of what I'm trying to technically describe, technically instruct people in the use of, or technically explain how it works.

10

No goddamn boss who's going to breathe down my neck and yell at me to hurry up accomplishing a task he couldn't do himself if his *ass was on fire!*"

Having said all this out loud, Mac involuntarily took a hasty glance around for microphones or spy cams jutting out of ceiling corners in his direction.

Bert smiled like a tranquil Bodhisattva. He took a piece of copier paper out of his shirt pocket, unfolded it, and handed it to his friend. "Have I got a deal for *you!*" He declared benignly.

This is what was on the paper, in Bert's sloppy handwriting. You've seen it already:

$$
\begin{array}{ll}
22 & 3.1 \\
26 & 81.2 \\
27 & 1.9 \\
28 & 9.6 \\
31 & 0.1 \\
32 & <0.1 \\
46 & <0.1 \\
78 & <0.1 \\
79 & 4.0 \\
\end{array}
$$

Well, Mac didn't get it. "What's this?" he asked.

"Some numbers that came out of a burst transmit file."

"Uhhh...what's that?"

"Satcom."

"Bertie...."

"Okay...*Satellite communication.*"

"What satellite?"

"I don't know, but—"

"*BERTIE!*"

"But! I've got a *suspicion* what satellite. I gotta go talk to The Amoeba."

"Yeah, okay...but you haven't told me what the *numbers* are!"

Bert rustled in his shirt pocket and dredged out a second piece of paper, which he unfolded. He smoothed out the wrinkles and laid the paper down in front of Malcolm. Here's what that item looked like:

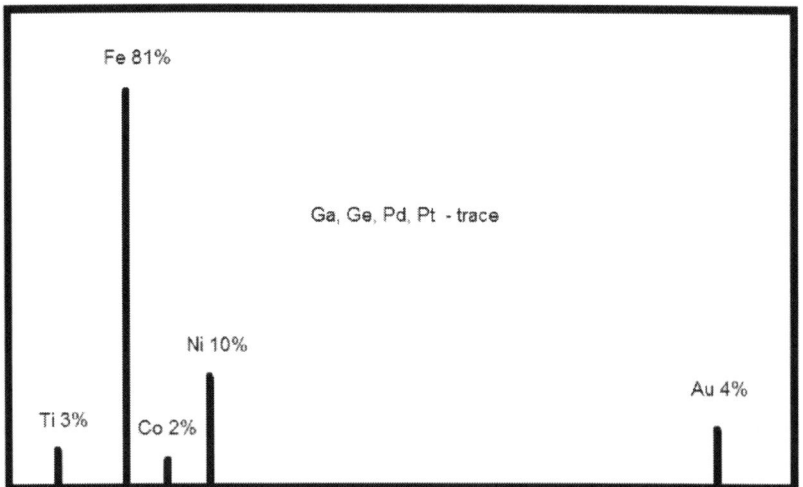

Fe 81%

Ga, Ge, Pd, Pt - trace

Ni 10%

Au 4%

Ti 3% Co 2%

Mac squinted at the tiny printing. Okay…a bar graph showing percentages…he wasn't *completely* math ignorant! "Percents. Bars representing percents. Oh hey! Same values as the right-hand column on this other page. What's 'Ti'?"

"Titanium. Element 22 on the periodic table."

"Yeah…and what's 'Fe'?"

"Jeez, Dooley! Didn't you ever study science?"

"In high school!"

"It's Iron. Element 26. 'Ferrum'…that's Latin for—"

"Iron! I get it! I studied Latin for three years, *tu tanta stulte!*" [1]

"—And the next one's cobalt, then nickel, then the trace elements are gallium, germanium, palladium, and platinum."

"And what's 'Au'? Element 79, I'm guessing. "

"Aurum, *si linguae Latinae ingenio omnino!*" [2]

Malcolm could not remember having encountered the Latin word 'Aurum'. "Er…I— Okay, so what's Aurum?"

"Gold!"

---

[1] **you enormous fool**

[2] **if you have any ability at all in the Latin language!**

BERTIE EXPLAINS HIS HYPOTHESIS

L ook here, MacDooley...here's a bunch of nine elements. The datafile I got had thirteen bunches of nine elements, listed by their Atomic Numbers, and each one paired-up with what has to be an abundance percentage. Then—"

"Why? I see you've got percentages on your crappy little bar graph, but why do these values *have to* be percentages?" Mac wanted to know.

"*Because for each bunch of nine, the values add up to 99.9, more-or-less, plus 'trace' elements!*"

"Which are the 'trace' elements?"

"*The ones whose percentages are listed as '<0.1'
...less than a tenth of a percent! Sheesh!*"

"Okay, okay! Don't blow a fuse, Bertie!"

Bert took a deep breath and calmed down. "So...why thirteen bunches? Each of the first twelve bunches is pretty much the same as far as nickel, cobalt, and the trace elements go. Iron varies a few percent. Gold varies between 3.2% and 6.5% percent, except for Listing Number Five, which has got 26.8% gold."

"Wow! What's with the 26.8% figure?"

"Must be a vein."

"Wow!...Wait! You said twelve bunches, but a minute ago you said there were *thirteen* groups in the datafile."

"The thirteenth group has the mean values for each element. The 'averages.' That's the table I'm showing you on this paper here. The one displayed on this bar chart."

Malcolm's eyes strayed of their own volition to that percentage figure for gold: four-point-zero percent. Whose eyes wouldn't? "Sooooo…" he answered cautiously. "So, what do you think these quantities represent?"

"Twelve element assays from twelve different sites. Probably pretty close together. Assays that were done spectroscopically or by X-ray refraction."

"Bertram…*where did you get that datafile?*"

"Outer Space."

"*What?*"

"I'll tell you later. We've got to go upstairs and ask The Amoeba what he thinks. Do you want to know what *I* think?"

"I'm *dyin'* to know!"

"Look here. Iron about eighty percent. Nickel at ten percent…that's right in the middle of what you'd expect. Cobalt, two percent…you'd generally expect more than a trace of cobalt in one of these guys."

"One of WHAT guys?"

"An M-type asteroid. Nickel-Iron asteroid. The Amoeba will know. Probably about a hundred meters mean diameter. Should weigh about four-point-three to four-point-six billion kilograms. Four percent of that works out conservatively to about one-hundred seventy-one million kilograms. That equals five-point-five BILLION troy ounces, Mac!"

"Of *GOLD? You tellin' me there's an asteroid out there made of GOLD?*"

"Yeah. Not so loud, Malcolm! Current spot price is $1266 per troy ounce, so that works out to about six-point-nine-six trillion dollars."

Malcolm was a little too excited to be hearing accurately. "Dollars? *SIX-POINT-NINE-SIX BILLION? DOLLARS?*"

"For God's sake, keep your voice down! Let's just call it seven, shall we? There are a few unknowns."

"Yeah, but SEVEN BILL—"

"Not BILLION, Malcolm. Seven <u>TRILLION</u> dollars. In gold."

"Habba-abba...*whaaaa?*...hamma..."

"The other metals aren't exactly chickenfeed. One-point-three BILLION dollars worth of iron. Even more than that for the cobalt – two BILLION bucks! Just under one BILLION dollars for the titanium and the gallium. Each! A comparatively paltry four hundred MILLION for the nickel."

Malcolm was gobsmacked. Utterly speechless.

"And you know what we're going to do? You and me, Malcolm? And maybe a few other trusty specialists?"

Mac had no energy left. He heaved a monumental sigh, then answered in a voice of profound weariness. "No I don't know, Bertie. What are we going to do?"

"We're going to help ourselves to a solid-gold asteroid!"

4

HOW THE AMOEBA GOT HIS NAME

When the Amoeba was seventeen-and-a-half years old and living in Taipei, his natal city, he had graduated high school with honors. This is scarcely odd because the Taiwanese school system seems to be organized like a vast, high energy, efficient machine for turning children into honor students, or coming near to murdering them in the attempt. Well...there *is* a time honored third option: training those kiddos into becoming first class factory workers, practitioners of blue collar vocational occupations, or soldiers. The Amoeba, under considerable parental pressure, had opted for the honor student path. And so, after placing astronomically high on his post-high-school University Entrance exams, The Amoeba had gone off to National Cheng Kong University for his Bachelor's studies in Computer Science and Electronic Design, followed by his Master's studies in more of the same. He had thereupon been awarded a stipend to travel to the United States and do his Doctoral studies at the Massachusetts Institute of Technology.

The Amoeba had not always been called such. His traditional Chinese name was **Ng Ying Wan**, and by this name he was known throughout his school years in Taiwan. If you want to become befuddled to the point of insanity, look up and thoroughly read a Wikipedia article on Chinese names. Chinese people can be known by surnames, given names, milk names, nicknames, western names, school names, courtesy names, diminution qualifiers, pseudonyms, temple names, era names...even posthumous names if they happen to be dead. Or anything up to and including *all* of these, strung together. Well so **Ng** was The Amoeba's *surname*...his family name, inherited from his dad. Think of this as the traditional American 'last name'…like maybe **Johnson**. And **Ying Wan** was The Amoeba's *given name*, two syllables being perfectly legitimate for a Chinese given name. Think of this like the traditional American 'first name' of somebody who is condemned to go through life with one of those hillbilly two-name names, like **Billy Bob** or **Suzie Mae**. In fact, The Amoeba took to spelling his given name **Yingwan**—no space—shortly after arriving in the United States for his Doctoral studies, to prevent people from calling him just plain **Ying** and assuming that **Wan** was an unimportant middle name or something. About a week after adopting that particular subterfuge, The Amoeba decided to swap his surname and given name around, becoming **Yingwan Ng** because Americans kept calling him **Mister Wan** or **Mister Yingwan** or, familiarly, **Ng**…and it doesn't bear considering all the weird ways in which the American tongue could mispronounce that perfectly common Chinese syllable **Ng**.

After six months in the United States, The Amoeba decided to just give up on the whole Chinese name bit. After all, he was a fluent English speaker, having studied the language diligently in Taiwan starting in preschool at age three, continuing through his undergraduate studies, ending at age twenty-two. He'd like to know how many *American* kids had studied Mandarin half as diligently, and become half as fluent as he had become in English! So he assigned himself a nice Western name that he'd taken a fancy to while watching a theatrical production of Hamlet. The name was **Marcellus**. When, after earning a Doctorate in aerospace communications hardware architecture at MIT, he had been instantly hired by ProCon Enterprises. The Amoeba had signed up under the name **Marcellus Ing**. His revered ancestors would be rolling in their graves, of course. But his revered ancestors didn't have to get along in the United States.

The Amoeba was a friendly, cheerful chap, and his fellow wage-slave engineers took to him enthusiastically, early on. They all had nicknames for each other, like Malcomb 'Mac' MacDooley and Bertram 'B-Koz' Koslosky and Jessica 'Casabas' Moonflower. In the company cafeteria or a local pizza parlor or at a convivial neighborhood microbrewery, when a bunch of ProCons were eating, drinking or yakking around a table, they agreed there had to be something other than **Marcellus** to call the new Taiwanese Genius Spacecraft Hardware Nerd in their midst. **Marc** was the simplest option. Pretty boring. There were advocates for **Marco**. One afternoon, the nickname **Mickey** was suggested, and since the suggestor was Jessica Moonflower, and since The Amoeba was quite fond of Jessica (from a respectful distance, of course!) and equally fond of the vintage Disney mouse (although not in anything like the same way!), that nickname had its appeal.

The Amoeba had very little heartburn over the japery associated with his cronies figuring out a nickname for him. In fact, the traditional Taiwanese process of one's peers deriving a suitable nickname for one, was a source of honor and pride to Taiwanese sensibilities! Have at it, peers!

So, six months after The Amoeba's start date, by which time his cronies had all become aware what a massive data sponge their Taiwanese colleague carried around in his dolichocephalic skull, someone suggested a somewhat more far-afield nickname: **Simcard**. This moniker still had its advocates. For a short while, the handle **Ing-corporated** was bandied about, but to The Amoeba's great relief, this grotesquery was howled down. Deliberation turned back to simple adaptations of the name **Marcellus**, sequentially in the form of **Marky**... **Mac**... **Marcel**... **Cellus**... **Cello**... **Cell**... **Wan-Cell**....

"How about *One*-**Cell**? offered a trollish microprocessor cross-compiler genius who had borne the burdensome but birth-certificate-official name of **Rosalind Butts** her entire life, including, formatively but *not* in a positive way, three excruciating years of junior high. It was whispered around that, ironically, Rosalind had been born into this intolerant world via a breech presentation. Without a doubt, Rosalind believed the rest of humankind should suffer along with her.

"**One-Cell Ing,**" MacDooley recited slowly, trying it on his tongue. "Hey, Marcellus...maybe you need a *villainous Superhero* nickname! We could call you *The Amoeba!*"

So there you have it.

5 _____

IN THE AMOEBA'S LAIR

So after finishing their tasty lunch, Mac and Bertie took an elevator up one floor and sought out The Amoeba lurking in his hideaway. He saw the two of them coming. "Hi, Mackus!" Dr. Ing sung out.

"Hi, Marcus!" Dooley ritually responded.

"Hi, Bertie!"

"Hi, Meebs!" Bertram responded, using The Amoeba's acceptable short-form nickname.

"So what's up?" The Amoeba waved toward his Guest Chair, then ducked into the currently unoccupied adjoining cubicle, stole its Guest Chair, slid it back down to his burrow and gestured for his guests to make themselves comfortable.

Bert fumbled with his two sheets of paper. "Um...the thing is, Doc...I've got a question for you."

"Shoot!"

"Are you familiar with a Mil Spec project ProCon might have contributed to in about 2001 or 2002 that involved twelve separate, simultaneous element assays, by mass, maybe on a— "

"Just a minute," The Amoeba interrupted, holding an index finger to his lips. He scooted his desk chair up to his computer. Clicked off the power. Reached around back and pulled out the Ethernet cable. Unplugged the power cable for good measure. Unplugged his antique, hardwired pushbutton telephone. Took out his personal cellphone and powered it down, then dropped it in his bottom desk drawer, stuffed a sweater in on top of it, and shut the drawer. Stood up, gave the work bay a 360° scan to make sure there weren't any coworkers within thirty feet. Scootched his chair considerably nearer to his two visitors.

Crouched down so all three of their heads were below the tops of the fabric partitions with respect to the line of sight from the security camera lurking in the corner of the work bay.

"It was called...*4599 Sarpedon-E*," Dr. Ing said, in a hushed voice. The project name was *Icarus*.

"Iron-Nickel asteroid?"

"Yep."

"Strategic Defense Initiative project?"

"Yep."

"Earth Crosser?"

"You bet."

"*Trojan* object?"

"Yep."

"Lagrangian Point Four?"

"Even better: Lagrangian Point *Five*! So, Bertie...if you know all that, what exactly are you asking me?"

"Couple more questions. Twelve probes? Like MIRVs...independently maneuvered? Autonomous?"

"That's right."

"Linked intercommunication?"

"That was the plan...."

"UHF encrypted downlink to Goldstone?"

"That's classified. But...yeah."

"Able to dock?"

"Magnet grapple, then auger, then spot-weld. Also classified."

"Jesus! Spectrographic or X-ray assay?"

"Both."

"Meebs...were they going to *re-orbit*?" Bert barely murmured these words.

The Amoeba leaned close to Bertram's ear to whisper the reply: "Highly classified!"

"But?"

"You bet your ass!"

Malcolm interrupted. "Wait a minute! Wait a minute! *What the hell are you two talking about?*"

"You want to tell him, or should I?" Bert asked.

"Be my guest." Meebs gestured grandiloquently with an open palm.

Bert turned one of his pieces of paper over to its blank side. He laid it out on Dr. Ing's desk, then held out a hand. Dr. Ing placed a ballpoint pen across Bert's palm, and Bert meticulously drew a diagram. In the center was the sun. Around the sun, some distance out, was the orbit of the earth, a lightly-shaded line. This was, for all practical purposes, circular. Out on the edge, he drew a small dot and labeled it "Earth". Then he moved to a position about one-sixth of the way clockwise from the earth, and drew a smaller dot, which he labeled, "Sarpedon-E". He enclosed Sarpedon-E in an oval blob, which he labeled "L5." Then he drew blobs for the other Lagrangean points, L1 through L4...but we don't have to worry very much about these because they don't have anything to do with Sarpedon-E. Then he drew Sarpedon-E's orbit as a heavily-shaded line, which was pretty close to Earth's orbit, but weaved inside and outside a few times. Just to clarify which direction Sarpedon-E and the Earth were rotating around the sun, he drew a couple of nice counterclockwise arrows superimposed over Earth's orbit. This made it clear that Sarpedon-E was 'chasing' the Earth, that is to say 'behind' the Earth as it made its way around the sun. Here's a reproduction of Bert's diagram:

23

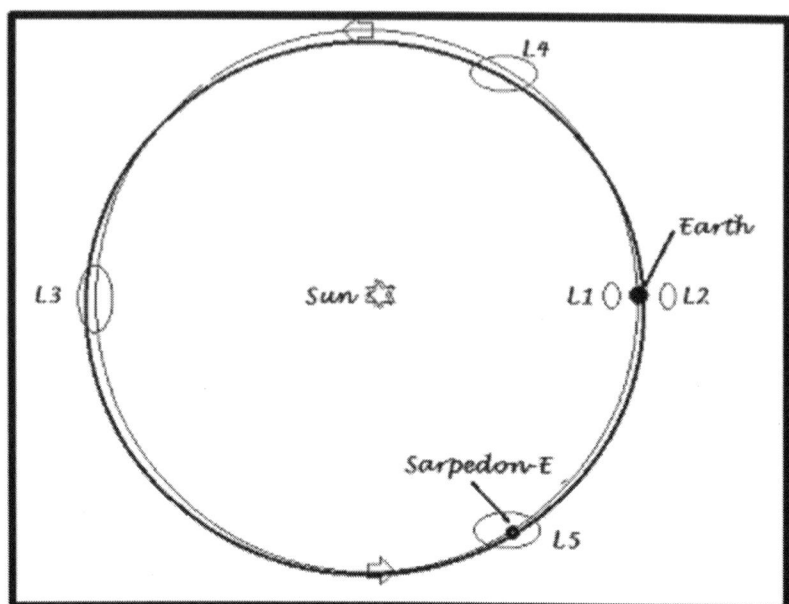

"Okay, Dooley…listen carefully." Bert began. "Here's the sun. Here's the Earth…lighter of the two orbits, nearly circular. See these five blobs? Those are points on the Earth's orbit where there's a neutral, or balanced, zone between Earth's gravity and the Sun's gravity, with respect to a third orbital body. That means the sun and the Earth exert just enough gravity in these zones that a third object can just ride along in that zone, tracking along Earth's orbit, more or less, in balance with the sun and the Earth. This—"

"A third object like this Sarp-whatever asteroid?"

"It's called Sarpedon-E…yeah, this asteroid of ours. Points L1, L2 and L3 were first postulated by a guy named Leonhard Euler in the mid-eighteenth century. Then in 1772, a French guy named Joseph-Louis Lagrange said there ought to be *two more* points, L4 and L5 in this diagram, each forming an equilateral triangle—Earth, Sun, Lagrange Point. Actually, this setup would pertain to *all* the planets, particularly the great big high-gravity ones like Jupiter and Saturn. L1 through L5 are called 'Lagrangian Points.' So Lagrange's hypothesis suggested—"

"But what's that got to do with—"

"Patience, Grasshopper. Lagrange's hypothesis suggested that astronomers should not be surprised to discover whole planets, or at least one or more 'little' planets—asteroids—hanging out in one or more of the Lagrange points now and then. You got to understand that there are all kinds of perturbations in gravity in the Solar System. So it's possible an asteroid could ride along in a nice stable orbit for a few centuries, then get jerked out by, like, a relatively close pass of Jupiter or Saturn, and go flinging off somewhere else. Well back to Lagrange. In his day, they didn't have telescopes good enough to check this idea out. But in the 1900's, they *did*! They started discovering new asteroids! In the same orbit as Jupiter, in the L4 and L5 Points! When they started discovering these objects, they named them after characters in *The Iliad*. Greek names for the L4 asteroids, Trojan names for the L5's. So they got to calling them, collectively, *Trojans*."

"What's special about—"

"An object at Earth's L4 point is traveling almost exactly as fast as Earth, in almost exactly the same orbit. It's *leading* the Earth by about sixty-one days. An object at the L5 point is *trailing* the Earth by sixty-one days. Now, see this heavy orbit line? Almost, but not quite, an identical orbit to Earth. So an asteroid at L5, rigorously we'd call it a Trojan Object, would drift inside, then outside, the Earth's orbit, if it were a nice crisp pencil line in outer space. So we call an object with an orbit like that an **EARTH CROSSER**."

"And Sarpedon is..."

"Yep," said Doctor Ing, The Amoeba. "L5 Trojan Earth Crosser."

"Yep," said Bertram 'Aries' Koslosky, the software genius. "Iron-nickel asteroidal Earth Crosser."

Dr. Ing knew a lot of unrelated trivia about Trojans of both types. He commenced to monologue. "They discovered a *Jupiter* L5 Trojan in 1977 that they named 2223 Sarpedon. In classical literature, Sarpedon from *The Iliad* was actually the king of the 'far-away Lyceans,' a Near Eastern people who lived on the River Xanthus. Sarpedon was reputed to be sired by Zeus himself! He had no quarrel with Menelaus and the Greeks, but he'd always pledged loyalty to Priam, king of Troy, so he allied with them in the Trojan War. Sarpedon was the first of the Trojan army to vault the Greek defenses and enter their encampment...whereupon he was killed by Patroclus, who was later killed by Achilles, who a bit later killed Hector, whose kid-brother Paris—the guy who started all this madness in the first place—killed Achilles by shooting him in the Achilles-heel with an arrow! At Sarpedon's death in battle, Zeus caused bloody raindrops to fall on the combatants as a sign of his grief."

"Soooo...Sarpedon?   The   asteroid?"   Dooley prompted.

Bert took over the tale.   "Yeah...I'm guessing the Department of Defense had astronomers secretly searching for Earth-orbit Trojans. They found a couple 'Greeks' at L4, but they weren't suitable. They found one in a very weird horseshoe shaped orbit, involving L1, L4 and L5...far too unstable an orbit for DoD's purpose. Then I'm guessing they found one that was juuuust right! And they must have named it Sarpedon-E. E for Earth. But that's top secret too. Am I right, Meebs?"

"Right. At least, Sarpedon-E *was* top secret."

Mac MacDooley was still bewildered. "But...what would the Department of Defense be interested in an iron-nickel asteroid for, a million miles from earth?"

"*Ninety-three* million, more-or-less.   They'd be interested because an object orbiting at L5 can pretty easily be persuaded to *de-orbit*, and then *re-orbit* right in close to good ol' Planet Earth...and even go into an *earth-centered* orbit, like a second Moon. A *geosynchronous* orbit, like, right over Moscow or Beijing.   With a little thrust, judiciously placed. By the way, Malcolm...I doubt DoD knows *anything* about Sarpedon-E—its element makeup, for example—except that it exists."

"But, you're suggesting they wanted to boost it with rockets or something like that?"

B-Koz and The Amoeba exchanged smirks. "Something like that!" Dr. Ing grinned.

"What for?"

"Remember SDI? The Strategic Defense Initiative? Can you imagine the defense value of a second moon in a nice geosynchronous orbit, practically invulnerable because it's made out of iron? As a base for ICBM interceptors?"

"*Our Trojan?*" Dooley goggled, already assuming proprietary grammar for the thing.

"Yep!"

"*Our four-percent-gold asteroid?*" Dooley cried dubiously.

"Yep," Bertram Koslosky affirmed.

"*Nobody said anything about GOLD!*" yelled The Amoeba, a tad too loud.

THE AMOEBA IS *IN!*

Bert Koslosky insisted they'd said enough, at least in precincts owned and doubtlessly monitored by ProCon's black-ops Security *apparat.* He slipped the piece of paper with the nine element abundance averages to The Amoeba. "Top Secret!" he cautioned Meebs. "Your eyes only!"

The three of them agreed to rendezvous at Bert's apartment. Seven-thirty that evening. Dooley and B-Koz headed back downstairs, far too wound up to accomplish much from ProCon's agenda for the rest of the day.

Dooley and The Amoeba arrived within thirty seconds of each other. When Bertie-K's doorbell rang, both his colleagues were waiting anxiously in the hallway when he opened his apartment door. "Come in, fellows!" he said cheerily. He had put out a plastic bowl of peanuts salted in the shell—the customary snack food for ProCon engineers—and a few cans of Mountain Dew.

Dr. Ing clanked his battered leather attaché case onto Bert's coffee table. He snapped the latches. Lifted out a thick document bound with DoD-standard brownish covers. Across the front was this banner:

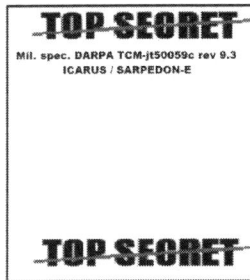

TOP SECRET

Mil. spec. DARPA TCM-jt50059c rev 9.3
ICARUS / SARPEDON-E

TOP SECRET

"Jeez, Meebs! That's a classified document! How the hell did you get that out of the ProCon building?"

The Amoeba made himself comfortable on Bert's sofa. "Well, first of all, it's not classified any more. See those thin red diagonal lines? They mean 'Not Classified Anymore.' In 2004—"

"But why?"

"I'm coming to that. In 2004, they— Wait, I better back up. In January 2003, the *Icarus* package was launched as a top secret military payload, carried into orbit on the *Columbia*, mission STS-107. Yes, that's right, that was the mission on which the *Columbia* broke up on re-entry and killed all the astronauts on board. Well anyway, the *Icarus* package was not very large. It consisted of a fairly small upper-stage booster rocket and a MIRV-like payload on top."

Malcolm interrupted. "MIRV? Like the ICBM nuclear warheads?"

"Very similar. Multiple Independently-targeted Re-entry Vehicles. I encountered a little bad news about these Vehicles in a testing phase addendum inserted into this MilSpec. The DoD referred to these vehicles as Positioning/Observation/Steering (POS) modules...but they were known informally in contracting circles as 'Pieces Of Shit' for their noteworthy unreliability in testing. Anyway, *Icarus* housed twelve identical vehicles for assay/boost functions, plus a thirteenth 'command' module (designated CM). In the boost phase, the payload was to be nudged into a trajectory just a bit larger in diameter than Earth orbit. So this wouldn't take a lot of energy, you understand. It would sort of drop behind Earth, running a little outside Earth's orbit, over a period of months, then another retrofire of the booster to bring it back down to something very close to Earth orbital velocity, right at L5."

"And right close to Sarpedon-E!" Bert added.

30

"Yes. Then, the idea was, all thirteen vehicles—twelve POS and one CM—would exit the MIRV bus, rendezvous with Sarpedon-E at precise locations, and fasten themselves onto the surface. First, with tethered magnets...Sarpedon's mostly IRON, after all! Second, once in contact with Sarpedon's surface, by laser-augering exploratory bore-holes at their attachment points, the material from which would be assayed to assure suitability for DoD's purposes. And last, by each vehicle's nice stout landing legs spot-welding themselves onto the asteroid. The twelve POS assay modules were to communicate with the command module, which was to collate data and retransmit it to Goldstone Deep Space Communications Center in the Mojave Desert. That's where ProCon comes in, by the way. We designed and fabricated the communications system."

Bert just had to interrupt. "Well...actually it was E-Duce Communications that was originally contracted to develop the comms, before E-Duce was bought out by ProCon. Back in 1998 when I first started with them in Albuquerque. That's how I happened to receive the element abundance datafile this morning."

"Okay. Wait a minute, Bertie. I want to hear what happened to that...that *Icarus* probe and its thirteen little vehicles."

Dr. Ing sighed. "That's the thing...no one knows! The shuttle crew was supposed to just chuck it out into space at a prearranged altitude and location, on their way to the International Space Station. The whole thing was so highly classified that none of the shuttle crew knew what *Icarus* was supposed to do. Then after *Columbia* broke up on re-entry, all the media attention was focused on that, and there was very little discussion of STS-107's missions. DoD and its subagency, the Ballistic Missile Defense Organization, haven't talked much about *Icarus* since 2004, but here's what happened.

"Seventeen Jan 2003: *Icarus* deployed from the shuttle bay, and the shuttle continues on its ISS mission. Eighteen Jan 2003: *Icarus* booster ignites, *Icarus* achieves transfer orbit, craft coasts toward L5, at halfway point, craft successfully reverses orientation and accomplishes retrofire burn to alter velocity and orbital radius. Two January 2004: *Icarus* nears L5, acquires Sarpedon-E via radar, then infrared optics. Accomplishes second successful retrofire burn and enters pacing orbit with the asteroid. Then follows twenty hours of autonomous surface scanning, rough composition analysis. MIRV cone jettisoned. Command module autonomously evaluates surface topology of Sarpedon-E, determines all landing sites for probes, communicates this data to Goldstone. And that's the last anybody ever heard from *Icarus* until this morning, when Bertie here received that datafile. Bertie, do you care to explain just how you accomplished that?"

"It's something I set up when I was at E-Duce. I never told anyone. About a year before the STS-107 launch. You've got to understand, I had *no idea* what the E-Duce communications software was meant to accomplish! But I was just starting out in my professional career, and back in those days, I was incorrigibly curious. So when they assigned me to set up the Goldstone end of the whole commo link, I just fixed the software to cc me any datastream that came from their 'client.' Apparently, the datafile got forwarded to my laptop because I've kept at least one of my e-mail identities unchanged all these years. I knew the project was space related, but I *swear* I didn't have the faintest inkling it would come from a solid gold asteroid!"

"Well how did you know all those details when you came to see me this morning?" The Amoeba gently insisted.

"Process of elimination…deductive reasoning."

"*Elementary, my dear Watson*, huh?" The Amoeba scoffed.

"Yep...I guess."

"Okay...what do you 'guess' happened next?"

"All thirteen modules must have deployed. Attached successfully. Performed their assays successfully. Communicated with the Command Module. Command module waited until the scheduled time to transmit the findings. Time arrived... and CM transmitted."

"But it didn't transmit until *TODAY!*"

"Yep. Mission clock hardware screwup...the 'scheduled' time was supposed to be back in January 2004, but it got fouled up and the commo went into sleep mode along with all other CM functions, and didn't wake up until early this morning. E-Duce didn't design or build the mission clock...someone else did. So what happened, Meebs, when the Department of Defense never heard another word from *Icarus*, fourteen years ago?"

"They went absolutely berserk. They'd put two-point-six billion dollars into the project up to that point. They tried a Command Module query...about a *hundred* CM queries! Got nothing. They tried commanding communications software resets. They tried ditzing with gain levels and antenna orientations, but couldn't get any confirming signals back from L5 that those commands had been acted on...or received, even. They tried all-system power-down/power-up reset...do you know how radical and desperate that maneuver is, from ninety million miles away? Nothing! Never heard another peep! Consensus was that the Command Module had melted down or crashed into Sarpedon-E or been stolen by aliens. After that, they sent teams of very intimidating auditors to every system subcontractor...I had to spend the scariest three months of my life dealing with those auditors! Well, eventually, Federal administrations changed, NASA chiefs changed...the whole star-wars enthusiasm died down,

33

Strategic Defense Initiative got shoved to the back shelf. And Project Icarus got written off as a swing-and-a-miss. They decommissioned all the ground support. Fired about fifteen hundred support staff. Welshed on paying a whole lot more dollars to a whole lot of subcontractors who'd already pocketed plenty. Surplused-off half a billion dollars worth of *Icarus*-related equipment to companies and universities and collectors, none of whom got to ever hear of even the *existence* of *Icarus* or Sarpedon-E. Some of that stuff never got any bidders and is *still* for sale. Two years ago I got a DoD memo declassifying all the old Mil Specs, so I got to draw red lines through those two TOP SECRETs. Actually, I was supposed to submit this Mil Spec for destruction, but I hate to give up old docs for projects I had a hand in. Bertie, I don't even imagine Goldstone knew, cared about, or even noticed that crappy little datafile you received. Probably auto-routed to you because you cc'ed it."

"I've got a question!" Mac interjected, practically bouncing off the sofa. "How the *Hell* did DoD propose moving that billion-ton piece of iron into orbit around Earth?"

Dr. Ing took this one. "Those twelve assay modules can provide the necessary thrust."

"They're, like, *rockets?*"

Bertram chimed in. "Not rockets like you imagine them. They're low yield, precisely calibrated, damped Uranium-hydride atomic bombs, Malcolm. Twelve of them. Just a guess!"

All three of them fell silent at this sobering observation. Their eyes were unfocused and faraway, contemplating nuclear Armageddons of assorted varieties. There was nothing for it but to have a drink. Mountain Dew had to do.

Dr. Ing came back down to reality first. "Oh, by the way, Malcolm…a while back you asked how I was able to smuggle this Mil Spec out of the building?"

"Uh-huh…"

"I just carried it out. In my attaché case. I may have discovered something that constitutes a weakness in ProCon's security procedures."

Bert pointed at the four-hundred-page document in Dr. Ing's hand. "Can I borrow that for a while, Meebs?" he asked.

"Sure. Bring it back to ProCon in an attaché case or something."

And relating to carrying sensitive stuff out of ProCon facilities in attaché cases: No, The Amoeba had not discovered anything new. Plant security operated on a caste system. If you were a blue collar, low paid, assembly line type, which the security guards staffing the exits could easily recognize by (a) overalls, sweats, jeans or other casual attire worn by these laborers, along with yellow color-coded ID badges, or (b) lunch pails, mini backpacks, grocery bags or gym totes carried in and out by these laborers to transport their coffee thermoses and lunch vittles, since these individuals were not exactly invited to partake of the corporate cafeteria. Well, on departing at the end of the day, these miscellaneous lunch containers consistently came under the scrutiny of the ProCon Gestapo. The production line types would hold open their lunch boxes and the Plant Security types would check for contraband. Once in a while, an assembly worker would randomly be asked to assume the position and undergo a pat-down. The 'caste system' nature of all this came into play inasmuch as white collar employees were not similarly discommoded… just waved on through. An engineer or middle manager was recognizable by virtue of more upscale clothing. And a necktie, perhaps. Or a suit coat. Carrying a briefcase or an attaché case, or an umbrella, even. If displayed at all, a blue ID badge. This class of ProCon employee could be systematically disassembling the plant from the inside out, and taking the looted parts home with them in their attaché cases, piecemeal, and no exit-door security guard would think to shake them down. Upper level management and their secretarial and menial staff had their own private 'honor system' exits with no security guards *at all*.

Malcolm had come into an acute awareness of all this about five years previously. At the time, his sister Gertrude was staying with him temporarily, along with her four-year-old daughter Ophelia. One Sunday morning, Malcolm was about to leave his apartment for the day. A friend from work was moving with his girlfriend to a different part of Hartford, a bigger and nicer apartment, and had dragooned Malcolm and a couple other guys to help schlep boxes and furniture. Gertrude buttonholed her brother before he could get out the door. "Would you mind watching Ophelia for me, Mal?" she pleaded. "I've got a job interview!"

Dooley groaned. "I'll have to drag her along! I'm helping Mark and Janie move today!"

"She won't be any trouble! Let her take her Barbie-dolls and she'll just sit in a corner playing with them. I'll send along some juice boxes and grapes and a peanut butter sandwich and you won't even have to feed her!"

So off Malcolm went, his little blonde-haired niece in tow carrying her brown paper shopping bag full of Barbies and snacks. Sure enough, little Ophelia contented herself with staying out of the way and playing with her half-dozen assorted Barbies. It should be noted that four-year-olds play with Barbie-dolls primarily by removing their clothes and accessories, fake breast-feeding them, and then tucking them into dolly-bed. Nightie-night, Barbie. Putting the clothes back on? …not so much.

After a long day of schlepping, Malcolm was driving home, his niece belted into the bucket seat to his right. Without preamble, the urchin started to cry.

"What's wrong, honey?" Mal asked.

"I left my dollies at that man's house!"

Malcolm made consoling noises. But it was late and he was tired and hungry and there was a lot of traffic so he was *not* going to turn around and drive back to Mark and Janie's new apartment. "Look, Ophelia…I'll phone Mark when we get home and ask him to bring your dollies to work. And then I'll bring them home to you…will that be okay?"

"When?" the child grizzled.

"Tomorrow. First thing, when I get home."

"All right," the youngster sobbed, reluctantly agreeing.

It all worked out as planned, so next afternoon when Malcolm headed out of the building on his way home, he was toting Olivia's brown paper grocery bag full of Barbies.

As he approached the exit turnstile, a khaki-shirted security operative with shoulders like a linebacker stepped out of the sentry shack. The guard stopped Malcolm with a billy club gently laid across the bright-blue tie adorning Malc's chest. "What's in the bag, Sport?" the guard demanded.

Malcolm swallowed hard. He'd never yet been selected for screening by security—ever! "Oh…ah…um… er…. Nothing, sir!" he responded.

The massive security guy stiffened. Malcolm watched the guy reach down and unsnap the cover of his sidearm holster. "Put the bag on the shelf and step back!" the guard commanded. Behind Malcolm, thirty or forty

ProCon employees, queued-up to pass security, craned their necks to see what kind of drama was unfolding.

The guard pulled the sack open and glanced in. He raised a massive paw, flexed his fingers, and dipped into the sack. Slowly, pinched between his thumb and forefinger, he drew out a buck-naked Barbie by her heel, a tiny scarlet D-cup Barbie brassiere dangling from her plastic fingers.

The guard's eyes locked with Malcolm's. His eyebrows went up and down Groucho-fashion a couple of times. There was a sussuration of indrawn breath from Malcolm's riveted co-workers. The guard dropped Naked Barbie back into the bag's depths and, wordlessly, waved a beet-red Malcolm out the gate.

Like The Amoeba's Mil Spec, Dooley should have stuffed his niece's *dishabille* Barbies into an attaché case.

VALERIA FIGURES IT OUT

Bert, Dooley and The Amoeba were dead wrong about who was spying on them. ProCon Enterprises had certainly installed computer monitoring software on every company computer, copy machine, telephone, fax, elevator and motion-operated toilet in the twenty-story World Headquarters, and every speck of data collected was indeed archived in a massive databank, located in an air conditioned room in the sub-sub-sub-basement. But that's as far as it goes. ProCon's security staff was more given to projecting a Strongarm Goon aura. This tended to lead Human Resources to hire strongarm boys, washed-up athletes, and market-variety goons for security operatives, the preponderance of whom would not know what to make of spy cam footage if it were reduced to fruit smoothies and they were forced to gargle with it.

However! There *was* a covert agency which took quite an active interest in what went on within ProCon Enterprise's World Headquarters. This agency was known as:

Ministerstvo Mezhdunarodnoy Tekhnicheskoy Odnorodnosti

or MMTO, which, for all those not particularly fluent in Russian, translates as The Ministry for International Technical Uniformity. MMTO's mandate was to accomplish international technical uniformity by spying, internationally, on other technically oriented companies and government agencies and universities in foreign lands, so that uniformity might be achieved by means of duplicating their goodies without going to the bother of a lot of research and development costs.

MMTO had facilities in eighteen different locations throughout Russia. One of these was in the city of Chelyabinsk. The MMTO monitoring facility looked like a three story version of Costco: windowless tip-up concrete panel-and-pillar construction on top of a vast concrete slab. There was a sign in big Cyrillic letters which would have read, had it been translated to big *English* letters:

YUZHNO-URAL'SKIY ZAVOD DETSKOGO PITANIYA

This means 'Southern Ural Baby Formula Factory'. Camouflaging a sensitive, secret, hostile facility with signs identifying it as a baby formula factory seems to have gained in popularity, worldwide, but almost no smart bomb or cruise missile or spy satellite is deceived by mere signs anymore. Further, the big antennas and radar domes on top of the Chelyabinsk MMTO facility were a bit of a giveaway.

One of the six thousand lowlevel data screeners employed within MMTO was a nondescript, twenty-six-year-old nonentity University graduate by the name of Valeria Anjelika Tamoritskaya. Valeria came from the poorer part of Voronezh, not very much south but almost two thousand miles west of Chelyabinsk. Her parents were nonentities. She had no siblings. Her University experiences were unremarkable, and she had few friends. She had never traveled outside Russia. All these considerations made Valeria a satisfactory candidate for a security clearance allowing her to work at MMTO. In Chelyabinsk, she had a meager apartment, no car, no washer or dryer, very few friends, two pairs of shoes (if you don't count her Russian-made wellies for winter mud-and-snow wear), a paltry wardrobe, no sweetheart nor any prospects of one, and a very meager salary on which to enjoy all this bounty.

Valeria's particular duties revolved around the fact that Chelyabinsk had had a close call with catastrophic obliteration by a large meteoric impact on 15 February 2013. There was a school of thought in the more conspiracy-obsessed of Russian academic circles that the Chelyabinsk Meteor had been a trial run of a weaponized redirected-asteroid technology, probably originating in the USA, based on no evidence whatsoever, beyond an ingrained paranoia which may not actually have been entirely unfounded. Anyway, Valeria's particular job was to be on the *qui vive* for suspicious foreign technological similarities to the Chelyabinsk Meteor.

A fruitful source for data on near-Earth asteroids was the European Southern Observatory, cooperatively operated by a bunch of European countries and the government of Chile...whose participation was fairly implicit since the actual Observatory in question was the La Silla Paranal Observatory in the Atacama Desert in Chile. Once every month or so, Valeria would have a look at intercepted e-mails from La Silla Paranal.

Valeria Anjelika was not what you'd call a raving genius, but she was pretty smart nonetheless...and *very* persistent. She had a few unusual talents. One of these was quirky to the point of spookiness: Valeria knew where things were.

We are not talking about her *car keys*! You may recall Valeria had no car. No, we are talking about things like the Planet Venus. Or like Ganymede, the largest of Jupiter's moons. Or like the US Department of Defense's KH-16 'Eagle Eye' spy satellite. All you had to do was give Valeria a set of celestial coordinates—viewer centered or Earth centered, horizontal or equatorial or ecliptic or sidereal, it made no difference—and Valeria would instantly point her right index finger in that direction. Her ability to point at faraway celestial bodies with uncanny accuracy was such that if her fingertip could emit a bright red laserbeam, it would streak across the empty void of space and illuminate the surface of the celestial body in question, dead-center. This ability of hers had been the source of endless amusement over the years, by University cronies and by astronomically-inclined fellow MMTO employees. *She points at planets! Like an Irish Setter at a pheasant!...har, har, what a laugh!* On a whim someone decided to check it out, and it was discovered that Valeria was seldom off the mark by as much as a half-degree of arc. The jocularity tapered off.

In this morning's packet of intercepts stacked up in Valeria's electronic in-basket, there was a communiqué from an astronomy graduate student doing night shift grunt work at La Silla Paranal. The highly technical message, in Spanish, was directed to the US National Aeronautics and Space Administration. It seemed to be seeking to verify a prior finding by a US observatory in Arizona, concerning an unpublished discovery of a smallish iron-nickel asteroid that had tentatively been numbered **1997HT$_2$**. A set of ecliptic coordinates were given for the grad student's recent confirmative sighting, and they were not in Spanish, but in numbers.

Valeria examined the coordinates. They looked peculiar. She jotted them on a notepad, then rose from her cramped cubbyhole and stepped out into the corridor. She walked down toward the elevators, where there was a tiny window no more than a meter square that afforded the only vista outside the immense MMTO facility. Valeria consulted her notepad, stood upright with impeccable posture, closed her eyes a moment, then unhesitatingly pointed off in the direction specified.

Very odd! she thought to herself. Right on the terrestrial ecliptic plane! More than that...right along the orbit, trailing Earth by almost exactly sixty degrees. *Wait! That's a Lagrange point! L-five!*

Valeria hustled back to her pathetic little niche and tapped on her computer for a while. Hmmm…let's search: newish Fe/Ni asteroid, possibly at Earth's L5. After a moment's rummage around massive intelligence archives, something popped up! An intercepted e-mail from Goldstone Deep-Space Communications Center to some address at ProCon Enterprises World Headquarters in Hartford, Connecticut, USA. She peered at the e-mail address: aries@singularity.com. And then she looked at the message.

Only a bunch of numbers.

Valeria was nothing if not determined. MMTO had an active interest in what went on at ProCon. The Russian industrial espionage agency had been clandestinely hooked into ProCon's internal security network since 2013 when the World Headquarters hi-rise had been opened. She riffled through the last forty-eight hours of e-mails and imagery. A million files! She activated a filter that focused on the occurrence of the letters 'L5'. This image popped up:

Zdorovo! Valeria silently exclaimed. Awesome! The image was part of a surveillance camera frame grab. She blew the view up to the entire frame, and saw the sketch that Bert had made in The Amoeba's office:

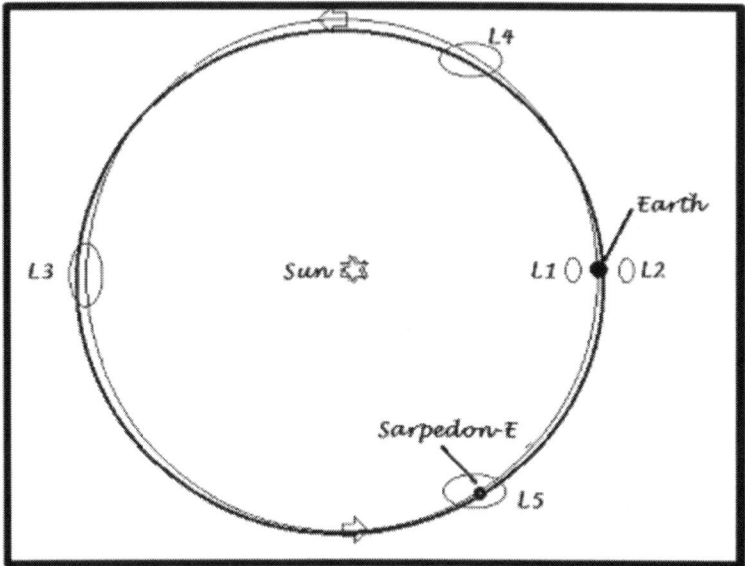

Valeria jotted down a few more sets of coordinates. The positional data she had on her pad was La Silla Paranal...Lagrangian Point 5...Goldstone...Hartford...The Amoeba's office. That dot labeled 'Sarpedon-E'...could that be the official, permanent name for 1997HT$_2$? Five points in three-dimensional space. A short while later, anyone out in the corridor near the elevators would have observed Valeria Anjelika Tamoritskaya pointing sequentially in one direction, then another, then a third, a fourth, and then a fifth, over and over, like a one-armed semaphorist doing a silent Macarena, trying to make sense out of a confusing enigma.

At something after eleven o'clock, Valeria lay in her meager apartment on her narrow, ill-sprung bed, beneath an insufficient blanket. Sleep would not come. Her mind would not let go of something. Those numbers from the American company...from the office of an Asian engineer peculiarly named The Amoeba. Those numbers ran through her fevered brain—the ones in the left-hand column. Twenty-six...twenty-eight...right on down to Seventy-nine. Two-digit numbers...no single digits nor any triple digits. A letter code of some kind? What could they mean? Where would she have seen such numbers? After forty-five minutes of dancing, singing, mocking two-digit numbers messing with her brain, Valeria was at the point of gibbering exhaustion. Her consciousness whirled down a black tornado toward the abyss of slumber, and, like Dorothy in Auntie Em's farmhouse, bizarre things whirled down the funnel with her: bicycles... cows... chicken coops... rowboats... classroom desks... blackboards... articulated plastic skeletons... posters of the Periodic Table of Elements....

YIKES! Valeria sat bolt-upright, all sleep banished. She groped for the switch of her bedside lamp. She squinted, trying to visualize the Periodic Table. The one in her high school chemistry text had been multicolored, and the middle elements were blue. Where was Element 26? First big, long row, right in the blue zone, in the middle. That made it a *metal*. Same with 27, same with 28. Get over to the right and Elements 31 and 32 are starting to get into those funny chemically-metalish elements which still lose electrons but have physical properties dissimilar to copper or tin...alkaline metals and metalloids. But hey! Every single number on that list is a 'metal'! Sarpedon-E has to be a *metallic* asteroid! The Chelyabinsk Asteroid was stony. So...a metallic asteroid of the same size would be, what? Four or five times as massive? *What* metals? Mainly iron! *Wait*! Iron is Element 26! And...and.... It wasn't any use...Valeria could not remember the elements corresponding to the rest of those Atomic Numbers.

Except Atomic Number 79.

Element 79 was *GOLD*!

GONNA NEED AN ATTORNEY

W e're gonna need an *attorney!*" Bertram blurted. He sprayed droplets of Mountain Dew down the sofa.

Malcolm wiped sugary droplets off his arm with the palm of his hand. "Why do you say that?"

"Well how else are we going to claim ownership of an *asteroid?* An asteroid that's been turned into a giant *space ship* by the Department of Defense? They're not gonna want to give it up!"

"They already *have!* Look, isn't it just exactly like when a ship hits a reef in a typhoon, and the captain yells 'All hands abandon ship!' and the crew jumps into the lifeboats and rows for their lives, but somehow the ship *doesn't* sink, and a couple weeks later a scurvy bunch of scalawags in a tramp steamer finds it derelict, floating on the ocean and takes it in tow and tows it to Dar-es-Salaam or somewhere? And sells it for scrap metal? Isn't it a *rightful salvage?* Law of the Sea? Or something like that?"

Malcolm gave his buddy a wry look. "And *that's* why we're gonna need an attorney?"

"Excuse me, gentlemen," The Amoeba interjected. "I happen to know a very good attorney!"

The attorney The Amoeba happened to know was not actually a *practicing* attorney. If one wanted to get technical, the attorney The Amoeba happened to know was actually a *disbarred* attorney. The Amoeba had no intention of giving up. "His name is...or *used* to be... Alonso Ribero-Nuñez. He changed it, though."

"Changed it to *what?*"

"Ummm…Saint Aidan Serpent's-Bane of Iona."

Silence for a long moment. "Saint Aidan?" Malcolm asked.

"Serpent's-Bane?" Bert asked.

"Of Iona. That's a little Scottish island in the Inner Hebrides. Used to be a famous monastery there, back when it was inhabited by archaic more-or-less Irish-like people." Meebs concluded. "It's a cult, sort of."

"A cult. Your friend the disbarred attorney belongs to a cult?"

"Well actually, he sort of *founded* the cult. He's the…oh, I don't exactly know what his title would be. Abbot? Chief Guru?"

"And…you want to seek *legal advice* from this guy?" asked Malcolm.

"He's a real good attorney! Or, he *used* to be! Before he got into snake killing!"

"Ah. That would explain the 'Serpent's-Bane' part.

"See, Alonzo—er, Saint Aidan grew up in Cave Creek, which is a suburb, sort of, north of Phoenix, Arizona. His daddy had a claim—silver, I think—a long way out in the desert southwest of Phoenix, in a nasty little cluster of mountains near a place that isn't even a town any more named Papago, not to be confused with Papago Peak or Papago Park, which are in the middle of Phoenix. Well anyway, when Alonzo was eleven he got bitten by a great big rattlesnake out in the desert near his daddy's claim. It was *uranium*, now that I think about it! Snakebite nearly killed him. Atrophied some leg muscles (snake bit him in the leg) so he walks with a slight limp. Put an end to his high-school football aspirations. Well as the years went by, Alonzo just got more and more pissed off at that rattlesnake in particular, giving him a limp and all, and the whole rattlesnake species, or genus or whatever, in general. Eventually, age forty-six, he was so obsessed that he started slacking off in his corporate lawyer responsibilities and screwing up big court cases and legal transactions. Got in serious trouble with the Bar Association. Eventually, he renounced his profession as an attorney and went back to the Papago mountains and took over his daddy's—his daddy was dead by then—his daddy's mineral claim and started a cult."

"Was Saint Aidan quite religious?"

"I don't think he's religious *at all*! Except, religiously committed to ridding the world of serpents, though. Starting with the Arizona desert."

"Ah. That would explain the Irish Saint name-change."

"Right. But, you'd be surprised how many devotees Saint Aidan Serpent's-Bane of Iona has amassed."

"And the cult is called…?"

Death to Serpents!

Malcolm was unconvinced. The notion of legal counsel was okay, but maybe a nice conservative law firm here in Hartford.

The issue was, who could they trust? Or afford? The Amoeba and St. Aidan went back a long way. Meebs assured his two partners that his old friend was not particularly crazy, except where it came down to venomous snakes, and would be entirely discreet as far as the whole Sarpedon-E thing went. It might cost them a small percentage to buy the ***Death to Serpents!*** cult's cooperation, but let's recall we are talking seven trillion dollars' worth of gold, here. Not to mention five-point-four billion smackers' worth of less significant metals. Plenty to go around.

"We've gotta buy off the *whole cult?*" Malcolm wailed.

"That would probably be the smartest approach. The rest of the Serpent's-Banes are pretty docile…but they're a lot crazier than St. Aidan. Anyway, the extra manpower might come in handy."

Bert was ready to get down to brass tacks. "Okay, you guys!" he exclaimed rather forcefully. "Exactly what are we going to do here?"

"Steal an asteroid?" offered Dooley.

"Fire off one or two of those abandoned nuclear thrust devices and get an abandoned asteroid into Earth orbit?" offered The Amoeba.

"Well, yes," Bertie confirmed. "You don't think it's going to be *easy*, do you?"

"Pretty easy, maybe…." Meebs mumbled.

"And, once we got it in Earth orbit, how does the entire rest of the world's population know—and accept!— that it's *our* golden asteroid? And, how do we get the gold mined out of the asteroid and get it down to the ground and into the bank? And, don't you imagine that seven trillion dollars worth of gold might totally screw up the gold market, and plunge the price down to a buck seventy-five a pound and leave us with big, fat *nothing,* almost?"

Malcolm had to admit he hadn't thought that far ahead.

The Amoeba emitted an embarassed throat-clearing sound. "Um…I take it you've got a plan, Bertie?"

"You bet I got a plan! Here it is: First! Us three have got to quit our jobs at ProCon!"

"Aw Bertie…." Mal whined.

"Man! I don't wanna…" Meebs wailed.

"Did you guys ever read the employment contracts you signed, back when ProCon hired you? Fine print! Intellectual Property clause! Says that everything you invent, develop, or think about, on or off the job, belongs to ProCon. Everything you obtain through your activities, efforts, ruminations, or daydreams *while on ProCon property* belongs to ProCon. Everything you stumble over, possess, cherish, inherit or are given can be claimed by

ProCon Enterprises, at their corporate discretion. I'm pretty sure there's a clause in there about your firstborn male child, if conceived while in the employ of ProCon. How do you think they are going to feel about a seven-trillion-dollar asteroid?"

"Gulp," Malcolm gulped.

"Gasp," Meebs gasped.

"Okay. So, letters of resignation! Tomorrow! Second thing! We are going to need some working capital. Tomorrow, after I resign, I'll open us a corporate account. Meebs, can your attorney friend, Saint Iona Snake-Killer get us incorporated?

"Yeah...I guess. I'll give him a phone call."

"You two clean out your savings accounts. Take out your ProCon profit sharing accounts. Withdraw your IRAs. Sell all your stock."

"Jeez, Bertie!" Mal complained.

"Do I *have* to?" Dr. Ing grumbled.

"*Seven trillion dollars*! We're going to need some *working capital*! Scrape up your scratch! Okay...next thing. We—"

"*Third* thing, Bertie," The Amoeba interjected, in the interest of orderliness.

"Hmm. Third thing! We..." Bert stopped, momentarily stumped. "Oh yeah. *Third* thing! We gotta divide up a few tasks and get cracking on them. I've been mulling over this remote Arizona cult with its hotshot albeit disbarred attorney. The benefits might outweigh the risks!"

Malcolm registered shock! "You want to invite this crackpot *in*? You think a snake-murdering ex-attorney will—"

"I'm not thrilled about the *attorney*, Mal. It's more the *cultists themselves*. And the nice, empty Arizona desert!"

"You're going to have to explain that!"

"I counsel patience, Grasshopper," Bert pronounced soothingly. "Anyway, I suggest the three of us fly on down to Arizona and check out **Death to Serpents!** I'll book us some air tickets and a rental car tomorrow. Okay, next— Sorry...*fourth* thing! We shouldn't have to worry about title to the *asteroid*...we only have to demonstrate ownership of the *gold*, once it's in our hands! I'll get back to this in a minute. Let me tell you how I think we can accomplish that."

"You mean, once the thing's in Earth orbit, how do we three experienced astronauts jump in our own private space ship and go up and use laserbeams to cut the damn thing up and bring it back down with our antigravity ray? Let's see...you were talking about four point three billion *tons*?"

"No, Dooley...five point five billion *troy ounces*. Still an awful lot of gold. No, my lad, you are thinking conventionally. This morning I brought up an article on my laptop. The article was entitled 'Asteroid Mining'. The author suggested six different techniques:

A. If the asteroid has a loose, rubbly surface, a robotic spacecraft could use an auger or scoop mechanism to actively grab pieces of material. *Yeah...not likely! Where are we gonna get an auger spacecraft?*

B. Send astronauts to dig a shaft-type mine into the asteroid, and transport the ore to a processing facility. *I don't see the economics penciling-out.*

C. If the asteroid is covered with loose, granular material, these can be robotically gathered by means of a magnetic rake. *The iron, maybe...but not the gold!*

D. Heat can be applied to vaporize the volatile materials. *Not helpful! We're not after **methane**, f'chrissakes!*

52

E. Something called the Mond Process, where you use hot carbon monoxide to extract atoms of iron and nickel, then extract these metals from the gas, which can be re-used, but leaving the rarer metals behind as a residue. *In space? At large-scale? Not bloody likely!*

F. Self-Replicating Robotic Spacecraft! We seed Sarpedon-E with these babies, they take a few weeks, months, or years to extract one metal or another and build a replica of themselves, complete with rocket fuel, then the replicas build replicas, and after a while the whole asteroid is reduced to replicas, so they zoom back home to Earth, whereupon we melt them down into their constituent metals. *Yeah...right! Nice practical solution, that!*

Malcolm was ready to rip his hair out in exasperation! "So none of these brilliant schemes have any chance of working because they are beyond current technologies, or vastly expensive, or just plain harebrained! How do you propose to extract seven trillion dollars worth of gold out of Sarpedon-E, Bertram?!"

"Easy! We just smoosh that big bastard down on Earth, somewhere remote and unpopulated, and *pick gold nuggets out of the crater!*"

9

VALERIA'S ANABASIS

Valeria Anjelika sat in her pathetic little booth, diddling with the keys of her computer, lost in contemplation. Soon, her dreaded supervisor wandered down the aisle behind her and noticed she wasn't doing very much. "Oh, uh, good afternoon, Comrade Tsepesh," Valeria said, by way of acknowledging the leering whiskery face hanging over her shoulder.

"And...what are you investigating at this moment, Miss Tamoritskaya?"

Valeria shrugged. "Nothing. Just stopping for breath, Vladimir Krovopitza."

The supervisor snorted. "Well, the Ministry doesn't pay you to breathe!" he hissed, before even thinking about what he was saying.

Valeria couldn't prevent a peal of laughter from bubbling out. "Vladimir Krovopitza," she giggled, "Do you suppose I could take my accrued holiday time?"

"Um...ah...that is to say...we are *very* busy just now! When would you plan to take your leave?"

"Oh, right away."

"Uh...how long would you be gone?"

"I don't exactly know. Quite a long time."

"And...where would you be going?"

None of your snoopy-nose business, Valeria thought. But she said, "Paris!"

"What do you want to see in Paris that we don't have in Russia?"

"The Eiffel Tower, naturally! Maybe a boat ride on the Seine."

Vladimir Krovopitza Tsepesh[3] attempted an expression of Solomon-like wisdom. "No. No, young lady...I cannot endorse a leave request just now. Perhaps in three or four months. But you must plan ahead! Choose your dates, fill out a request form and submit it to me at least six weeks ahead. Is that clear?"

"Perfectly clear, Comrade Tsepesh. In that case, I quit."

"*WHAT?*"

"I hereby tender my resignation effective this instant. Good-bye!" Valeria scooped up her worn-out red leather shoulder bag, clicked off her computer and monitor for a last time, and skipped rather lightheartedly toward the stairwell.

While busing uptown, Valeria thought things over. *That may have been a little impulsive*, she thought. *But it's about time I did something impetuous!* As the bus plowed through piles of slush on the potholed roadway, Valeria added up her resources: her final paycheck, her grocery-and-emergency money, a paltry bank account, a slim stack of low interest government securities inherited from her late father. A few pieces of jewelry she might sell expeditiously with not too many questions asked. Perhaps a hundred-ten thousand rubles, taken altogether. She pondered the details: *Okay... here's what it will be. A few clothes in a backpack, her passport, maybe her digital camera. Don't forget the English phrasebook. Grocery money out of the sugar bowl. Stop at the bank to close out the account, cash the paycheck, redeem the securities. A quick, anonymous stop at a certain 'antique shop' she knew about, to peddle the jewelry. Then the bus station: redeye ticket to Moscow, then— Wait! NO! Go by bus and train, it will take days and days! If the Ministry gets a whiff of*

---

[3] **Vladimir "Bloodsucker" The Impaler**

this, they'll have the KGB on me! It's got to be air! Or...or high-speed train. Okay...flight to Moscow. Say, nine thousand rubles. Flight, Moscow to Paris...ought to be fifteen thousand rubles. Tres Grand Vitesse *through the Chunnel to London...maybe fifty-five hundred rubles. London to New York...*bozhe moi, *that will be fifty thousand rubles if it's a kopek! Eighty thousand rubles, Chelyabinsk, Moscow, Paris, London, New York! That leaves me thirty thousand if I'm lucky. That's...let's see...four hundred and fifty dollars, US! Will they let me in with that little money? I guess we are going to find out!*

The bus stopped at her dingy apartment block and Valeria jumped out into the Chelyabinsk snow slush for very nearly the last time.

Two hours later, Valeria arrived by bus at *Aeroport Chelyabinsk*, north of town. Twilight was approaching. She hurried inside, concerned whether there would be ticketing agents still on duty. She had taken Aeroflot flights between Chelyabinsk and Voronezh a couple of times, when her father was still living, but she was hardly a seasoned traveler. She pushed through the heavy glass doors, into the terminal's bustle and noise.

Long lines snaked back from the *Aeroflot* ticket desks. Valeria tapped her foot with impatience. An hour later, the line attendant waved her toward a wicket thirty meters down, practically at the end of the long counter.

The agent was a red-faced, gruff-looking individual wearing a rumpled *Aeroflot* uniform. "Destination?" he growled.

Valeria wanted to get her routing straight, but she was not certain whether she should book through. Her thought was that she might perhaps wish to book one segment at a time to keep her ultimate destination confidential. *Oh, what the hell!* she thought. *At this point, I'm a tourist, and tourists go to New York all the time!*

56

"Umm...here's what I was thinking. Chelyabinsk to Moscow, then Paris, then TGV to London, finally to New York."

The grumpy agent tapped his keyboard, squinted at his computer display, scribbled on a pad. "Cost you about ninety-five thousand rubles. Almost four days in transit. Tell me, *Milochka*, do you wish to stop over at any of those cities?"

I'm not your 'dearie'! Valeria thought. "Well...no, not exactly. Can I get to New York any sooner?"

"Certainly! And, a lot cheaper! *Aeroflot* to Moscow, KLM Moscow to London, Delta London to New York! Fifteen hours...sixty-two thousand rubles. Departs in six hours."

"Oh, that's a lot better! Let's book it!" Privately, Valeria gloated...this would leave her more than seven hundred US dollars as pocket money!

"Not so fast, *Dorogaya*![4] Do you have a visa?"

"Umm...no. Not yet."

"What is the purpose for your visit?"

Valeria expected someone would ask this question. She groped in her travelbag and came up with a letter she had ingeniously forged. The letter, handwritten in English, read as follows:

---

[4] **sweetheart**

> *Small cabbage-head mine,*
>
> *I wait for you almost not can! Inside of letter is money dollars for you buy ticket to ride inside of airoplane. Also inside letter a littlebit surplus money dollars for you spend on espenses in travel also nize preety sexy clothings for wear you! Arrive you New York Aeroport, telephone to me immidiate! I drive big expensive American car and I collect you at Aeroport and we drive to big church in city downtown, there we getting MARRIED!! Loves you outrageously!!*
> *YOUR*
> *Doctor Marcellus Ing*

Valeria showed the letter to the ticket agent. "I'm getting married! In New York...to a *doctor!*" she exclaimed, affecting an ingenuous, maidenly simper.

Her clerk comprehended not a syllable of English. But he bought her subterfuge nonetheless. He glanced right and left to see if he could exchange a confidence with his client without being overheard. "Listen, *Litso-kukli*[5], getting married in the US is a problem! After I sell you this ticket, I will fill out some documents and send you down to Customs. You'll have to talk to a US Immigration Agent if you want to persist with this getting-married business. Do you have any pre-approved Fiancée Visa paperwork? No? That's trouble! Take you a couple months and fifty-thousand rubles! Do you have an affidavit from your US doctor attesting that he's not already married? No? He will have to get an attorney on his end, and that's weeks and weeks of hassle. Do you have medical statement attesting you don't have AIDS or gonorrhea? No? They

---

[5] **Baby-doll**

58

won't let you go marry somebody until you get that document, and that takes about three months!"

"What am I going to do?" Valeria pleaded.

"You are a *tourist* instead of a bride! As of this instant! Ten minutes with the US Visa agent, five hundred rubles application fee, tourist visa for US, good for twenty-five days. Just marry your doctor friend in New York and you can stay forever!"

"As a tourist, won't I need a *return* ticket?"

The agent scratched his scalp, then smiled deviously. "I make you a wedding gift! I will give you a return ticket for flights that do not exist. You can show it to the US Customs agent in New York but it won't get you on any airplane, so I lose no skin."

"That's very kind—"

"Five thousand rubles. By the way…do you speak any English?"

"Ungleesh werry floo-wint aire me!" Valeria pronounced carefully, in what she supposed passed for English.

Six hours later, US Tourist Visa in hand, Valeria found herself strapped into a Tupolev 154M, its engines roaring for takeoff, ready to sky-up for the first leg of her adventure. She peered out the tiny Perspex window and rehearsed what she'd say to herself on the *next* flight segment when she got her first glimpse of the English Channel: *Волна! Волна!*, signifying her joyous and miraculous escape from a hostile land, just like Xenophon's homeward-bound Ten Thousand had cried out when at last, from a hilltop in Trebizond, they spied the familiar shores of the Black Sea: The sea! The sea!

10

THE AMOEBA HAS A VISITOR

A little after two o'clock in the morning, The Amoeba was woken out of a sound sleep by the nonstop, repetitive ding-donging of his doorbell. Groaning and rubbing his eyes, he rolled out of bed and padded barefoot toward his apartment door. Halfway there, he realized he was wearing a disreputable pair of saggybottom, gap-fly boxer shorts and nothing more. He about-faced, padded back to his bedroom, fought his way into a threadbare plaid bathrobe, scuffed his feet into a pair of slippers, and resumed his short shuffle toward responding to the interminable doorbell.

Meebs was about to just haul open the door when a shiver of suspicion washed over him. He took his hand away from the knob. He screwed his eye into the peephole. There was a shabby looking woman out there, her right finger on the doorbell button, her left hand clutching a beat-up green travelbag. She didn't look too dangerous. Meebs opened the door and asked, "What can I do for you, lady?"

"Dockatorre Eeng you?" the woman asked in a thick foreign accent.

"Er…yes, I am Dr. Ing."

"Valeria Anjelika Tamoritskaya. *Komitet Gosudarstvennoy Bezopasnosti!*"[6] Valeria flashed a totally bogus ID card with the big letters **KGB** on it that she had forged with a gold-ink pen and a black felt-tip marker on the plane ride across the Atlantic. "Ondarr arrestament, you!"

---

[6] **Committee for State Security**

Dr. Ing, who had never in his life had a run-in with the law, turned bright red and began sweating bullets. "Ah...er...what's this all about?"

"*Rabotitz* you?...ah...ProCon? Worrrk?"

"Yes. Well, no. That is, yes, but I've just recently resigned."

"Freends you, Meelcumb Mick...MuckDoodley? Beert Krapotskinski?"

"Never heard of them!"

Valeria rummaged in her travelbag and produced a creased MMTO surveillance document, sufficiently classified that she would have never gotten out of Russia unarrested had it been found in her brassiere cup, wherein she'd smuggled it onto the *Aeroflot* jet. She thrust the paper under The Amoeba's nose. It clearly stated, in Russian, that The Amoeba, Meelcumb, and Beert had been covertly observed in a meeting in The Amoeba's office several days ago. A grainy photo facsimile verified the fact. She rummaged in her travelbag again and came up with a barely legible surveillance facsimile of Bert's sketch showing the five Lagrangian Points, the Sun, Earth, Sarpedon-E, and its amazing Earth-crossing orbit. "Aha!" Valeria pronounced, in view of this damning evidence. "Ondarr arrcstiment!"

"Well that's— The KGB cannot just bust in at two in the morning and— See here! You *can't* arrest me!"

"You teeleephun the Beert, the Meelcumb!"

Actually that wasn't a bad idea. Meebs turned on his heel, strode back into the bedroom, and returned with his cellphone. Before he could begin to dial, the presumptive KGB agent stopped him. "Gives *voda* me!" she insisted.

She wants a **drink** *at this hour?* Meebs was too rattled not to comply. He stepped behind the breakfast bar into his inadequate galley kitchen, fumbled an Old-Fashioned glass out of the cupboard, groped in his liquor stash for a half-full bottle of Grey Goose, and poured the KGB agent a couple fingers of warm vodka. He handed the glass to the woman.

Bottled water! Valeria thought, her travel-parched throat twitching. *Nice! But decadent!* She took a big swallow. Bugged her eyes. Projectile coughed the length of the breakfast bar. "*Voda* I say! Thees Vod-KA!"

Chagrined, Meebs spilled the rest of her vodka into the sink. Turned on the kitchen tap and ran the idiot KGB agent a glass of Hartford's finest metallic-tasting, calcium-laden tapwater. Then he set about rousing Malcolm and Bert, and getting them alerted to this major crisis.

Half an hour later, his two cronies showed up at Dr. Ing's door. The Doctor ushered them in, made introductions. "This is Agent Tamoritskaya of the KGB, right off the plane from Russia, who evidently has been sent here in secret to arrest us."

"*WHAT?*"

"Hey! That's—"

Meebs made placating gestures. "Doesn't make any sense. Anyway, take a look at her credentials." He gave Valeria the international hand signal for 'show-me-your-credentials,' and the Russian girl produced her fake KGB ID card.

"Obviously a crude fake." The Amoeba scoffed.

"I'd say so," Dooley agreed.

"No question," Bertie seconded.

The three of them turned on Valeria. "So...what do you want?" The Amoeba confronted her in an icy tone. "Tell us the truth and it will go easier on you when the FBI gets here!" he lied.

"Piss off...uhhh...." *Damn! I've forgotten the next word!* Valeria thought, suddenly panicked. "Piss off...."

"No! Maybe *you* ought to piss off!" Meebs hissed. The three asteroid conspirators drew together threateningly.

In another moment, they were likely to commit violence on the slight frame of their feminine *faux*-KGB visitor. At the last second, however, the missing word popped into Valeria's beleaguered brain.

"ECK-shin!" she yelled. "Piss off ECK-shin! What I am want, piss off eck-shin, r-r-reegairds Sarpedon-E!"

"We're gonna need a Russian translator!" The Amoeba mumbled.

As it turned out, Dooley had an idea! "Guys...you are *not* gonna believe this! I know someone who can help us! One of our co-workers, right there at ProCon!"

"Who? Who, already?"

"Jessica Moonflower!"

"*'Casabas'?*"

"Yeah! Last month at that after-work retirement party for...for.... Well, I forget the guy's name. Some midlevel manager in the Financial Software Group. Anyway, our girl 'Casabas' got a little tight on punch, and she admitted to me that back in the 'Eighties just about the time *Glasnost* was kicking in, her mom had been a twenty-year-old hairdresser in Sochi. On the Black Sea? In Russia? Well, and she was struggling along on a shitty salary and dealing with one boyfriend after another that just wanted to bang her senseless and didn't want to commit, or even give her any jewelry or anything, and so she'd advertised for an American husband in the Washington Post, and Jessica's dad, who was sixty-seven and had just gone through a horrible divorce, sent her money and brought her over as a mail-order bride, and had gotten her knocked up in record time, the result being Jessica! She told me her mom's name...it was Tatyana Loo...Loo... Loo-NEETS-veh-tock! I don't know how that's spelled in Russian, but the name means 'Moonflower', but it's actually the flower of the plant *Datura innoxia*, which is in the nightshade family, and is highly toxic and seriously hallucinogenic, which I happen to remember because it's sort of appropriate to Jessica, don't you think? She legally took on her momma's name, that is, the English translation of her momma's name, when her dad kicked the bucket, because his name was 'horrid and unpronounceable', as Jessica puts it. Maybe we ought to call Jessica 'Looney' instead of 'Casabas'... because 'Casabas' is pretty insulting if you think about it, and anyway I can't usually bring myself to call her 'Casabas' to her tits I mean to her face. Oh, and Tatyana Moonflower had *really* enormous jugs before they kinda let go and sagged, according to Jessica, so that's where she got hers, I guess."

"Dooley!" Berty hollered in exasperation. "What's the point of that ridiculous story?"

"*Jessica Moonflower speaks Russian!*"

Valeria had been listening to Dooley's drivel. But she had not understood much of it, with the possible exception of the word 'Russian'. So, naturally, she imagined they were talking about her. When Dooley got to the part about Jessica's mother's enormous bazongas, he'd made the international hand signal for 'enormous bazongas.' Valeria had glanced down at her own meager pair, shapely enough but no larger than half-peaches. Or maybe apricots. She'd decided Dooley wasn't talking about her after all, lost interest in his monologue, and yawned cavernously.

"Hey you guys!" Meebs interjected. "Miss KGB has just got off an all-night plane ride that crossed about twenty time zones. Let's let her sleep it off. Dooley, in the morning you call Miss Moonflower before she has a chance to get off to work, and get her over here. Promise her a sumptuous breakfast, with mimosas. Promise her three hundred bucks to translate for us." He turned his attention to Valeria. "Agent Tamoritskaya...do you have a hotel?"

"*Chto?* Er...Huh?"

64

"Hotel! Hotel!"

"Ah…*hooteel*! *Nyet*."

"Would you like to sleep here?" Meebs illustrated this suggestion by pulling Valeria by the coatsleeve to his bedroom door and pointing to his rumpled bed, then pointing at her and making the international hand sign for 'sleeping'.

"Niveer I slip weeth you, nesty boy!" Valeria exclaimed in high dudgeon.

Meebs clarified his suggestion by retrieving his favorite pillow from his bed, throwing it on the couch, and by means of a lot of pointing and gesticulating, leading her to understand that *he'd* take the couch, *she'd* take the bed.

At nine o'clock next morning, a Tuesday, Malcolm showed up with Jessica Moonflower in tow. Since she had called in sick for work, she'd taken the liberty to dress casually: painted-on, raggedy, ripped denim shorts and a vee-neck top that was obviously a pub souvenir from a Wet T-Shirt contest. A stupendous amount of renowned Moonflower cleavage was on display.

Bertie, who had seen no sense in returning home and had consequently slept the balance of the night on Dr. Ing's carpeted living room floor, greeted them at the door "Hullo, Miss Moonflower," he mumbled gallantly.

"Well hi there, Bertiekins!" Jessica chirruped. "Where's this Russian chick?"

"Uh…let's let her sleep. Would you like some coffee?"

"Rather have a mimosa. Oh hell, coffee's okay I guess. Hey, Dr. Ing! Got any Bailey's for my coffee?"

Meebs was shy around women. The more gorgeous they were, the shyer he got. So he bustled off to the other side of his breakfast bar and went about organizing for breakfast. Scrambled eggs, toasted Wonder Bread, supermarket orange juice from a bottle. Highly creative gourmet provender.

The three conspirators and their hired translator were busy crunching toast and making small talk when Valeria came padding out from the bedroom rubbing her eyes. She had not yet dressed very much, other than fine, high quality coarse Russian cotton undergarments she'd occupied for the past thirty-six hours, but she showed no modesty in the least. Dr. Ing issued her a cup of coffee and slunk back into the kitchen to hide his scarlet cheeks.

"Ah! *Eto dolzhno byt' vashim gostem Rossii! Dobroye utro , dorogaya ledi ... menya zovut Dzhessika, no vy mozhete nazyvat' menya 'Casabas'!*"[7] Jessica exclaimed.

Valeria's eyes came out on stalks at the sound of her native tongue. Then she smiled broadly and began, finally, to relax. The two girls put their heads together and began yakking away in high-speed Russian.

"How are we gonna get the KGB off our backs?" Malcolm asked his buddies.

Bertie scoffed. "She's no agent! How do we get *her* off our backs?"

"She knows too much!" whispered The Amoeba.

"Are you suggesting we *whack* her?"

"No, no! Of course not! We may have to let her wet her beak a little, is all." Meebs had a penchant for gangster flicks, and admired the argot.

Neither Bert nor Mal were enthusiastic about letting Valeria in! They had both come to think of Sarpedon-E's seven trillion five-point-six billion dollars' worth of mineral bounty as their own.

---

[7] **This must be your Russian guest! Good morning, dear lady. My name is Jessica but you can call me 'Casabas'!**

"Look…it's not as if we won't have plenty of money to spend! We're just going to have to share some of it, to buy some cooperation!"

At this instant, Jessica Moonflower abruptly quit listening to Valeria gabble, and broke into the boys' deliberations. "What's this about a shitload of *mineral wealth*?" she insisted. "If Valeria's in, *I'm* in!"

Oh crap! The hook was set…Miss Moonflower was never going to let herself be tossed back! The five of them spent the next hour going round and round as to how much of a cut Valeria and Jessica were going to settle for. The deliberations shaped up that the two ladies were a unified bargaining block. The gents, in an unspoken agreement, danced around the subject of exactly how many dollars' worth of mineral wealth were involved. Jessica notwithstanding, Valeria was no fool. She imagined it would be a *lot* of dollars.

Originally it was Bertie's asteroid, and he was miffed at the ladies' audacity. Their non-negotiable, rock-bottom line came to eighty thousand bucks, split fifty-fifty. After recent expenditures on travel for the Arizona expedition, the working capital account was down to only about three-fourths that amount. If negotiations fell through, the ladies were prepared to immediately go public with what they knew, their lack of factual astronomical details notwithstanding. "We can't go that high!" Bert insisted.

"Impossible! Outrageous!" Malcolm agreed.

"Wait, fellows. I've got an idea!" This from The Amoeba, always the idea man. "Let's see if they'll take a 'futures' share. Let's let them have the nickel!"

Jessica was eavesdropping, at least to the extent of hearing that last word. "Not so much as a *NICKEL*?" she shrieked. "You chintzy skinflints are gonna be soooo sorry!" She put her head together with Valeria and jabbered away in Russian. Pretty soon, both pairs of feminine eyes were snapping fire.

"No, wait! You don't understand!" Meebs soothed. "I said 'nickel' like the *metal* nickel! A substantial part of the minerals we're going for is nickel! About ten percent...and it's worth a *lot* of money!"

"How much?"

Without thinking things through, The Amoeba blurted it right out. "Three hundred and sixty-seven point seven million dollars."

Jessica gaped like a speared frog. Then she and Valeria jabbered in Russian nonstop for at least ten minutes. "Okay!" Jessica said at last. "We'll take the nickel!"

"Great!" Dr. Ing agreed. The other two smiled their acquiescence.

"A couple more items. First: Val and I are going to go with you guys to Arizona...the Asteroid Association pays expenses."

Dr. Ing grumblingly agreed, while Mal and Bertie just grumbled. They had tickets to fly in two days, and at this late date, a couple more air tickets were going to cost a bundle.

"First class seats, you guys! And second: So she can stay in the USA, one of you three is going to have to *marry* my good friend Valeria!"

11 _____

Death to Serpents!

The blazing Arizona sun glared down on gritty desert soil festooned with cacti. Little, lumpy cacti like watermelons studded with fish-hooks. Middle-sized, branchy cactus bushes with dense golden fur of thorns, inviting one's caress like the blonde pelt of a purring, long-coated lap cat...except for the golden fur being comprised of a zillion tiny prickle-sharp thorns as brittle as spun glass, once into your flesh. Great, huge saguaro cacti like enormous vegetable Greek columns, their flutes bristling with thousands of three-inch nails honed to needly points.

On the ground in the meager shade of an ocotillo, a four-foot diamondback rattlesnake lay coiled, lazily absorbing the morning's heat. Except for sensory cells beneath the snake's belly scutes which were exquisitely tuned to detect vibrations running through the soil surface, the creature's hearing was not particularly acute. Its sense of smell was another matter. A slender black tongue, deeply forked, flicked out to sample the air. The creature tasted the coppery flavor of dirt and minerals, gritty with the nuance of weathered granite. There was a crisp chlorophyll essence of dessicated foliage. The tinge of water, but nowhere near the surface, and not in ready liquid form: bound up in the moist cells of cacti, safe and unobtainable within their thick, sticker-studded green skin. And...one more taste!

Human!

Cautiously, the serpent unwound. It elongated, thrust its angular diamond head out into full sunlight.

Then, undulating slightly, it slithered out from under its ocotillo bush.

"May Almighty Jehovah's vengeance on all wicked Earthly serpents be *DONE*!" a harsh voice bellowed. The rattlesnake started to vibrate its rattle-tipped tail in alarm, but felt itself seized by that selfsame tail! It was swung into the air! Around, and around again! The creature's weak eyes watched its desert environment whirl past, and its tongue frantically flicked outward, seeking by its keenest sensation to analyze what was happening to it! Around, around ...SPLAT!

A grimy human form, barefoot, clad in filthy sackcloth, wild locks straggling, stood up with the dead rattlesnake's tail clutched in his hand. The smashed head peeled away from the rock onto which the raggedy man had dashed its reptilian brains. He held the yet-twitching trophy at arm's length, shoulder-high. The pinkish mouth gaped, and venom dripped from the vicious white fangs.

"Four feet at least!" the serpent killer gloated. "Praise the Almighty!"

A distant noise, growing in volume, foreign to the desert stillness. The snake slayer looked up from his kill. Over where the roadway ran, a billow of dust. At its head, glinting in the harsh light, a bright blue vehicle. As it approached, its lines became distinct. A minivan! As the vehicle passed fifty yards away from the viper's-bane hermit, the grizzled character could see the car held five or six occupants. It was headed in the direction of the Cloisters.

"Nonbelievers!" the filthy old man spat.

Earlier, at the car rental counter, Dooley had been elected to handle the paperwork. He'd had to surrender his perilously overburdened credit card to be swiped for security. He'd had to provide his driver's license and insurance particulars to cover the rental car. Adding insult to injury, a majority of the Asteroid Associates had declared him to be Designated Driver for the duration of the Arizona expedition. Therefore, Dooley took each jagged rock that leapt up out of the gravelly track they were following, and rapped the rental car in its tender undercarriage, as a personal affront. BANG! a rock would say, rapping the oilpan. OUCH! Dooley would say, under his breath, and pull his head down as if into his ribcage turtle-fashion, wincing visibly.

"There it is!" The Amoeba yelled. He was Designated Navigator, crammed into the front seat on the tranny-hump between Bert (shotgun), and Malcolm (driver). The women had the complete leisure of the backseat, and had done without the encumbrance of seatbelts, bare legs drawn up so the two of them were knees-to-knees, chattering away in Russian. A pile of suitcases and backpacks filled up the van's rear spaces. "There!" Meebs repeated, extending a pointing finger in front of Dooley's face. "Turn left!"

No sign…no mailbox…no gateposts. Just a dim sandy pair of ruts wandering out into the cactus fields. Dooley navigated the van onto the ruts, shifted down to second gear. Immediately, the vehicle began dragging its belly on the gravelly, mounded center of the lane. *There go the shocks!* a panicky Dooley fretted. *And the tranny…the leaf springs…u-joints…differential! Maybe, the floor pans!* Rental-agency-confiscated dollar signs whirled past his mind's eye like fruit on a runaway slot machine.

The dirt lane rose over a gentle mound, entered an arroyo. Around a pile of boulders, into a box canyon. And there it was: the Cloisters of St. Padraig Serpent's-Bane *na hÉireann* [8]

The place didn't look like much. Mud-plastered adobe walls with a few dark-brown timbers framing up the

---

[8] **Of Ireland**

doorways and windows. Two-story central portion. Stuck-on wings left and right, probably monastic cells and chapels and refectories and whatnot. Whole thing roofed in corrugated metal starting to rust seriously in the unforgiving desert sun. Big stone chimney rising up out of the whole affair. The front door was an impressive slab of Sugar Pine, hand carved in bas-relief into a large, curvy rattlesnake, loopy-knotty like an image from the Book of Kells. The serpent's head was being trod upon by a sandaled foot.

Malcolm coasted into a weedy cul-de-sac and shut off the engine. At that instant, the Cloisters door was yanked open and a female figure rushed out to confront the visitors. She was toting a very large double-barreled shotgun. The woman was four-and-a-half feet tall and was wearing scuffed pink cowboy boots. Highly tooled. Fringes around the tops. Silver toe-adornments. Other than that, she was stark naked.

"*FREEZE, SCUMBAGS!*" the tiny apparition shrieked. Bertie was in the lead, so it was he who had the double-barrel thrust into his belly. Malcolm chivalrously pushed the ladies behind him for their safety. "*Trespassing Scumbag Disbelievers! I'm gonna gutshoot the whole lot of you with double-O buckshot!*" The insane woman's itchy finger tightened on her dual triggers.

A hairy hand the size of a catcher's mitt drifted out from beyond the doorjamb, reached around the lunatic gunslinger's torso, and wrapped itself around the shotgun. The twin barrels were slowly lifted away from Bertie's abdomen and from the madwoman's grasp. "Now...Sister Brigid! We've discussed this, haven't we? This is no way to greet guests."

The tall, wide, large-bellied form of a priestly man, robed and cinctured like a monk, the fellow whose hand had disarmed Sister Brigid Scumbag's-Bane, emerged from the door's shadows. "Well hey, Dr. Ing!" the priest said cordially. "Welcome to The Cloisters."

"Hello, Alonso," Meebs replied. Then, noting the pained look that flashed across the priest's bearded face, Meebs corrected himself. "That is, Saint Aidan Serpent's-Bane of Iona."

At St. Aidan's invitation, the visitors edged past the now-disarmed and docile form of Saint Brigid, renowned Patroness of Ireland, shed for the present of her cumbersome ecclesiastic robes. *Perhaps in consideration of the desert climate*, Malcolm imagined. *Or maybe an act of contrition.* They entered a large room set up as a refectory, with split timber benches that looked as if they might have been obtained from a Forest Service campground via a deed of midnight pilferage.

Valeria drew Jessica Moonflower aside by her sleeve and mumbled some Russian in her ear. "Excuse me, Mr. Saint Aidan. My friend here wants to know why Saint Brigid isn't wearing any clothes except them cowboy boots," Jessica asked.

St. Aidan glanced toward Brigid Patroness as if surprised to notice her nakedness. "Well…it's just a matter of personal preference, my dear. We try not to be too judgmental here at The Cloisters. Ah…you yourself may feel at liberty to consider clothing optional…and your foreign girlfriend too. The clothes-free option *does* permit a very nice tan!"

"Oh. That's nice, I guess." Jessica's thoughtful expression suggested she was perhaps entertaining the possibility.

St. Aidan showed his visitors to their cells. There were only three visitor's accommodations, side by side off a short hallway, very spare. In each cell there was a low bed fashioned out of a pair of army surplus mattresses on a juniper log and woven rope frame. No bed linens beyond a folded khaki blanket across the foot of the mattresses. A bedside table with a single candle waxed onto a plate. "Two to a room, I'm afraid", St. Aidan advised his guests. "You can work things out as you prefer. Okay then! I imagine you will want to freshen up! Out the back there you will find the Necessarium. One bucket of water each, I'm afraid…we are somewhat limited in terms of our water supply. You may share buckets and wash cooperatively, of course! We will have midday refection at…well, at midday! You will hear the bell!" St. Aidan Serpent's-Bane made his departure.

"I'm not bunking in with any of *you* guys!" Jessica declared. "Neither is Valeria!"

The three guys did the remaining arithmetic within about two seconds. Malcolm pondered the eighty long, hard miles they'd driven since the last motel.

"Hey, before you guys go wash off the sweat, I got something I want to show you!" Jessica Moonflower crowed. "I know none of you think Valeria is good for anything, and you only let her in on the action because otherwise she's blowing the whistle, and me too I guess because the only real use I am is to keep Valeria on a short leash, right? Well, watch this!" She turned to her girlfriend and rattled off a little Russian.

"Okay! One of you choose a planet or something!"

Dooley spoke up first. "Venus!" he said in a pissed-off tone.

"*Venera!*" Jessica translated. Valeria responded with a rapidfire Russian question.

"She says, what time is it?"

"Eleven forty-seven a.m. Mountain Standard Time."

"And, what's our lassitude and lawn-attitude?"

"Latitude and longitude?"

"Yeah I guess."

Dooley dug an Arizona US Geologic Survey map out of his backpack. "Umm...latitude thirty-three point one North...longitude one-one-three point two West."

Valeria chattered some more. "She says, what's the side-something accordionesses of Venus?"

"Sidereal coordinates?"

"Yeah! I guess! So I'm real stupid!" Jessica grumped.

This took a little consultation among the guys. The Amoeba thrashed around in his pack and came up with an iPad. Tapped and fumbled for a while. "Here it is!" he said at last. Valeria grabbed the pad, examined the numbers, then cavalierly tossed the pad back to Meebs. Without a moment's thought, she extended her left hand and pointed off over her shoulder. "*Yest' Veneroy!*" she declared.

The three genius engineers goggled. Dooley pulled a compass out of his backpack and shot an azimuth. Bertie got a pencil and eyeballed the vertical angle of Valeria's pointing finger. The three of them performed a few quick trigonometric calculations on paper and in their heads, examined the crude result, then used Dr. Ing's iPad to check their answer.

"Amazing!" whispered Bert in an awed voice. "She's within seven-tenths of a degree!"

"Oh, bullcrap!" Dooley cried out. "Try her on Jupiter!"

In the next while, Valeria accurately pointed out the positions of Jupiter, Neptune, the moon Callisto, three geosynchronous communications satellites, and the star Beta Pictoris. She could have gone on all afternoon, but a gong stridently ringing in the central Cloisters announced the serving of Midday Refection.

The five of them went to lunch dirty.

DESERT PROVENDER

What awaited in the refectory was not exactly lunch. **Death to Serpents!** didn't *eat* lunch. They ate *a meal*. Just the one. At midday. If there were leftovers, any resident brother or sister was welcome to browse...the doors to the pantry were open to all. There was no refrigeration, so leftovers were a risk perhaps. Leftovers were better eaten promptly than tossed out, where **Serpents!** might make a meal of them.

The five Asteroid Association members, as Jessica had named the outfit, filed into the refectory. The refectory was actually the living room. And the auditorium for large public meetings, which **Death to Serpents!** had never actually held one of, yet. And a dormitory, if it should come to pass that **Death to Serpents!** ever exceeded its current roster of six friars and friaresses (let's call them *members,* shall we?), and one Abbot. So once a day, the multipurpose great-room became the refectory by the addition of a pair of sawhorses and a big sheet of ¾-inch plywood covered with a tablecloth.

St. Aidan was already in attendance, although none of the members yet. It was his week to set the table. He directed the five Associates to places as they came in. Dr. Ing at the left of the big carved chair that was obviously reserved for the Abbot, and Jessica Moonflower on the right. Valeria next, to facilitate translating. Then Bert and Mac.

St. Brigid, still naked except the cowboy boots, but scrubbed clean for refection, ambled in. "Hi, Nonbeliever Scumbags," she mumbled politely as she found her way into a vacant seat next to The Amoeba.

"G'day, Miss Saint Brigid," Meebs mumbled, reddening in embarrassment. He tried with little real success to direct his eyes away from her saucy nipples.

St. Aidan attempted a casual comment to ease the strain. "Actually, we all have...ah...nicknames, I guess you'd say. Heaps less formal that Saint This and Saint That. St. Brigid is familiarly known as *Naked Bree*. When she's not on serpent-killing duty, she's our cleaning wench and scullery maid. She came to us three years ago, severely addicted to methamphetamine, but we have made significant progress. Haven't we, Naked Bree?"

The young woman snarled silently beneath a hooded brow.

"Er...what is *your* informal name?" Bertie had to ask.

"*Venerable*. 'Cause I'm the Abbot, you see?"

"Do you have 'duties' too?"

"Psychological counselor. And, of course, Abbot. Table setter, one day in seven."

Three more Brothers and one Sister trooped in, scootched back chairs, and sat, mumbling generic greetings. It left one chair and one place setting unclaimed.

"Okay..." the Venerable Abbot said. "As long as I'm doing introductions. That fellow there is The Redoubtable Cruithnechán Serpent-Slayer. He's kind of a lunatic, because he's had eight bouts of sunstroke. Or is it nine?"

"Eleven!" the Redoubtable Serpent-Slayer muttered. The Asteroid Associates had not yet seen The Redoubtable, but he had seen *them*! In their van, just after he'd killed a four-foot diamondback out in the desert near the road.

"Eleven! Right! Eleven bouts of sunstroke. We call him *Crewneck*, because...what the hell, who can pronounce that Irish name? He's a full-time serpent slayer. Our very best!"

Venerable pointed out the next brother. "And that's Lay Brother Andrew the Scot, or *Andy-boy* as we call him. Our newest member. Andy's a salaried part-time government employee, and as such is our main source— actually, our *only* source!—of revenue."

"So Andy-boy! Jessica Moonflower joshed. "What do you do for the Gov'mint?"

The boy mumbled something, awed by the enormity of Jessica Moonflower's bosom.

Jessica imagined she'd heard Andy-boy say his job title was 'Fecal Lector' but she couldn't imagine what kind of job that was. Washing out portapotties, maybe?

The other four Asteroid Associates heard 'Fecal Lector' as well. None had the nerve to beg Andy-boy's pardon or ask for clarification.

"Okay then! That brings us to our young Sister there. She ran away from home somewhere far-away when she was fifteen. She won't tell us where, so we took her in. Her therapy is coming along pretty well. At first we called her *Bega the Virgin*. But that was before she discovered her vocation. So now her monastic name is *Bega, Whore of the Desert*. Her duties are assistant cleaning wench and sexual gratification provider. Oh, and her informal name! We just call her *Honey-Bee*! Sometimes, pronounced *Horny-Bee*."

"One more, Venerable." Dr. Ing prompted.

"Oh yes…of course! Every spiritual following eventually has its Martyrs, doesn't it? This young fellow is Martyr-to-be Coirpre Creoumh, known as *Croom*. Poor fellow is suicidal. Can't let him Serpent-Slay on his own, because he's apt to let them give him a good bite. Most of the time, I assign Croom to building maintenance and repairs, so we can spend a little extra time every day on his therapy and otherwise keep an eye on him. And you're going to meet one more member of our little monastic family…our Provisioner and Master Chef! Currently in the

78

kitchen putting on finishing touches. He's Finnián Findloga, who we call *Fin Fin*."

Chef Fin Fin chose that precise moment to make his entry. He was lugging a large whiteboard easel onto which he'd penned the bill of fare for today's midday refection. This is what the whiteboard looked like:

MENU du JOUR

Hors d'oeuvre
>   Sauterelles en croute sans jambes, frites
>   en jus d'agave

Plat Vert
>   Pagales de poire epineux, sautees

Amuse-Bouche
>   Pepins 'Mesquite' avec sel

Entree
>   Rondelles de 'Poule' a Sonnette en sauce
>   au poivre epice

Plats d'Acompagnement
>   Pomme de terre suppleant des racines varies
>   Fleurs de jardin sanspluie

Un Doux
>   Fruite frai de cholla a sauter

Boissons
>   Breuvage extrait de nopale
>   Margarita Pulque mettre en fut

If this looks pretty yummy, it is because it is in *FRENCH*! French can make "shit pie" look delicious. Let's try!

Specialite de la Maison: TARTE de MERDE A LA MODE

What the bill of fare would say if Fin Fin had written it in English, and had been brutally honest, is:

TODAY'S MENU

Appetizer
  Battered Grasshoppers, de-legged, fried
    in Agave juice
Salad
  Pan-Fried Prickly Pear Paddles
Palate Cleanser
  Salted Mesquite-Tree Seeds
Main Dish
  Sliced Rattle-'Chicken' with lots of Pepper
Side Dishes
  Fake Potato from Various Roots
  Desert flower-Blossoms
Drinks
  Nopali Cactus Juice
  Leftover Cactus-liquor Margaritas

"Looks yummy!" Jessica Moonflower enthused. "I'm so hungry I could eat a plate of lizard tails! Let's start with some of those Margaritas and a bunch of fried sauterelles!"

ST. AIDAN OFFERS LEGAL ADVICE

So let me get this straight. There's a huge asteroid hurtling toward the Earth and you want to stake a claim to its *iron content*?"

Obviously, Dr. Ing had not revealed all the Sarpedon-E details. "That's essentially correct, Venerable," he reassured the Abbot.

Detritus from midday refection had been cleared away, and the order's members had gone about their assigned monastic duties. This left the Abbot and his five guests around the table, discussing earnest topics while sipping cactus-juice Margaritas.

"You aren't a little bit concerned about wiping out *all of humanity*?"

The Amoeba made deprecating noises. "It's not *that* big! Besides, there are methods to…ah…control the energy of impact."

"What ways? Parachutes? Retro-rockets?"

"No…no…. Primarily, orientation…and clever use of Earth's rotational velocity. But it should impact with no more than one point one megatons of energy."

"*ONE-POINT-ONE? MEGATONS?* …Okay then, where is this asteroid liable to smash down?"

Dr. Ing gestured vaguely out the open window at an infinite prospect of empty desert. "We were thinking out there."

St. Aidan Serpent's-Bane made choking noises for a while. Then he harrumphed theatrically. "Well here's the legal viewpoint. Except for things like my mining claim here, that's mostly unencumbered Federal land out there. You will have to make application with the Bureau of Land Management for a special-use permit to stage your meteoric impact. Let's call it, 'landing' rather than 'impact.' I'm quite certain it will be something entirely new, so BLM may have to involve Congress in enacting some pertinent legislation."

"Uh…Congress? Won't that take some time?"

"A couple years. Then there's the Environmental Impact Statement. Have you ever written one of those? Or participated in the preparation?"

"No…."

"Three years at least. Six more for review and revision. I can tell you right now that the archeologists alone will resist bitterly—your asteroid is liable to smash a lot of already-broken Anasazi pottery and ancient cliff dwellings. Don't get me started on the wildlife people! And you can anticipate resistance from the Public, once they get wind of your project!"

The Asteroid Association exchanged gloomy glances.

"Well look here, Venerable! What if we just obtain rights for iron ore *on the ground*? Then we go about our business like nothing's happening until, *BLOWWIE!* Out of the blue, a big iron/nickel meteor smacks down, right on our claim. What good luck! But, look at this deed of mineral rights, folks! All that iron belongs—"

"And nickel!" insisted Jessica Moonflower.

"All that iron and nickel legally belongs to us!"

"And…none of us ever heard anything about… ah…*coercing* that asteroid to crash?" the Abbot asked.

"We never!"

"Noooo, no!"

"Not a thing!"

"Mum's the word!"

"*Meloch! Nichego! Pustyak! Gluposti!*"[9]

---

[9] **Nothing! Nil! Trifling! Fiddle-faddle!**

"All right…because, otherwise we'd be guilty of conspiracy to defraud the Government, harming public lands without a permit, arson, mayhem, misuse of Government property, failure to file an Environmental Impact Statement, and a gross act of terrorism."

"*Terrorism*?" Meebs almost shouted, aghast.

"*One-point-one megatons*, Yingwah!"

"Well what are we going to do?"

"Keep our mouths shut tight about the coercion thing. Nobody knows nothing. Let's start the wheels turning to secure a mineral-rights claim. Over the next few months, it would help if you guys look like a bunch of ore prospectors. Or steel-refinery entrepreneurs, or something. Set up offices in Phoenix. Take some Community College courses in metallurgy and geology. Make a few forays out into the desert and pick up some ore samples. You know, iron-ore and…and…"

"NEEKEEL!" Valeria yelled.

"Yeah, nickel. All that activity will give you guys some legitimacy. Meanwhile, I'll ride herd on the BLM to get the permit put through. While we wait, I guess I'll have to contact the current mineral-rights holders. People with specific claims, like my daddy had on this place. We'll need for them to execute sublease agreements to us for their rights to iron. Yeah ladies…and nickel! Shouldn't take too long, considering it's the Federal Government."

"How long?"

"Eighteen months. Two years, tops."

Down the table, Bertie Koslosky was waving his hand in the air like a third-grader who had to pee.

"What's up, Bert?" The Amoeba asked.

"Eighteen month's won't work!"

"Why not?"

"Because, before we left Hartford, I used ProCon's electronic letterhead, you might call it, to send a brief, encoded, halfway-anonymous dispatch to Goldstone Deep-

Space Commo Center, requesting an automated control-signal beamcast on a particular frequency!"

"Come on, Bertie! None of us know what you're talking about!"

"To the Icarus command-module. To schedule the de-orbit!"

Audible gasps from five horrified throats. "Why, Bertie, *why*? Did it work?" Dr. Ing asked apprehensively.

"Why? It didn't seem to me there was any reason to wait. We-all were doing a lot of talking but not much acting, so I just sort of took the initiative. As to whether it worked, I got an automated message from Goldstone about four minutes ago. Don't worry...I had it routed through five consecutive anonymous intermediaries, so no one will trace it to me. Probably." Bertie held up his iPhone. Tiny numbers sprawled across its display. "Three out of three successful device detonations. On-the-money de-orbit. Transition time works out to one hundred eighty-nine days. We don't have eighteen months, let alone two years."

Audible gasps from four sets of vocal cords.

"Er...Bertram, when you say 'detonations'...what exactly do you mean?" This from an ashen-faced Abbot.

"Atomic devices. There are twelve of them welded onto the asteroid in various places. Three of them were detonated at a very precise instant, when the asteroid—which is tumbling around two separate axes of rotation—was exactly aligned. This disrupted its orbit and put it on an intercept trajectory with the planet Earth."

"*A-bombs?* Won't they be able to detect those blasts, and wonder what the hell's going on?"

"*Eti idioti? Nikogda za million let! Oni ne mogli nayti svoi sobstvennyye shary s obeikh ruk, yesli oni svetilis' v temnote i svisteli!*" Valeria scoffed. All eyes turned to Jessica Moonflower.

"She says, 'Those idiots? Never in a million years! They couldn't find their own balls with both hands if they glowed in the dark and whistled!' She means the Russky scientists, I guess."

Bert felt inclined to clarify. "You gotta understand, Abbot! These are a particular kind of nuclear device. There was a lot of experimentation back in the 'fifties. The AEC and the Pentagon wanted to develop *low-yield* atom bombs, that could, like, be fired from artillery pieces or tanks, and go off at ranges of a thousand yards or something, without blowing the tank or artillery crew to smithereens. They used uranium hydride, instead of pure uranium. That damped, or slowed-down, the chain reaction. But instead of just reducing the instantaneous explosive energy, they got only a very small, slowish yield. They called these slow reactions *fizzles*."

"And so...?"

"Well, the asteroid's nuclear devices are *not* Atomic Bombs...they're specialized Atomic Fizzles. Set one off and it emits a directed jet of energy that lasts maybe eight or ten seconds. Like a short-lived, super-thrust rocket. Equal in energy to a half-kiloton nuclear explosion, but actually only a fizzle. This is good, because a low-yield fizzle is not considered a nuclear detonation with respect to either the 1967 Outer Space Treaty or the 1996 Comprehensive Nuclear-Test-Ban Treaty...and anyway a fizzle doesn't produce the same electromagnetic pulse as an A-bomb, so it's not gonna trip any sensors. So we're probably okay setting two or three of them off at a time in order to rocket Sarpedon-E around, without the CIA or the KGB—the *actual* KGB [he glanced disparagingly toward Valeria, who had the decency to blush]—coming after us. Well, after the POS modules bored into the asteroid's surface performing the element assays, the atomic fizzle devices were inserted into the boreholes, about six feet deep. So, when they go off, there's about two tons of vaporized iron/nickel/cobalt ejected in a pretty precise direction at about twelve percent lightspeed, generating half a billion pounds' thrust for a few seconds."

Everyone had a slow, meditative pull on the dregs of their Cactus Margaritas, digesting the implications.

"Venerable..." began Dr. Ing, hoping to salvage ground lost to his imprecision with the facts of Sarpedon-E. "Can we get a mineral-rights claim that specifies iron and nickel...but also includes associated other elements in trace quantities?"

"Like, copper and tin?"

"Yeah. Somewhat like those."

Valeria elbowed Jessica Moonflower. "Casabas..." she whispered, *"Chto, sobstvenno, yavlyayetsya nikel'?"*

"Oni delayut monety iz nego."

"Skol'ko stoit?"

"Pyat' tsentov."

"Pffft! I my sobirayemsya, chtoby poluchit' trista shest'desyat sem' millionov dollarov stoit iz nikh?"[10]

---

[10] **Casabas...what, exactly, is Nickel?**
They make coins out of it.
Worth how much?
Five cents.
Pffft! And we are going to get *three hundred sixty-seven million dollars'* worth of them?

DIVIDE AND CONQUER

There were still six or seven good hours of daylight left. Abbot Aidan suggested the whole bunch of them pack into the rental-van and go pay a visit on The Hermit.

"Who's he?" 'Casabas' Moonflower asked. After refection, she'd slipped down to her cell and changed into something more comfortable: ass-hugger shorts and a bright-orange spandex bandeau top four sizes too small for her bosom. But stretchy. She'd considered going 'Naked Bree' above the waist, but hadn't quite worked up the nerve. Valeria had borrowed a few items of clothing from Jessica, and was more coolly and provocatively attired as well.

The Abbot pointed off toward the northwest, where craggy mountains loomed. "An old codger who lives in a canyon up there. No one seems to know his name. Works a hard-rock mine claim, looking for gold." The Venerable's eyes roamed over the two ladies. "Girls…" he began falteringly, "maybe you'd be more comfortable not coming. I doubt the Hermit has laid eyes on a woman in five years or more, and he's apt to be…uh… *inappropriately forward* to ladies of your particular qualities. How would it be if you rode to the BLM office with Andy-boy and asked for a printout of all current mining claims in, say, a two-hundred-mile radius of Papago?"

"Is there a road, at all?" asked Dooley, changing the subject.

"Sure there's a road! Perfectly adequate road! Sort of a road."

THE GIRLS VISIT THE BLM

A ndy-boy owned a rust-eaten pickup truck, the only operating motor-vehicle in the possession of *Death to Serpents!* This was because his job with the BLM required him to drive forty miles to the BLM office, sign in, don his Fecal Lector uniform, then drive, ironically, a *serpentine* route performing his Fecal Lectoring duties. His route only took about three hours to drive, so he told the girls to take care of their BLM business, then walk a quarter-mile down to the Desert Blossom Café and Pub and make themselves comfortable until he got off work and could collect them for the drive back to the *Death to Serpents!* monastery.

The pickup jounced along the washboard secondary road on its way to the highway. Andy-boy gripped the wheel like a drowning man. This was because Valeria Anjelika had called shotgun, placing Jessica Moonflower jammed into the tranny-hump position with her soft, warm shoulder pressed up against Andy boy. Do the math!

In blessed reprieve from the washboard jolting, the pickup reached the blacktop of Poco Dinero Road. A question which had been eating at Jessica Moonflower since midday refection popped into her seemingly-vacuous head. She turned sideways to face Andy-boy, substituting her left-hand breast for her left-hand shoulder, with respect to contact with Andy-boy's right-hand arm. The poor lad almost took the pickup into the right-hand bar ditch.

"Andy-boy," Jessica crooned, "I'm dyin' to know exactly what's a Fecal Lector do for the BLM. Won't you tell me'n Valeria, please honey?"

Andy-boy swallowed hard. "Uh…okay, it's not that much, Miz Moonflower. I…uh…they…uh…"

"Relax, sweetiekins! We ain't gonna bite!" She gave his right-hand arm a little squeeze, accompanied by a little bosom-pressure which very nearly took them into the left-hand bar ditch.

"Uh…well, they got a canvas bag with a big padlock on it, and a slot. I pick that up at the BLM in Gila Bend. That's where we's agoin' right now. I gotta put on a badge says I'm a certified Fecal Lector so's folks know I'm a Fed'rl Agent, sorta. Then I drive around to them campgrounds. Uh…bein' City Folks, you know what 'campgrounds' is, Miz Moonflower? 'N Miz Valuh…Vuh-leer-uh?"

"We know all about campgrounds, Andykins!" Jessica reassured him. She gave him a little reassuring pat on the thigh, causing him to goose the accelerator radically.

"Yeah…uh…well, BLM's got six campgrounds. Folks needa pay a fee. Twelve bucks a carload, ever night they camp out. I gotta make sure they's only got one car at each camp spot, an' they got their *re*-ceet on display. More'n one car, they's gotta pay a sep'rate fee for each vee-hickle. So I drive all through that campground, checking *re*-ceets. Then I go back up ta the entrance station. There's a big information kee-yox, see? An' there's a boxful of campin' fee env'lopes. I gotta make sure they's plenty a' env'lopes. I got a whole box a' them env'lopes back there in the jockey-box…so's I can fill up the kee-yox dispenser, iffen I need to. They's a slot where they stick the env'lopes, oncet they've stuck their money in an' written their name an' taken their *re*-ceet. I got a special key lets me open up a trapdoor for the *re*-ceet slot. That's when I do it!"

"Do what?"

"Dump'm in my bag! Collect the fees!"

Collect the fees. Fecal Lector. Fee Collector.
Jessica Moonflower might have been something of a
mental lightweight, but she wasn't completely ditzoid. She
opened up two inches of gap between her shoulder and
Andy-boy's, and sat silently with her hands folded in her
lap, all the rest of the way to the Gila Bend BLM.

She thought she might need to have a couple
cleansing, restorative Margaritas later on at the Desert
Blossom Café and Pub. Maybe three or four.

The girls sat in a pair of Guest Chairs with their
bare legs demurely crossed. On the other side of a cluttered
desk was the District Geologist. In front of him was a
stuffed brown Pendaflex folder containing a pile of mining-
claim affidavits. He had tried to explain that records such
as these for operational mining claims on BLM lands
weren't normally made available to members of the general
public who lacked proper credentials. Valeria, speaking
Russian and all, did not comprehend this explanation.
Jessica, not *wanting* to comprehend things contrary to her
wishes, simply allowed the Geologist's words to enter her
left ear and proceed out her right ear. This ability may well
have been the genesis of the belief that Jessica was an
airhead. She twiddled the fingers of her outstretched,
upward-oriented hand in the international hand signal for
'why-don't-you-just-give-me-the-damned-information?'

The District Geologist knew when he was beaten.
"If you'll be kind enough to wait here, Miss…uh…
Moonbosom, I'll make photocopies for you. Oh! Sorry!
Flower! Miss Moon*flower*!"

Jessica and Valeria exchanged smiles of triumph.

Twenty minutes later, they were snugly ensconced
in a corner booth at the Desert Blossom Café and Pub. The
early-evening rush was on in the 'pub' part, and the girls'
bottoms had barely brushed their banquettes before a pair

of complimentary, brimming Margaritas appeared in front of them, courtesy of a winking, gesticulating benefactor who looked like he'd just blown in off the desert unshaven and unbathed from four months of heavy prospecting. Jessica smiled and nodded politely, and acknowledged the yummy Margarita with a little lift of the salt-rimmed glass. She took a tentative sip and dismissed the whiskery benefactor from her thoughts.

"A lot of claims!" observed an amazed Valeria in Russian, pawing through the forms. With her free hand, she dipped half of the Arizona-style Philadelphia Cheese-Steak sandwich she'd ordered into a small bowl of beef stock and took an avid bite.

Jessica was not about to talk business before she'd downed that icy concoction in front of her. *The guys will make sense of it,* she decided. She gestured toward Valeria's untouched Margarita. "Have a sip, Valeria! Or would you rather a nice icy *Stolichnaya*? We oughtta do some serious drinking while the opportunity lasts!"

THE BOYS VISIT THE HERMIT

The rental van jounced over jagged rocks whose size, angularity and viciousness was reminiscent of large, savage, feral Chihuahuas. Dooley's jaw ached from clenching, which helped very little. "How much farther?" He whined, then added, "And tell me again why we've got to visit this hermit guy!"

"He holds a mineral claim. Only a hundred sixty acres, but smack in the middle of sixty thousand square miles of uninhabited desert wilderness. Uninhabited, except for **Serpents!** We want to obtain exclusive rights to surface deposits for the entire sixty thousand square miles."

"Surface rights?"

"Of course! We'll write up the application to include:

'incidental ore and metallic materials, including but not limited to iron (Fe) and nickel (Ni) and their usually-associated trace elements, which may be obtained without hard-rock mining or blasting techniques, that have accumulated within the surface twenty feet of unaggregated soil depth via weathering, solifluction, glaciation, waterborne erosional forces, and miscellaneous Aeolian, atmospheric, condensational, and/or meteoric depositional processes.'

How's that sound?"

"Alonso, you are a cunning and articulate bastard! I see how you slipped those 'trace elements' and that word 'meteoric' in there!"

The Venerable Abbot Alonso-Aidan chuckled with self-satisfaction. "Now all we got to do is get the Hermit to sign off on it. He's got one of the major, producing prior claims, and as far as the BLM is concerned, it will queer the whole deal if he balks. One thing, fellows! Nobody better utter one specific word, or he'll close up like an oyster!"

"What word?" Dooley asked, wincing, just as a particularly fractious road-rock hurled itself at the van's crankcase.

"GOLD!"

At the behest of Saint Aidan's pointing finger, Malcolm swung the van hard aport into what appeared to be a slot canyon. The roadbed, not so hot to begin with, took a turn for the worse.

"This is a *creekbed*!" Mal hollered.

"Nonsense! It's been a road since the days of the covered wagons! It only turns into a creekbed when it rains!"

"How often is that?"

"Never!"

"What...*never*?"

"Well...hardly ever."

Feeling effectively reduced to a bit-part in *HMS Pinafore*, Malcolm clammed up and turned his attention to driving. The jagged rocks weren't so bad, since he'd become used to them during the last twenty hellish miles of what passed for road. But in between rocks, there were patches of sand that bogged the wheels and made them almost spin out. Mal Dooley wondered if anyone had thought to bring a few five-gallon jugs of water in case they got well and truly stuck and had to hike out of here. For that matter, how would he explain a bogged-down rental van abandoned in a remote desert arroyo and in need of towtruck-retrieving to the rental-car folks?

Miraculously, there was a firm set of tire-tracks leading them up and out of the arroyo, over a rise, and into a spacious playa. On the far side, perhaps half a mile distant, the ground rose abruptly into sunbaked mountains of extruded metamorphic stone, jaggedy and foreboding. A small miner's cabin squatted amid the cacti, looking so typically like a miner's cabin it was as if someone had contacted Paramount Studio's property department and ordered-up a miner's cabin.

"That's the place!" the Venerable St. Aidan admitted, with joy and relief in his voice.

Mac was appalled. "You didn't know! You've been just *guessing* where we were supposed to be going!"

"All's well that ends well!" the Venerable observed cheerily. "Gents…you'd better let me do the talking."

The Hermit greeted them by bursting out the door of his cabin brandishing an enormous shotgun. *Déjà vu all over again*, Bertie reflected, as he deftly took up a sheltered position behind The Amoeba. As an afterthought, he peeked around Meebs, and down. *Yep…tooled cowboy boots!* At least they weren't pink, and the old coot had the decency to be wearing clothes.

"Ah…hi there, Old-Timer! Remember me? I'm Aidan! I live down in the valley a mile north of Papago? With a few…ah…therapy patients of mine? Do you suppose we could dispense with the shotgun?"

"These fellers some more of your Crazies, Holy-man?" the Hermit asked.

"No, not at all. Visitors. From…from the City, out East. Geologists!"

That caught the codger's attention. "What's a passel of New-York Perfessers snoopin' around my claim for?"

"Well that's why I brought them up here! This is Dr. Marcellus Ing. And those are his associates: graduate students MacDooley and Koslosky. Gentlemen, this is our local expert in hard-rock mining, Mister...ah...er.... Do you know, Old-Timer, I can't remember your actual name!"

The aged miner grounded the stock of his firearm. He seemed to swell with dignity. "Willard Gouldfarthing Smithson, M.S., at your service. Graduate Mining Engineer, Colorado School of Mines, Class of Nineteen and Fifty-One! When folks ain't calling me *Hermit* or *Old-Timer*, I'm partial to bein' called 'Wig'! And yeah, it's Smithson like James Smithson, Oxford Perfesser and benefactor of the Institution bears his—bears *our* name, out in the District of Columbia. Shirttail relative, back a coupla centuries! He'd been a lineal ancestor, maybe I'da inherited some of them riches!"

The boys murmured noises of collegial greetings.

"Okay, monk-boy! You stay out here in the sunshine. Bring ya a glass a water in a bit. Rest of you *mineralogists*, welcome to my abode! Let's palaver about something *real*...like scratching paydirt out of a tightfisted ol' planet!"

The inside of the stereotypical miner's cabin was a reeking sty...not surprising when you consider the probable habits of a decrepit bachelor hard-rock miner with very little time, energy or water to spare for such niceties as keeping the place clean. There was a rickety table of sorts, burdened with a half-dozen interesting ore samples and a couple haggled-open cans of potted meat, evidently a recent meal but now being squabbled over by about five hundred bluebottle flies. There was a single chair, obviously Wig's perquisite. There was also a bench, conceivably wide enough for two bottoms. And a small wooden keg which had once held a lot of ten-penny box nails but now was essentially empty if you don't count cobwebs and their resident spiders and insect-mummies. Guest seating for three. The boys sorted themselves out.

W. G. Smithson. ejected a pair of heavy-gauge buckshot shells and propped his shotgun beside the door. A considerate host after all, he rustled around in a cupboard and produced a half-empty—or was it half-full?—bottle of cheap whiskey. From another cupboard, two fairly-clean jam jars, a tin can, and a coffee cup. Graciously, he kept the tin can for himself. "Let's have a drink, gentlemen!" the ancient Mining Engineer proposed. "Then you tell me what you'd like to know!"

Room-temperature whiskey which was pretty vile in the first place presented some difficulties getting down. Nevertheless, the Asteroid Associates did their well-mannered best. Dr. Ing felt obligated to take the conversational lead. "Well, Mister Smithson, we—"

"Wig...please!"

"Of course. So, Wig, my colleagues and I specialize in cataloguing of exoplanetary mineral specimens, and—"

"Meteorites. I ain't no tenderfoot, fellers!"

Meebs smiled tolerantly. "So I'm learning! It's a relief...you cannot imagine how difficult it is sometimes, trying to communicate with the geologically ignorant. Well, Wig, we have two concerns you can help us with, if you will."

"Shoot!"

"First of all: we'd like your assistance in locating any meteoric impact remnants you might have encountered in the surrounding topography, like—"

"Like Barrington?"

"Oh goodness no! Something even a tenth the size and a lot more weathered than Meteor Crater up near Winslow would have shown up in air photos or satellite imagery long ago, and would be thoroughly picked over.

Smaller cratering than that...astroblemes of ten meters diameter or less. Or tektites, maybe. Actual bolide fragments, even—I see you are fond of picking up unique specimens, Wig," Meebs said flatteringly. He hefted one of the tabletop rocks to illustrate the point.

"Uh...nope. Nosiree, not the sort of stuff that interests me, gents. I'm a hard-rock man. Spend half my life down in one a them holes I got bored into that mountain up there. When I prospect, I got a nose for one thing only, and that's *gold*! Sorry I can't be of help, fellers. Now...you said *two* concerns."

"Uh...yes. I did. The second one is more a contractual request than a professional one. You see, we are hoping to do extensive field surveys for meteoric residues in these topographies. The Bureau of Land Management insists we obtain a mineral acquisition permit. As part of that process, BLM insists we obtain permission from claimholders of record, such as yourself, to search for specimens on unclaimed lands adjacent to your own, so that—"

"But ifn you stay offa my claim, what diff'rnce do it make?"

"Well Wig...as the BLM Geologist explains it, there are no identifiable boundaries to your claim. Or to any other claims, many of which are unoccupied, unlike yours, and as-yet undeveloped, unlike yours. If we obtain permissions ahead of time, it circumvents the possibility of egregious misunderstandings before the fact, if our field researchers were to accidentally stray onto claim-constrained lands. Does this make sense?"

"Jeez, you college-types sure do like to spin a fruity sentence, Perfesser! Yeah, though. Makes a passel of sense. You got my hand on it!" The old codger thrust out a callused paw.

"W^{o}n$_d$e^{r}f$_u$l, $_w$o^{n}d$_e$r^{f}u$_l$!" Dr. Ing said, his hand being pumped vigorously up and down. "Now, if we can just jot down the fundamentals and get your John Hancock, we'll get out of your hair. A handshake's more than good enough for me...but with the BLM, we're dealing with the Federal Government, and they need signatures."

Wig Smithson, graduate Mining Engineer, got a bit squinty-eyed over the contested confidence. "Errr...what sorta fundamentals?"

"Oh...like, what compensation we might negotiate if we happen to encounter valuable meteoric specimens on land that proves to be within, or even adjacent to, your claim boundaries. And...and enumeration of the types of mineral materials we are seeking. These would include stony meteorites, carbonaceous chondrites, M-type meteorites comprised of iron, nickel, cobalt...and, naturally, their associated trace metals."

"Associated trace metals such as what?"

"Oh...titanium, germanium, cobalt, palladium. That sort of stuff."

"What about...*gold*?"

"Oh, I suppose there could be insignificant traces of precious metals such as that."

"Nope. You gotta exclude the gold. Gold's mine."

"But.... Well, but we wouldn't be able to specifically enumerate *all* the relevant trace metals, Wig! We would have to—"

"No deal. Any meteor's got gold in it falls on my claim, it's mine! Tell you a little something, fellers. There's a whole lot more of that nasty-ass desert land under claim out there than you might suspect. *All* of 'em is gold claims! They ain't bein' actively worked on a day-to-day basis, necessar'ly, nur lived-on, but there's a passel a old coots just like me, or maybe even a gooddeal more cussed rattlesnake-mean, and none a them's gonna see things any different'n me. Not a one of those claimholders is apt to budge an inch on his right to every speck a gold on his claim! Sue you seven ways from Sunday, he expects you've flimflammed him on the subject of gold. All the way to the Supreme Court! All the rest of it's fine with any prospector...happy to cooperate with geological science 'n research. Just...not the gold!"

The disconsolate Asteroid Association trio made as gracious a retreat as they were able, after making weak promises to Wig to see if the BLM would go with watered-down permit specifications. They collected the Venerable Abbot. "What did you find out?" he begged them.

"Tell you in the van," Meebs muttered from the side of his mouth. The three ersatz Meteorite Geologists forced smiles onto their faces and waved farewell to Wig the Hermit.

"Man oh man, Meebs!" Bertie whispered as they walked toward the van. "That was some performance back there in that cabin! *Bolides! Carbonaceous chondrites!* Where'd you come up with that stuff?" Bertie was sincerely impressed.

"I've been doing my homework," The Amoeba admitted sulkily.

As the van skittered and bumped down the arroyo, The Amoeba outlined the old codger's intransigent position regarding certain trace-minerals. To-date, nothing had been said to his friend Alonso, or to any other member of **Death to Serpents!** on the subject of gold, and Meebs thought it might be prudent to keep it that way.

"Well, *shit!*" their disbarred attorney the Venerable St. Aidan opined. "That's going to make the whole 'permit' thing very damned complicated!"

The four of them rode down out of the mountains in dejected silence as the late-afternoon sun settled redly toward the Arizona desert landscape.

NIGHTY-NIGHT

Valeria and Jessica Moonflower had arrived back at the **Death to Serpents!** compound just as evening settled over the land. They waved Andy-boy off to the member's dormitory-cells and he dutifully plodded off to bed. Truth to tell, the two ladies were still unforgivably tipsy on the Desert Blossom Café and Pub's highly potent Margaritas.

"Let's see if there's any of them sauterelles left to snack on!" Jessica giggled in slurred Russian.

"Jessie! That is not food! It's *bugs!*" Still feeling light-headed on strong drink, Valeria had an amusing flight of surrealistic fantasy focused on biting the heads off living, chirping, squirming grasshoppers.

"Don't care! They're pretty tasty!"

"And anyway…aren't you still stuffed with cheese and jalapeño nachos? And Coahuila Caliente Chicken Wings? I sure am!"

"Okay, okay. …Aw hell, Val! Maybe just a few fried crickets? Then let's go out to that there Necessarium, collect our buckets of water and have us a bath in the moonlight! I'll wash your back if you wash mine!"

Valeria, who'd felt like the sweat dripping down her back for the last few hours was eroding arroyos in the layer of dust aggregated on her skin, agreed enthusiastically.

The girls, giggling like a pair of brownie-scouts on a midnight summer-camp cookshack raid, minced barefoot across the cloister toward the Necessarium wearing nothing but inadequately-sized bath towels. They rounded the partition. There, as promised, were five buckets of Guest Water, lined up on a wooden bench standing on the duckboard bathing-floor. Five somewhat small buckets.

Each only about two-thirds full. On the adobe wall behind the bench was this admonitory inscription:

WATER is Precious
to All GODLY Purposes

First cometh: *The preparation of food and drink*
Next cometh: *The cleansing of our bodies*
Next cometh: *The cleansing of dishes*
Next cometh: *The cleansing of garments*
Next cometh: *The cleansing of floors and lavatories*
Last cometh: *Water for birds and amiable rodents*

Spare not a drop for
SERPENTS!

"Huh!" observed Jessica Moonflower. "Wonder where the brushing of our damn *teeth* cometh in!"

When, half an hour later, the boys dragged their hot, weary asses back into the compound in the starlit dark of the evening and bailed out of the rental van, there was a cacophony of unladylike screaming coming from the Necessarium. Curiosity proved more compelling than good manners, and the three of them quick-stepped across the cloister toward the Necessarium, then peered around the adobe partition to see what was up. There in the moonlight were Valeria and Jessica Moonflower, stark naked, profligately flinging dippersful of water and snapping one another with wet, rolled-up towels, shrieking with laughter.

"Well you boys wanta cleanse your bodies, better strip down and get on in here quick!" screeched Jessica, her gleaming, water-dripping boobies bouncing adorably in the moonlight. "There's only just enough water left for two or three *amiable rodents!*"

An hour deeper into the night. Valeria and Jessica, lay awake, sharing their austere bed, snuggling together for warmth, shivering themselves dry and whispering. Valeria lay on her side, curled up fetally, with Jessie spooned close behind.

The Russian girl smiled with contentment in the dim light of the cell. "I am so happy, Friend Jessica!"

"Why's that, *Kukla?*"

"I am in America. Arizona! Cowboy and Indian Country! We had wonderful day, had BLM bigshot eat out of hand regarding permits. We eat *ochen' vkusnyy*[11] Pfeellee cheesy pepper beefs and hot-hot-hot Mexican bean-food! We drink delicious Mexican lime drink... better than iced vodka! Valeria's head spin like...like our Earth-crosser neekeel asteroid! Around two separate axises at same time! We go crazy in Necessarium with *all* our water...our late-arrival boys only get a little splashed! Now, I nice and warm, with Best Friend Ever having her arms around me and big sexy *sis'ki* snuggling in my back! This best day ever, in Valeria's life!"

"You think Dooley and Bertie are having as nice a time snuggling in the next cell over?" Jessica giggled.

"Mmmm...it's just sad, thinking of them. And Doctor Amoeba all by himself!"

Jessica Moonflower pulled away and sat up. "Hey *sestra*, that gives me a big idea!"

---

[11] Very delicious

"Big…" whispered Val, cupping a hand under one of Jess's spectacular breasts. "Dear Friend…if only my little bumps were one-half so splendid and *bol'shoi*."

"Well maybe we can fix that! You gotta tell me, *Prelestniy*…are you getting very much *snocheneya* these days? Much fek-fek?"

Valeria blushed in the moonlight. "Uhhh…not too much."

"*How* much?"

"Not much at all."

"*Any?*"

Valeria covered her eyes with her hand and shook her head.

"*Bozhe moi, Sladkiy Pirog*[12]…do you mean…are you *devstvennitsa*?"

Valeria made five or six short little nods behind her hand, like a Russian woodpecker. "*Da!*" she answered in a small squeaky voice. "Virgin!"

"Well hey, Angel! All you gotta do is give those little sweeties some *nourishment*! Pump them up with estrogen! You gotta turn your endocrine system loose on this little shortcoming, and those girls are gonna come alive!"

"Do you think?"

"Why, lookit me! How you think I grew this yummy pair of casabas? Plus! You get to have a full-up sexy blast! Every night if you want! *Twice* a night! Five or six weeks, you'll be size thirty-four C! Three months, Sugar, you're gonna have a hard time standing up!" Jessica Moonflower bounced up and down on the miserable army-surplus mattresses, her thumbs softly stroking her friend's petite bosom. "Okay, now all you gotta do is choose."

"Choose?"

---

[12] **My God, Sweetie-Pie!**

"Yeah, choose! You got two of them right next door…another one just along the hall. I was you, I'd start with Bertie!"

"*Start* with?"

"Well you gotta get one of them to say I-do with you, so you can stay in the USA! They promised! Articles of Partnership! *Lyubovnika*, you might's well take *all* the candidates for a test-drive! Now, choose!"

"Well…I like Bertie. He's…he's *kulturny.*[13]"

"Yeah…and he's pretty cute! Bet he's hung like a stallion. Little secret: *all* the quiet, brainy ones are!"

"But I don't know how to—"

"Don't worry! You come with me! *Tetushka*[14] Jessica'll take care of everything." Jessica Moonflower leapt out of bed, wiggled into a silky camisole, and stretched out her hand to Valeria.

"But…what if none of the boys like me? No one makes me his bride, Immigration will ship me back to Chelyabinsk. KGB arrests me, I get no neekeel, I get no nice warm Arizona sunshine anymore, only nasty sloppy Siberia slush snow for the rest of my miserable life!"

"No way, *lubimaya devushka*! If all three of them are so stupid, *I'll* marry you!"

"You would do that? It is *legal*?"

"It's not even squawked-about anymore in Connecticut! Legal in all fifty states. Thank you, Supreme Court!"

"But…. Jessie, you aren't *lesbian*, are you?"

"Um, not particularly, but get those hooters grown-up a little and we might hafta re-evaluate! No, it doesn't matter anyway! There's *no test*! You don't hafta produce a doctor's certificate! But honey, I like people with penises an awful lot! And I'll bet you will, too, once you make the

---

[13] **Cultured, polite**
[14] **Auntie**

acquaintance! Last resort: you'n me, big Lez wedding in
Hartford! Then we'll buy a big house on Narragansett
Bay—"

"Pay for it with NEEKEELs!"

"Yeah! Have our own private swimming-pool,
filled with—"

"NEEKEELs!"

"And all those sorry SOBs are gonna have to come
around beggin' to play with the two of us! But right now,
Sugar Pie, let's you and me go see if Bertie's still awake!"

Valeria had a sudden thought. "But what about the
Doodley?"

"Honey, you let Auntie Jessie and the Casaba Twins
worry about him!"

The girls peered sneakily around the hanging piece
of blanket, which is what served for doors to the guest
cells. Malcolm and Bertie had pushed a fold of their
skimpy bed-blanket down into the crack between their two
single mattresses. This afforded each of them privacy in
exactly half the bed, and a little less than half of an
inadequate blanket apiece. To further promote isolation,
the two of them had their heads faced in separate
directions. The arrangement was sufficiently awkward and
uncomfortable that neither of them was sleeping.

"Oh, boyzzzz!" Jessica murmured in silky tones.

Both the guys sprang up like tripped mousetraps.

"About the bedroom assignments: we got a better
idea!"

Malcolm was suspicious. They probably wanted
him and Bertie to go sleep in the van, so the girls could
have a whole bed apiece. On two seconds' reflection, that
plan didn't seem so bad!

"Valeria's lonely. And, she's scared of spiders!
And she's cold. She needs one of you nice big strong brave
men to give her some protective cuddling or she can't get

106

any sleep at all. Bertie, you got the job. Hop up, *Chelovek,*[15] and take her with you."

"Uhhhh...where are *you* going to sleep, Miss Moonflower?" Mac asked.

"Let's pull that tucked-in blanket up outa the mattress crack so we can share it, and I'll show you, Honey! *Spokoynoy nochi,* Valeria!"

"Nighty-night, Jessie!" Giggling, Valeria took Bertie by the hand and tugged on him to get his feet moving. By the time the two of them made it back to what had been the Lady Guests' Shared Cell, a peculiar noise was emanating from what had until a minute or two ago been the Men Guests' Shared Cell:

SQUEEka-SQUEEka-SQUEEka....

Bert's mind whirled! Valeria whisked off her camisole and pointed Bert in the direction of the bed. "You get een!" she directed. "Beertie, you-me make sweet fek-fek, *da?*"

"Um, er...Miss Valeria, I'm not very, uh—"

"You *nicogda*...uh...niveer do thees weeth Roosian geerl before?"

"Uh-*uh!*" Bert conceded, rather hastily.

"Weeth *any* geerl?"

"Er...nope!"

"Weeth *boy?* Weeth *goat?*"

"*Valeria!*"

"Niveer mind, Beertie! We learn togetheer!"

In a remarkably short time, another peculiar noise emanated from their cell as well, singing a sweet duet with Malcolm's and Jessica Moonflower's little loose-bedjoint serenade:

---

[15] **Man, guy, fellow**

SquaDEEka-squaDEEka-squaDEEka....

Dr. Ing was deeply asleep in the third Guest Cell. In his slumber he dreamed a strange dream. Dressed only in white cotton boxer shorts and a ten-gallon Stetson, he, Marcellus Ing, rode a handsome pinto mare with flowing mane across a burning desert landscape. The saddle's fine tooled-cowhide leather creaked—SQUEEka, squaDEEka—with the horse's gait. Suddenly a band of warpainted Apaches sprung from behind boulders. Arrows filled the air! From out of a distant canyon, the sound of bugles as the United States Cavalry rode to the rescue! Too late! Arrows protruding like porcupine quills, Cowboy Ing had been laid low. Troopers hoisted his inert frame into a slivery buckboard, and for good measure tossed in the still-warm, naked corpse of a slaughtered savage. The buckboard set off toward an unknown destination where medical attention awaited the grievously-wounded cowpoke. In the rocking, squeaking wagon, Meebs felt the Apache's body gently moving against him...but he was paralyzed, too wounded to separate himself. After a while, it seemed that contact with the corpse was...not unpleasant. Except, that is, for a couple of heavy objects which banged against his shins. Cowboy Meebs strained to glance downward. The cadaver wore a pair of hand-tooled pink leather cowboy boots.

"*What?*" Cowboy Ing cries out. Is he still dreaming or is he awake?

"Shut up, Disbeliever Scumbag!" Naked Bree says, not unkindly, and soon a third voice joins the gentle midnight chorus:

SqueedleEEka-squeedleEEka-squeedleEEka....

VALERIA'S BIG IDEA

Valeria was up with the dawn. She seemed to be dancing in the cool morning air, slippered, out in the middle of the tile-paved cloister, slowly spinning on light feet like a fairy ballerina. A bright beam of the orange rising sun shone through a high clerestory, illuminating the center of the small courtyard like a spotlight. Valeria stood in its radiance, holding her left hand loosely, close to her body. But her right hand, with its index finger extended, made graceful sweeps across the pale morning sky, one side to the other, then back again.

Those who were coming to know her understood this was *not* dance...unless one were of sufficient poetic nature as to term the ponderous, ancient, celestial sarabande of the planets and stars to be dance as well.

Suddenly, she stopped in frustration. She turned on her heel, preparing to stalk off in search of Bertie. But he was no farther away than the colonnade, half-hidden in the shadow, an audience of one. In secret and silence he had followed to watch her dance since shortly after she'd risen and left their blissful bedchamber.

"Valeria," Bert called softly.

"Beertie! I...I come joost now, feend you!"

"I thought maybe you might be. What is it, Val?"

Her brow creased. "Hokay. Look thees. Lagrange Five is theere...the Sarpedon stairt theere." She strode back to the cloister's exact center, took a ballerina's First Position, closed her eyes a moment...then gracefully rose on her toes *en pointe*, turned to her left about forty degrees, brought her right hand up in an elegant gesture, and pointed precisely off into the morning sky at the Lagrangian Five zone, abode of the Trojans.

"*Khorosho.* Then, Beertie, yetzsterday you geeve me coordeeneetsy's wheere the Sarpedon gets retro boostings, *da*?"

"*Da*...I mean, yes."

Again the supple ballet movements, this time ending in a gesture toward a different direction. "Thet ees pless for slowdoown boostings. Now look thees, Beertie. The Sarpedon traveel...uh...uh...*simmetrichnyy* orbeet arc, *da*? Soory! Stupidnika me...cannot remember Eengleesh word and no Jessica to heelp!"

"Symmetrical?"

"*Da*! Seeymmeetreecal! So look thees, Beertie!" This time, Valeria's dance was a sweep of three moves: starting at L5...then the perigee retrofire...then destination. She pirouetted to repeat the graceful sweep four times.

She isn't doing the calculus! Bertie mused. *She's like a human orrery...a medieval clockwork celestial mechanism that just knows where things are, in her very nature. And she dances her comprehension! I am in the favored presence of thoroughly unique genius! Beautiful...so beautiful!*

"Do you see, Beertie? Do you see?"

"Well...it's going to wind up parked, or more-or-less parked, at Lagrange Two. Except! We plan to give Sarpedon one more little bump and it comes down out of the sky. *Splat!*"

"Joost afteer the Sarpedon she do heer last Eerth-Crossing!"

Bertie goggled! She was right, of course! Bottom-to-top earth crossing of Earth's orbital path! Why hadn't he seen that little orbital nuance? "You're right, Sweetie! Is that what—"

"Beertie...iss *bol'shoi* problem! You do retrofeer at last meenoot, KGB see! CIA see! Is *ATOMNOYE*! Atomeeck! We geet in big troobool! Also, the Sarpedon cannot *splett* eento Areezoona! Mooch more Nyorth, *tozhe* Weest! Most leekleey, Pisseefeek Otsyan!"

"But—!"

"But no woorries, sweet *lyubovnik* Beertie! Veery small change, where you do retro boostings, we smeck down the Sarpedon in mooch betteer place!"

"Where?"

"I show you! Stend heere!" She moved Bertie by the shoulders until he was centered in the sunbeam. "You are Eerth! You turn sloowlye, like *bol'shoye* blue pleneet! *Nyet...Nyetu*!! Ootheer way!"

Bertie slowly began to pivot counterclockwise.

"*Da, da*! Now...I be Sarpeedon!" Valeria backed off, rose on the points of her toes and held the flat of her hand out. She danced toward the slowly-rotating Bertie making 'shhhh' noises like their asteroid swooshing through outer space. She approached Bertie on his sunlit side and splatted her hand into his belly. "**Pfssshht!**" she cried loudly, grinning.

"Theere!" Valeria beamed. "You see? The Sarpeedon splet down een the Areezoona, or eef oonlooky een Otsyan, een bright dayleet! Eerth rotating thees way, Sarpeedon going thet way! Double speed...*big* splett!"

"Uh-huh. So—"

"*Nye khorosho*![16] Thees path mooch betteer! You turn ageen like Eerth!"

Again her celestial dance, this time starting with a finger extended to L5, then to an ever-so-slightly altered perigee retrofire point, then...

Again Valeria went 'shhhh' with her palm outstretched, and closed in on Bertie. But this time, instead of slapping him on his sunlit side, she passed *behind* him , into the shadow, moving her hand closer and closer to his turning body. "Afreeca! Sarpeedon cross Eerth Oorbeet,

[16] Not good!

inseed to outseed! Grebbed by Eerth grevitiye!" she murmured. "Heer…Oostreelya!" The path of Valeria's ballet took her curling around Bertie, who was still slowly revolving. " Now, *bol'shoye* Pisseefeek Otsyan! Sarpeedon eenteer atmosphere, cross Eerth Oorbeet sooth to noorth!" She started swooshing again, and slowly lifting her palm up Bertie's frame. "Heer Sarpeedon he flee's ooveer the Alyeska! Coorves, end stairts sooth a leetle. Now…now…" Bertie, facing into the sunbeam, felt her gently slap her palm into the middle of his back on his shady side. "*Poosh*!" Valeria said, very softly.

"Meedle of neeght! Eerth rotating *thet* way, Sarpeedon going *thet* way also! Sarpeedon smeck into Eerth…only *nye* so heerd! And in deark! You chenge retrofeer pless, *da*? "

So simple! If you hook around the globe's *dark side*, you reduce the net velocity of impact by two thousand miles per hour! "Honey, can you tell me where that impact point is?"

"Thet pless ees best pairt! You geet mep, I show!"

"Okay. Ummm…Malcolm has one! He's got a pretty comprehensive atlas! Two pages in the middle, showing all of North America."

"Ees the Mal Doodley steel slipping weeth the Jessica, *da*?"

"Yeah…I guess."

Valeria smiled sweetly. "You-me go back into the bed, meck hot lovey unteel they weck up? *Da*, Beertie?"

"*Da…ochen' khorosho!*"[17] Bertie answered in bemusement at himself. That pillow-talk thing was no myth!

Death to Serpents!, under Abbot Aidan's relaxed guidance, observed a very loose rendition of the Liturgy of

---

[17] **Okay! Very good!**

the Hours. Usually, a bit of plainchant at Matins, just to loosen up the old lungs in anticipation of another day's holy labors, then a prayer or two at Midday Refection. Some thumping-good hymns from the Protestant camp before bedtime, mainly because they were in English instead of Latin or Greek, everyone knew the words, and The Redoubtable Serpent-Slayer liked to play guitar.

All the membership except Naked Bree were lined up in the cloister square, ready to go. This morning they were running late. The Venerable Aidan paced worriedly. "Aren't they up yet? Lay Brother Andy-boy, go have another look, will you please?" St. Aidan resumed pacing while the young fecal lector dashed off to the visitor cells.

"Nope! Still snorin' away, all six of 'em!" Andy-boy reported.

"Well okay...we can't wait forever. Let's just all do the *Kyrie* and see if that gets them stirring."

"Maybe with guitar? With the amp plugged in, this time?" Croom the Serpent-Slayer suggested.

"I could go fetch muh drum-set!" Andy-boy volunteered.

Abbot Aidan smiled irreverently. Rock-out plainchant! Why not? "Sounds good to me! Let's do it!"

An avalanche of sacerdotal hymn, instrumentally accompanied, washed over the sleeping Asteroid Association plus Naked Bree, blasting them awake. From the Cloisters, the ancient Greek chant sounded in caterwauling voices:

Kyrie eleison
Christe eleison
Eleison, eleison
Ach moro eleison
Eleison amartoli
O bampas sas oh [18]

The singing finished up with a hand-clap doo-wah chorus, a lot of chord vamping and staccato on guitar, and two minutes of drum solo.

Dr. Ing wandered out, itching his frowzy scalp, just as the sect members finished up, Naked Bree trailing behind him and looking a trifle unnatural wearing Dr. Ing's dirty shirt from the day before. "Good morning, all!" Meebs greeted the congregation

"Well, glad to see you survived the night, Marcellus!" St. Aidan said in cheerful tones, only carrying a hint of subtext. "I've had the Whore of the Desert put out the water ration a bit early today. It appears your female contingent did a quite thorough job laundering themselves last night...perhaps the gentlemen might want to have a wash *first* today. Fair being fair, and all! We've an

---

[18] **Lord have mercy**
Christ have mercy
Mercy, mercy
Baby, have mercy
Mercy on your
Wicked daddy oh

especially-festive offering from Fin Fin at midday refection!"

A muzzy-eyed Jessica Moonflower appeared, clad in a wrinkled silk camisole. "Don't you worry about us, Aidan-Sugar!" she sang merrily. "We all six gonna have a nice group washin', so that water's gonna get used 'n reused 'til it don't know which way is up!"

"Oh…uh…er…."

"And we ain't leaving a single drop for no *Serpents!* "

After cleansing and ablutions, turned out in their alternate unsoiled set of clothes, the Asteroid Gang assembled in the Refectory for a little private discussion. It was still a good while until Midday Refection, so they pushed a bunch of chairs off into a corner for their confab, and let Fin Fin and St. Aidan prepare the table. Naked Bree snarled at her Abbot when he directed that she might wish to take up her scullery maid duties, *vis a vis* the mountain of pots piling up in the scullery. She'd spent the morning so far clutching The Amoeba's arm, evidently having decided to terminate her therapy and switch alliances. As an indicator of indecision about the 'naked' thing, she seemed content to retain Meebs's shirt, but was disinclined to button it up higher than her navel.

Fin Fin struggled out from the kitchen with the day's *menu du jour* whiteboard. Here is what it looked like:

MENU du JOUR

<u>Hors d'oeuvre</u>
>   Petits oeuf rotis de tortue de desert

<u>Plat Vert</u>
>   Saule fanee laisse avec du beurre de
>   chevre sauvage

<u>Entree</u>
>   Entrecotes cheval quart grille sur charbon
>   de bois Mesquite –puisque vous qui
>   sont philistins insistez, en Anglais:
>   Grilled Porter-house steaks

<u>Plats d'Accompagnement</u>
>   Pommes de Terre Frites "Magiques de la
>   Cuisine" a Gauche au-Dessus de Hier
>   Gousses a Partir d'un Arbre Inconnu que
>   le Chef a Trouvee par le Arroyo,
>   Bouilli

<u>un Doux</u>
>   Miel avec des Sacres Fourmis sur les Petits
>   Biscuits Graham

<u>Boissons</u>
>   Breuvage Extrait de Saguare
>   Margarita Pulque Mettre en Fut, car ils ont
>   ete un Tel Success Hier

"Wow!" Jessica Moonflower goggled. "That's even better than yesterday! Look at that entrée! Hey Mackie, what's all that mean, Honey?"

Malcomb squinted at the French. He did not particularly speak French. "Blah blah blah in French...then there's a little bit in English—says...

Grilled ♫ ⚿rter-ho♈ьse Steaks

"That's what I thought...Porter House Steaks! Grilled! Wow, I jus' *love* a good Porter House! Medium rare, all juicy 'n crisscross grillmarked, with a little strip of fat around the edge...nice big tenderloin side to it! Maybe some mushroom slices fried in butter, piled on top? Hope they got a big bottle of A-1!"

Bertie sniffed. "What're those weird letters?"

Andy-boy had just bustled into the room on his way to the kitchen carrying a couple of hefty buckets of slightly pre-used water intended for the cleansing of dishes. "Oh no, Miz Jessica...them ain't Porter House Steaks a-tall!"

"Oh yeah, Sugar? Then what are they?"

"Wull...there's this dude ranch has a permit to op'rate on the BLM. Once a month, I gotta c'lect fees from them guys, dependin' on how many head a livestock they got grazin' on the home spread, 'n how many dudes they taken up into the BLM wild'ness. Wull anyways, couple days ago, one a them dudes who don't know no more 'bout ridin' a horse than he do 'bout drivin' a submarine, goes 'n lets his mount stick its off foreleg down a prairie-dog burra, 'n the pore critter—nice ropin' horse too, he'n his rider took second place at th' State Fair last summer—wull, pore critter snaps his cannonbone!"

"Uh-huh?"

"Er…uh-huh *what*, Miz Moonbr—Moonflowers?"

"Uh-huh so what happened to the poor horse?"

"Oooohhhh! Wull…they hadda shoot it."

"And what's that got to do with Porter House Steaks?

"Oh yeah! Sorry there, Miz Jessie…sorta forgot why I was tellin' the story! Point is, they *ain't* Porter House Steaks. They's *Quarter Horse* steaks. Wull, its been real nice jawin' with yuh, Miz Jessica. I gotta get these buckets a water into the kitchen b'fore they evap'rate! Bye!"

Here's what the entire menu would have looked like, if Fin Fin had had the decency and brazen honesty to write it out in English:

Today's Menu

Appetizer:
> Small roasted eggs of desert tortoises

Salad:
> Wilted willow leaves with wild goat butter

Palate Cleanser:
> Oven-baked bitter desert squash seeds, with
> pepper

Main Course:
> ♌♎rter-ho♊se steaks grilled over Mesquite
> charcoal

Side Dishes:
> Fried "kitchen mystery" potatoes left over
> from yesterday
> Pods from an unknown species of tree the chef
> found down by the arroyo, boiled

Dessert:
> Honey the damned ants got into, drizzled on
> Graham crackers

Beverages:
> Saguaro Cactus juice
> Cactus-liquor Margaritas, since they were such
> a big success yesterday

Notice that there does not appear to be *any* degree of honesty which would move Fin Fin to reveal in English the true identity of those *entrecôtes grillées.*

"Mal, Sweetie..." Jessica Moonflower cajoled. "Honey-pie, you s'pose we could all pile in the van 'n go have lunch at the Desert Blossom Café 'n Pub?"

Assent was instant and universal:

"Yeah, let's do *that!*"

"Good idea!"

"Let's pack up and go!"

"*Da! Pravilnye!*"[19]

Seven minutes later, almost the entire Asteroid Association, plus Naked Bree, were clustered around the van, all packed to go, waiting for Malcolm and the van-keys. He was being slow, throwing up in the Necess-arium...something about Andy-boy's revelation concerning the steaks had hit him wrong. Over by the snake-carven wooden front door to the *Death to Serpents!* retreat, Dr. Ing pumped The Venerable St. Aidan's hand with gratitude and farewell, then turned away to rejoin the rest of his team. Relieved that her catch was returning to her grasp, Naked Bree crowded in close to Dr. Ing. She was toting a burlap grain-sack full of her meager belongings. In her other hand, her fearsome two-barrel shotgun.

"Ah...perhaps we'd better leave this behind, Miss Bree," Dr. Ing opined. After a brief struggle, he succeeded in disarming her. He walked the firearm back over to the Abbot.

"I believe this belongs to you?" Meebs said, extending the gun.

"Yes...I suppose it does. And you'd better take these. St. Brigid Patroness's Driver's License...State of New York, expired. And also her medical and treatment records, such as they are."

---

[19] **You bet! Truly!**

"Thank you, Alonso. I'll be in touch!"

The rental van fired right up, and the six of them headed out the rock-studded lane, bidding farewell to the **Death to Serpents!** abbey and cloisters.

Incidentally, a *genuine* Frenchman would never have scrupled at refecting on grilled Quarter Horse steaks....

SYMPOSIUM AT THE DESERT FLOWER CAFÉ AND PUB

S o forty-five minutes later the six of them had secured a nice corner table in the air-conditioned shady-side room of the Desert Flower Café and Pub. The first pitcher of Margaritas—blended, with salted goblet rims— had been poured out and largely swilled down in sustained, nonstop gulps. The next pitcher—rocks, non-salted rims— was on order with the pub's barman. The Desert Flower management remembered Valeria and Jessica Moonflower from the previous evening, in light of the ladies' infectious Yee-Haw Southwestern high spirits and generous tipping, and the waitstaff was under orders to treat the Asteroid Association with special munificence. A huge platter of nachos—*meat* nachos...certified ***cow meat*** nachos—was even now wending its way on a waitress's shoulder toward their table, and an order of six *Enchiladas de Pollo Especial con Guacamole* along with twelve *Chile Rellenos Acapulco* had just been liberally topped with cheese shreds and red sauce, and slipped into the mesquite-fired blast furnace back in *la cocina. ¡Muy delicioso, pero un poco de mas o menos engorde!*

Naked Bree had been persuaded to button up Dr. Ing's shirt. At present, she was intensely busy with a basket of tortilla chips and a bowl of blazing-hot salsa, evidently her favorite food, not a speck of which she'd seen for more than three years. Hot sauce adorned her face like garish clown-makeup. She hadn't addressed the matter of intimate wear, and a flit of breeze from the air conditioning briefly revealed this shortcoming to Jessica Moonflower across the table. Our girl Jessie slipped out of the windowside banquette and came around to the chair Naked

Bree had shoved up next to Dr. Ing's. She crouched down so she could share confidences with Bree. "Honey, you gotta wear some kinda undies in a classy café like this," Jessie whispered.

"Ain't got any!"

"Well I better loan ya some of mine. Hey Dooley, lemme have the rental van keys."

She was back in a few minutes. "Here, Babydoll. They's more-or-less clean!" She handed Naked Bree a wadded-up pair of hot-pink silk drawers. Unselfconsciously, Bree hoisted up her shirt tail, stuck her cowboy-booted feet one at a time through the leg holes in the undies, and pulled them on up.

"Why, that wasn't so hard, was it, Sweetheart!" Jessica declared proudly.

"No'm."

"Guess we gotta call you 'Dressed Bree' from now on."

"Just 'Bree'…if that's okay."

"Just-Bree then."

"C'n I have some more these chips?"

"Sure, Honey! Anything you like." Jessica winked. "And after lunch, me'n Valeria're gonna take you clothes shopping. With Dr. Ing's credit card!"

Ting-ting-ting-ting-ting! The Amoeba tapped on his empty Margarita glass with his fork. Misinterpreting this maneuver, Just-Bree picked up the hefty Margarita pitcher and poured him another. Meebs addressed the assembly. "Well, ladies and gentlemen, we must have a brief symposium. I note with amusement that the word 'symposium' was coined in ancient Greece, and means something like 'Let us all get together naked and drink a lot while listening to music, and then have a little philosophic conversation.' So—"

"Not sure about the 'naked' part, Meebs!" Bertie volunteered.

"Anyway…we've had the 'drink' part, and the jukebox is handling the 'music' part. So it's time we move on to the 'philosophic' part. Stars, planets and celestial bodies are pretty philosophic. So let's talk about Sarpedon! Valeria, can you give us an update on Sarpedon-E's position and trajectory?"

Valeria stood, then backed up a bit so she could be seen by everyone. She assumed First Position and closed her eyes for a moment.

"Thees Lagrange Five…" she pointed.

"Heer Sarpeedon…" pointed again.

"Eend heer, reetro-feere…" she winked at Bertie to confide that it was their *revised* retro-fire location to which she pointed.

"Eend heer, Sarpeedon smeck into Eerth!" A broad, sweeping gesture far northward, seeming to extend from one horizon to another, with a fillip of her hand at the end to represent her coming-up-the-darkside maneuver.

"Wait!" Malcolm interjected. "I thought we were bringing it down out there in the desert!" He waved vaguely southward.

Meebs took this question. "Two considerations suggest a change in plans, Mal. First, if you consider what we ran into yesterday, both out at that miner's digs and also the girls' findings at the BLM, we gotta admit that the Arizona wilderness is a lot fuller of miners and mining claims that we ever imagined. Second is that we are going to need a very large piece of completely uninhabited real estate to aim Sarpedon-E at, because we need to allow for unforeseen variables and inaccuracies. So we—"

"Bigger than the *Arizona desert*?"

"Bigger. Completely uninhabited, more-or-less."

"*Is* there any place like that? You aren't thinking Antarctica or the Greenland Icecap, are you?"

"No, Mal...but that isn't a bad idea...except for Antarctica being extraordinarily inaccessible. Greenland too, for that matter. Let me tell you what Valeria came up with this morning."

Jessica Moonflower smiled proprietarily at the mention of her little protégée's name.

"Okay...where's that map?" Bertie handed it over and Meebs moved tacos and empty plates and Margarita glasses to make a space. "Here's the candidate impact zone. See this rectangle? Sixty-five or seventy miles wide, four hundred ninety miles long. Not a permanent human dwelling in the entire area. No villages, oil camps, mining operations, parks, hunting lodges, pipelines, dams, power transmission lines, roads, radar installations or farmland. In summer, there's some travel by boat or floatplane along the fringes, and maybe some hunting or scientific expeditions. Nothing at all seven months of the year when no sane person would venture into this whole region. It's probably the biggest, emptiest, most completely isolated piece of land on the planet! Barring Antarctica, of course, Malcolm. But this zone is *not* solid ice three miles deep! Flat relief, thin soils overlying solid glacier-flattened rock, or muskeg and permafrost. All that is frozen solid clean down to China for eight months of the year. Usually no more than twelve inches of snow in the wintertime. Midwinter, by the way, is when we'll be plunking Sarpedon-E down!"

Jessica Moonflower and Malcolm gazed in awe at the red-penciled rectangle. Meebs, Valeria and Bertie had concocted the plan, so that rectangle was no surprise to those three.

"Canada! The Canadian Arctic! That's *brilliant*, Meebs!"

"Better thank Valeria, Dooley...it's her idea."

"So...we gotta send somebody up to Ottawa to negotiate mineral rights with the Canadian government?"

"Well…no. The redline rectangle isn't exactly under the control of the Canadian national government."

"*What?*…uh…well then, *who*?"

"In 1999, the Canadian government finalized a promise they'd been pushing around for decades. Back in high school, we all probably saw a vast region of Canada on our classroom globes, a region north of all those familiar provinces, that was marked as 'Northwest Territories.' If you took in the details, part of the NWT around Hudson Bay was shown as 'Keewatin,' or 'the Keewatin District.' Well, most of the very sparse population up there is Inuit. They've been promised Province status and a lot of governmental self-determination for a long time. That's what happened in 1999. A great big swath of the Canadian Arctic got broken away from the Northwest Territories, and became **Nunavut**. It's the largest single subdivision of Canada, but more-or-less the least populous. It's the fifth-largest country subdivision in the *world*…bigger than Texas or Alaska. Bigger than both of them put together!"

"So where do we have to go, to get the…the Nunavushians to grant us a mineral license?"

"Capital city. Iqaluit." Dr. Ing put a finger on Malcolm's map at very nearly the farthest-north seat of government on the entire globe, a little dot at the northern extremity of Frobisher Bay on Baffin Island. "We've got to divide up the tasks again. Bertie's run across an item we don't want to pass up. It's a piece of surplus gear being sold off by the General Services Administration in D.C. It's listed as 'Narrowband UHF Encoding/Decoding Data/Control Inter-transfer Module pursuant to Mil. Spec. TCM-jt50059c project, discontinued Apr 2003' "

"Whoa! That's the Icarus Project!" murmured Malcolm.

"Yep. Bertie says they're surplusing a useless single-purpose deep-space commo set. It's probably the backup to the Goldstone equipment, specialized for use with the Icarus Project. It's mounted in a small covered trailer. It was intended to be activated at Fort Meade, parked inside a secure communications compound. All we gotta do is hook it up to a parabolic dish bigger than about eight feet diameter and we can talk directly to Sarpedon-E without the risk of going through Goldstone anymore and just hoping no one notices. Is that about right, Bertie?"

"Right, Meebs."

"How long do we have, to put it in service?"

"Seventy-eight days, more-or-less. We need a couple days to check it out, then it's gotta be ready to go operational by the retro-burn scheduling deadline, sometime in October."

Mac was intrigued. "How much does GSA want for it?"

Dr. Ing studied a GSA website display on his iPad. "Revised minimum bid as of this morning is...uh...cripes! Only three hundred bucks! We gotta act fast though...they've got a special push going on, clearing old junk off the books. The closing date for the Module is...next Tuesday! If it doesn't sell, they'll scrap it."

"Okay...I'll do it!" Malcolm volunteered.

"I wanna go with him!" Jessica Moonflower chirped.

Hmmm...might not be a bad idea, Meebs thought. He'd noted how a little exposure to Jessica seemed to reduce various male desk-jockeys to slobbering idiots. "Valeria, will you be all right without your translator for a couple of days?"

"Ee'm being Noombeer One all reeght!"

"Then it's settled! Jessica and Mac head for the GSA in Philadelphia and buy that Module. Bertie, Valeria and me, we head for...for Iqaluit, where we make connections with someone in the Nunavut equivalent of the BLM. Now look, guys! It seems likely to me we may wind up being forced to negotiate. But once we let out of

127

the bag what Sarpedon-E's got up its sleeve, I'm betting we won't get it *back in* the bag...and we could wind up on our asses out in the frozen tundra without a nickel."

"No neekeel?" Valeria intoned mournfully.

"Only if we're stupid, Honey!" Meebs reassured her. "Let's order one more pitcher of Margaritas before we've got to get serious!"

As the last round of Margaritas was being absorbed, Dr. Ing flagged the other two guys over to a nearby unoccupied table. He had a whispered private conference with Mac and Bertie. "The 'gold' thing is going to slip out sooner or later, fellows. What do you think about letting the girls in on it? I think they've both proved their mettle, don't you?"

"Valeria knows already, I'm pretty sure," Bertie murmured.

"Wouldn't put it past Jessica," Mac offered. "She plays quite a bit dumber than she actually is. And, anything Valeria knows, Jessica's found out."

"Okay. You guys let them know the mineral truth about Sarpedon...we ought to cut them in as equal shares, don't you think? All in favor, say aye."

"Aye."

"Aye."

"Me too...aye." Meebs confirmed, making it unanimous.

"What about Saint Brigid?"

"Oh lord!" Meebs moaned. "She's sort-of like an orphan puppy that followed us home. A mascot or something. Guys, we can't just abandon her here. How about we just take her along for the time being, if we can keep her in clothes?"

"What you mean 'we'?"

"Oh okay!...'me.' "

"No equal-share partner?" offered Bertie.

"Nay," voted Mac.

"Nay," voted Meebs. "If it comes to it, I'll give her something out of my share. Assuming this thing doesn't all go completely to rat-shit and there *is* some kind of share!"

Malcolm squared his shoulders to the task of talking to Jessica and Valeria about the gold. He waved Dr. Ing and Bert back to the table where the girls had just poured themselves the last of the Margarita. "C'n we have just one more pitcher, Meebsie?" Jessica wheedled. "We don't need to be at the airport for hours 'n hours!"

"Okay...I'll get the waitress to put in the order. But right now, Miss Jessica, Mac has something he wants to tell you and Valeria about...why don't you take your glasses on over to that table there, and I'll come over and top you up when the pitcher arrives. Gotta be the last one, girls! Can't have us needing to carry you onto the airplane!"

"What's up, Dooley?" Jessica asked. She sneaked Mac a little kiss with some lime-flavored tongue in it.

"Hi, Doodley-doo!" Valeria slurred, a bit in her cups.

"Well, girls, we were just talking about something we probably should have told you a lot sooner. You see—"

"Is it about the gold?" Jessica Moonflower asked.

Mac goggled. "Uhhhh...well, yes!" he managed at last. "When...how....?"

Jessie laughed merrily. "Valeria's known since before she left Chelyabinsk! You remember that little bar-chart Bertsie drew up? She had a copy of that! Worried her way through that problem, finally remembered what 'Au' stood for We figured there must be a couple billion dollars of gold in Sarpedon-E, so giving us the whole nickel share was really pretty nice of you guys!"

Valeria tugged on Jessie's sleeve and the two of them had a short, intense conversation in Russian. When she was done, she gave Jessie the international hand signal for go-ahead-and-tell-him.

"Okay. Val says, she's always been perfectly happy with splitting the nickel with me, 'cause no one's ever been that generous with her in her whole life, and even if only half the nickel gets recovered, and even if the estimate of nickel content is off by fifty percent, and even after splitting it with me, she still might probably wind up with forty or fifty million dollars worth of nickel, and that's 'bout eleven thousand times as much as she was earning every year, back in Chelyabinsk, and we already agreed somebody's gonna marry her, she's leaning toward Bertie, so she can be a *novaya grazhdankiya Amerikanskaya* forever—that's a new American citizen—and she's never gonna have to go back to cold, icy, snowy, ugly Chelyabinsk ever again, so why should she care how much gold there might be in it for you three guys?"

Valeria tugged Jessie's sleeve again. She whispered *"Spasibo bol'shoye!"* in Jessica's ear.

"She also says 'Thank you enormously!' Look...she and I talked about what fun this is, an' how nice you guys are treating us, an' how neither one of us never did anything half so exciting before, an' how even if that stupid asteroid crashes in the ocean an' we lose everything, we're probably never again gonna do anything so bold an' adventurous in our dull little humdrum lives, so we don't really care about the gold!" She paused to take a big slurp of Margarita.

"Jessica, there's *seven trillion* dollars' worth of gold in Sarpedon-E."

Jessica Moonflower projectile-sprayed her mouthful of Margarita down the front of Malcolm's shirt. Then she commenced choking. Valeria pounded on her back for a while. In a breathless voice, Jessie tried to rasp 'What? SEVEN **TRILLION** DOLLARS?' but it came out like *"Whaaa?* SHHF-N **TSHILYIN** GALL'RSH?"

130

"We want you two to come in for equal shares. Split everything five ways."

"Wubbout guh gnickrl?"

"The nickel?" Mac asked.

Jessica nodded, wide-eyed and slack-jawed, dribbling Margarita.

"Oh, I guess you can have that, too. I get the impression Valeria's pretty attached to the nickel."

Valeria nodded, wide-eyed and slack-jawed.

MAC AND CASABAS IN PHILLY

After a grueling three-legged flight from Phoenix Sky Harbor International to Dallas/Ft.Worth International to Atlanta Hartsfield-Jackson International to Philadelphia International, crammed together for the final two-hour leg in parsimonious coach seats in the middle block of a two-aisle aircraft, all the fun buzz had gone out of Jessica Moonflower's midday Margarita refection. Malcolm wasn't much better off, although his travel expectations had never run to First Class seating anyway. The aircraft made a bouncy landing at half past nine in the evening, and it was another forty-five minutes before Jessica's light-blue, flowery hardside suitcase came conveyering up out of the terminal's bowels and was disgorged onto a carousel. Malcolm had been travelling carry-on since they left Hartford several days earlier.

Mac had taken the time earlier to reconnoiter by GoogleMaps. They'd booked rooms—that is to say, *a* room—at the Rodeway Inn City Center, about five miles from the airport, and no more than three or four city blocks from the Strawbridge Building, home of the General Services Administration divisional office holding sales responsibility for Bertie's satcom hardware. Mac figured they'd use cabs for ground connections, rather than mess with a rental car.

At the cab stand, there was the usual lineup of Checkers and Yellow Cabs, a smattering of Ubers, and three or four upscale hotel limos. A few cars back, there was a modest gunmetal-gray limousine sporting a discreet cab-light on its roof. The light indicated 'car available.' Stuck to the inside of the windshield was a small, frilly decal identifying the vehicle as a licensed taxi. Malcolm happened to be aware that any vehicle in Philly displaying a hack license was constrained by law to charge the same rates as the grungiest, most beat-up, cigar-smoke-stinky taxi. He handed his carry-on bag to Jessica and asked her to wait a moment. Then he strolled down to where the limo's driver lounged against a pillar smoking a Marlboro.

"Are you available?" he asked the driver. "To the downtown Rodeway?"

"Gnrrghh," the fellow replied, noncommittally. Evidently the guy wasn't too thrilled about a modest, fifteen-buck crosstown ride for two fares on some kind of budget business trip.

"Extra fifty bucks in it for you. My lady-friend would love to ride in a limo." Malcolm indicated Jessica Moonflower with a jerk of his head. The cabbie's eyes briefly came out on stalks at the sight of Jessica. He tossed his glowing cigarette into the gutter, straightened up, swung open the passenger door and said, "Your chariot awaits, m'lord!"

Mac strolled back over to Jessica and indicated the spiffy limo. The driver scuttled over and grabbed her suitcase and Mac's carry-on bag. It was all the driver could do to prevent himself from grabbing Jessica, too.

Malcolm had only been in Philly three or four times before. He didn't much care for the city's brash bustle, its mix of stately old buildings and crappy slums. The limo ride to the Rodeway was not exactly unpleasant, hardly what you'd call scenic, and mercifully short. "Here we are!" the cabbie proudly announced over the intercom.

Well, the City Center Rodeway Inn attempted to radiate classic style, but only seemed to succeed in looking like a tired-out pile of bricks set amongst a row of tatty groundlevel businesses as far up and down Walnut Street as the eye could see, in the dim light of streetlamps. Nevertheless, they were met cordially and efficiently by a liveried bellman. The desk clerk checked them in with aplomb, late-arrival reservations waiting and prepaid, thanks to Dr. Ing's efficiency with on-line travel planning. They were whisked up to a perfectly adequate room on the third floor, street side, where a nice chilled bottle of Chardonnay and a pair of wine flutes awaited them, compliments of the hotel.

Jessica flung the drapes open. Directly across Walnut Street, a two-story red neon sign blinked, declaring **GARAGE** in a strident vertical arrangement. Jessica flung the drapes back closed. "Dooley Sweetheart," she begged. "Pour me some of that wine, won't you, Angel? I'm gonna get out of these creepy, sweaty clothes and go in that necessarium to take me a forty-five minute shower, nice'n hot!"

"Okay. Sounds nice!"

"Wanta come too?"

An hour and a half later, still wrapped in bath towels, Jessica Moonflower sat perched on the end of the bed, flipping through the room service menu. On the Atlanta-to-Philadelphia leg of their flight, she'd been served a plastic-wrapped bagel at least two weeks old bearing a slice of Velveeta and a smear of what looked like radioactive mayonnaise, which after unwrapping and examining, she'd wisely decided not to eat, so by the time they'd gotten settled into the Rodeway and all finished showering and whatnot, she was pretty hungry. She scanned the burgers and sandwiches section of the menu. Her eyes came to rest on the following item:

Philadelphia Cheese Steak Sandwich on a Fresh-Baked Sourdough Hoagie Roll with Caramelized Onions and Crunchy Green Pepper Slices, Served with Fresh Beef Au Jus and a Side of our Chef's Special Creamy Coleslaw.

Well, when in Philadelphia! She recalled that Valeria had lunched on a Philadelphia Cheese Steak Sandwich a couple days ago in Phoenix, and had raved that it was the best, most delicious edible substance she'd ever imagined existed. Surely a Philadelphia Cheese Steak Sandwich in Philadelphia would be even better than the Phoenix, Arizona rendition of the same item. Her mind made up, Jessie grabbed the phone and punched-in Room Service.

The following morning the two of them reluctantly untangled themselves from each other and arose. Malcolm groped for the bedside clock-radio. Eight-seventeen. Not bad. They had a ten-thirty appointment with a guy at GSA. "Want the bathroom first?" he asked Jessica.

"Huh-uh...you go."

Mal was perched on the Seat of Ease when the bathroom door opened and Jessica wandered in, eyes closed as if she was sleepwalking. She'd shucked her nightwear, which had been a navel-length, gossamer-sheer silk tee-shirt. She was now dressed in a pair of tight, lime-green, French-cut undies and nothing more. She ignored Malcomb. She leaned over the sink, squinted at her visage in the mirror, tugged on some tiny wrinkles at the corners of her eyes. "Ugh!" she observed. She turned on a blast of water and proceeded to scrub her face with a washcloth until she was satisfied with the result. She pirouetted away from the sink, gave an astonished and still-seated Malcolm a little kiss, and all but skipped out the door, leaving it wide open.

135

So much for modesty! Mal reflected.

In the lobby, the hotel offered coffee, miscellaneous juices, and fresh toasted bagels with non-radioactive Philly cream cheese. The two of them found a table looking out over a bustling Walnut Street, and munched their way through a light breakfast. Malcolm chivalrously went for refills on coffee. Upon returning to their table, he set the filled cups back in the saucers, and before sitting himself down again, bent over to give Jessica a little kiss for no particular reason. She threw her arms around him and pulled him in for a more comprehensive smooch. "Honey-pie, I just *love* traveling with you!" she gushed.

They had plenty of time, so they strolled the three blocks eastward toward the Strawbridge Building on Eighth Street. Along the way, they were accosted four separate times by unrelenting panhandlers, and once by a lunatic street-preacher who sought determinedly to save their thrice-damned souls as they scurried down the sidewalk trying to escape. And at Seventh Street the crosswalk light changed on them when they were two-thirds of the way across, and the traffic just started up again at warp-speed with horns blaring, forcing the two of them to scramble for their very lives. They reached the Strawbridge Building shaken but more-or-less intact.

The Strawbridge Building, if it had had bars on the windows instead of glass, would have borne a fair resemblance to a high-rise federal penitentiary. Stone-block construction designed by an ill-paid architectural burnout in the nineteen-twenties, its unornamented streetside facade reached upward ten stories. It was the sort of building you'd choose to leap off of, if your last friend in the world had just died lingeringly of pancreatic cancer, and then your dog had been run over by a locomotive when you were walking home from your deceased friend's funeral. In the rain.

Jessica and Malcolm elevatored up to the tenth floor. Wandered timidly down a long, wood-paneled corridor, strikingly similar to the one Dorothy and her three companions, in Oz, wandered down on their way to the Wizard's Inner Sanctum. They pulled up at an oaken door with a gluechip glass window panel sporting 'GSA' in gold-leaf. The sounds of languid typewriters and clattering Xerox machines came from within. Mal cautiously operated the knob and pushed the door open. The two of them entered, scarcely breathing.

They found themselves in a small reception area. Naugahyde chairs, old magazines, out-of-date GSA sale catalogs. The reception area was empty of all other would-be GSA supplicants. One wall was semi-opaque glass from waist height up, and behind the glass vague forms could be seen moving about. There was a big red call-button on a narrow counter underneath the glass. It was apparent that a segment of glass could be slid back to afford interaction between whatever portal-guardian held sway on the glass's far side and those in the waiting room seeking an audience. Gingerly, Malcolm reached out and pressed the button. A faint, faraway buzz sounded.

Creeeeeek! The glass slid back. This had been accomplished by a plump woman in a purple dress wearing a tag identifying her as Ms. Miranda Stürm. "Yesss?" she queried the two of them, theatrically.

"Uh...I'm Malcolm MacDooley and this is my colleague Miss Jessica Moonflower. We have a ten-thirty appointment with...uh...Mr....uh...Ratcliff! Richard Ratcliff."

The window creaked closed.

"Colleague, huh?" Jessica whispered.

"Well I was gonna say 'girlfriend' but 'colleague' sounded more professional."

"Colleague is pretty cool, Dooleykins! Girlfriend is nice, too. How long you think Mr. Rats is gonna keep us waiting?"

Malcolm shrugged. He was just about to sit down when a side door opened and the presumptive Mr. Ratcliff beckoned them in. "Any trouble finding us?"

"No, no...we overnighted about three blocks away...our plane from Phoenix got in late."

"Oh? You live in Arizona?"

"No...Hartfort. Connecticut. Our enterprise is engaged in surveying a large tract of Arizona desert land in connection with an MIT study on mineral distributions *vis a vis* meteoric impacts." All this was Malcolm's razzle-dazzle BS, intended to establish some reasonable excuse to buy the arcane UHF communications gear GSA had for sale.

"Here we are!" Mr. Ratcliff gestured them into a small glass-enclosed office with a pair of Spartan guest chairs, an overflowing steel desk, and a black synthetic-leather swivel chair, obviously Mr. Ratcliff's. "Can I get you some coffee, Miss Moonflower? Mr. MacDooley?"

"We're fine, Honey!" Jessica assured him. "We both drank about a gallon of coffee at the hotel, 'n me for one might need to go visit the necessarium before we're done here! But you're real sweet to ask!" This was Jessica's razzle-dazzle BS, intended to get Mr. Ratcliff slobbering and breathing hard.

Malcolm jumped in. "Well, Mr. Ratcliff! I bet you're a busy man, so let me get to the item we are interested in." He pulled out a xerox of the catalog item listing: **'Narrowband UHF Encoding/Decoding Data/Control Inter-transfer Module pursuant to Mil. Spec. TCM-jt50059c project, discontinued Apr 2003. Contact Philadelphia GSA Office.'**

Ratcliff went ticka-ticka-ticka on his keyboard and an exact copy of Malcolm's item listing popped up on the computer display. "Mmm...yes, it's available. Shows as having been on the market without bids for...ummm... seven years six months. That means I'm authorized to make a direct sale here and now. Electronics don't always store well in non-airconditioned warehousing, so I have to advise you it would be an 'as-is' sale. Another thing: this commo hardware is surplus from some kind of Defense Advanced Projects thing that got de-funded or something. Point is, the communications technology is sixteen or seventeen years out-of-date. And also, there's no technical documentation."

"Oh that's all right. We've got a couple of genius grad students who'll just wade into it and reconfigure it to our project needs."

"Um, okay...just so you understand. Another thing: we wouldn't be able to ship or deliver an item this insignificant. You'd have to pick it up in...ummm, let's see...Massachusetts! The whole thing's trailer-mounted. Only weighs about fifteen hundred pounds, so you can probably haul it with a pickup or SUV. Oh...I see it's got a parabolic antenna dish roof-mounted on the trailer...that'll add about three hundred pounds. See...here's a photo of the unit."

"What is the appraised price for the antenna?"

"Mmmm...doesn't show a price. Oh heck, I'll just throw it in with the electronics and trailer. Minimum bid shows as three hundred dollars, but I've got some leeway. Say..two-fifty for the works?"

*This was **easy**!* Malcolm thought to himself. *Why haven't I ever bought anything from GSA before?* "Well I think that will be satisfactory, Mr. Ratcliff. We can handle the transaction in cash, if necessary."

"Cash always works! Mrs. Stürm will be the cashier, and will give you the—"

"Hold on a second, Richie!" Jessica Moonflower interjected.

Oh lord, is she gonna put her foot in the deal? Malcolm stewed.

"Yes, Miss...uh...Moonblossoms?"

Jessie smiled tolerantly at the GSA junior administrator. "Well I was just having a glance at all the fine print on your screen there, Sweetie. Seems there's more to the item than the publicly-available website advertisement shows."

"Uh...er...that is..."

"See right here? 'Ancillary equipment: twelve robotic assay/receiver units plus one master controller unit for remote sensing. Seems to me that stuff could be pretty useful. Dontcha think, colleague?"

"Yep! Oh yeah! Uh-huh, you bet!" Mac agreed.

Mr. Ratcliff reddened. He did *not* want to disappoint Miss Moonboobies, the most ravishing client he'd entertained in a long, long time. "If you'll just give me a moment...." He scrabbled frantically through the pages in a dossier, then rattled his way through several more pages of computer display. "Oh! I see what the issue is! I...that is, my staff...cannot seem to locate the receiver units and their controller. Evidently, they've been temporarily mislaid in our extensive warehousing system. I'm certain they'll turn up eventually, and we will advertise them when—"

Jessica rapped a glamorous fingernail on Ratcliff's computer screen right under the entry discussing the missing units. "Can't an efficient, can-do type of fella like you just sell these thirteen units to us *on spec*? We sure could use them, 'n we'll just take the risk they turn up sooner or later. How 'bout it?"

"Well, it's not without precedent..."

"Of course, you gotta give us a good deal on 'em!"

Jessica and Mr. Ratcliff haggled a bit. Ratcliff was way out of his league. Jessica wound up negotiating a killer price: $400 for the lot: trailer, dish-antenna, transmitter electronics, twelve temporarily-missing assay/receiver units, one temporarily-missing master controller unit.

"Well okay then! We'll just—"

"One more thing, Mr. Ratcliff. 'Bout them thirteen units...says here, 'suitable for welded attachment onto iron/nickel/cobalt metallic base' " Jessica tapped the words on the GSA computer screen again for emphasis. "Is the base for these units provided? Like this nifty trailer that comes with the commo unit?"

Ratcliff fumbled some more. After a while he gave up. "Sorry, it doesn't say."

"Well can we have the base or bases included with the assay units? If they're not already base-mounted, those bases should be stored along with the units, and if the units turn up, shouldn't the base or bases as well, don'cha think?"

"I guess so...okay, let's assume so."

Jessica had Ratcliff on the ropes. "How much?"

"Oh...we'll just throw the base or bases in. No charge."

"Nope...we'll pay fair 'n square up front, 'n accept the risk the dratted things won't show up. That way there's no problems down the line. Like f'rinstance if them bases turn out to be Mil-Spec solid gold or somethin'...like them three-thousand-dollar Galaxy airplane toilet-seats a few years back!" Jessica laughed merrily. Malcolm joined in. Even Ratcliff lightened up and had a good laugh. Solid gold bases...what a hoot!

"How about we say sixty dollars for the bases, all of them together?" the GSA man volunteered.

"Mr. Ratcliff, Sugar-pie...you got yourself a deal!"

Ten minutes later, Malcolm and Jessica Moonflower were riding the elevator down. All Malcolm could do was murmur "Oh boy oh boy oh boy oh boy!" All Jessica could do was grin smugly.

They left the elevator at the streetlevel lobby. Mac took a quick look around. Nobody in sight. He grabbed Jessie by the shoulders and planted a hot, hard kiss right on her mouth.

"My goodness, Mister MacDooley!"

Malcolm waved the GSA papers. "This here..." he babbled. "This here is a US government deed of ownership to a trailer-mounted deep-space UHF encrypted communications uplink/downlink, with parabolic antenna. Honey, back in 2001 the gov'ment spent *seventeen million dollars* on that one-of-a-kind, custom-engineered trailerful of Mil-Spec electronics! An' we just now paid two hundred and fifty bucks for it! But it doesn't stop there!" Suddenly sensing that there might very well be surveillance cameras and eavesdropping microphones on-duty in the lobby of the GSA building, Malcolm strongarmed Jessica out into the street and about fifty feet down the block. "It doesn't stop there!" he repeated. "Then you negotiated the purchase of one deep-space long-duration hardened 'control' descent unit, plus twelve more 'assay/transmit' units, *each of which contains a top-secret semi-explosive nuclear device*! And, that goofball GSA guy up there doesn't know where those units are, *but we do*! *Spot-welded onto Sarpedon-E*! Which makes Sarpedon-E, in its entirety, the 'iron/nickel/cobalt base or bases' you'n him were wrangling about! Which means, these papers here in my hand are a bought-and-paid-for *bona fide US Government deed of ownership to Sarpedon-E*! Which we happen to know, *but GSA doesn't*, is worth seven trillion dollars and change! *And we just paid sixty bucks for Sarpedon!* Total of four hundred and sixty bucks to the US Government for the whole works! Look! Look...here's the receipt to prove it! In *our* names! You'n me, Honeybun! Plus, the other three as 'participating owners in equal measure!' With a big purple GSA seal stamped on it! I love you so much I feel like I'm gonna *bust!*" Malcolm was so wound up his voice had ascended into the high-pitched squeak of an amiable rodent.

Jessica smiled sweetly. "Shucks, Lamb. Isn't nothin' but some highly-honed shopping skills! Your Babykins is a darn fine shopper! But I'm gonna prob'ly take out that 'I love you so much' line and wave it in your face every so often!"

They strolled with light feet all the way back to the Rodeway Inn. Every panhandler that accosted them got five bucks and a couple of nice smiles. They packed up, checked out, then limousined half a mile westward to the Rittenhouse Hotel, perhaps Philadelphia's finest. Malcolm reviewed the available accommodations and settled on an upper-floor balcony suite overlooking Rittenhouse Square Park. Enormous heart-shaped bed. Pink spa-tub with gold-plated dolphin spigots. Big complimentary basket of fruit, flowers and candy. Nine hundred forty dollars for the night. Before following the bell captain to the elevators, Mal had put in an order for a nice bottle of chilled Dom Pcrignon, a platter of Caesar salad, smoked oysters, sevruga caviar on buckwheat blini with multifarious fixings, and assorted cheeses. And a very emphatic 'Do Not Disturb' hanger for the door.

THE OTHER FOUR'S ADVENTURES IN IQALUIT

When the Amoeba had tried to book four airplane seats from Phoenix to Iqaluit, the capital of Nunavut Territory, he ran into a little trouble. The Phoenix Airport ticketing agent he'd been dealing with by phone when he'd booked Malcolm and Jessica through to Philadelphia had been courteous and efficient. Two travelers to Philly all booked, no problem. So after getting the two of them in a cab to the airport, Meebs had called the same ticketing agent back, on his private extension. Affairs turned to booking four places on a flight to the Far North of the Canadian Arctic. The agent had taken down Dr. Ing's particular wishes in terms of travel dates (starting with an immediate departure), destinations and seat preferences. Then there had been a long interval of silence except for computer keyboard clatter conveyed through the telephone: ticka-ticka-tick-tick.

"Ummmm..." the agent said at last. "Um, there appears to be some difficulty getting you-all to that destination, Dr. Ing."

"I'm right this moment looking at Iqaluit on Google Maps on my iPad..." the Doctor replied. "There's a great big airport right there in town."

"Well...frankly, Dr. Ing, I've never even *heard* of Iqaluit. Or Nunavut, for that matter. Is it a very small town?"

"Not particularly...maybe seven thousand inhabitants or so. By Arctic standards, that's huge! It's the capital of Nunavut, for heaven's sake! Nunavut's one of several Canadian Arctic territories. In area, it's bigger than all of Western Europe!"

Some more keyboard typing sounds. "Okay...got it. Here it is. Two Canadian airlines serve Iqaluit...Canadian North and First Air. Both connect out of Toronto, and we can pretty easily get you booked through, departing this evening, from Phoenix to Toronto...except for a not-so-great connection in Chicago. Let's see...you and your three colleagues travelling Phoenix to Iqaluit, staying five days, then return flight Iqaluit to Hartford, Connecticut. Four adult coach fares, including all relevant taxes and airport fees comes to" ...ticka-ticka... "just a moment" ...ticka...TICK. "eleven thousand one hundred thirty-two dollars and sixty-four cents. That's US dollars."

"Excuse *MEEEE*?" Meebs shrilled.

"Eleven thousand one hundred dollars and change. Two thousand seven hundred eighty-three dollars and sixteen cents per traveller."

"There's gotta be some kind of *mistake!*"

Tick-ticka-tick. "No...that appears to be the correct fare."

"Is there any more *reasonable* fare if we travel out of Hartford on some other day? Like, maybe two or three weeks from now?"

"No...doesn't appear to be. Both airlines quote nearly identical fares, with no significant premium for short lead-time bookings. Shall I book these seats for you?"

Dr. Ing was flummoxed by eleven thousand bucks. "You know," he assured the ticket agent, "Last year I was at a weeklong conference in Los Angeles, and my company insisted I travel immediately to Reykjavik, Iceland, to take care of an emergency...then back to the conference a couple days later. I booked a ticket on eight hours' notice, round-trip, LA to Reykjavik and back to LA again, and it cost me eight hundred and fifty-seven dollars. You've just gotta be wrong about that fare to Iqaluit, 'cos it can't be half as far as LA-to-Reykjavik, and Iqaluit sure as hell isn't very much farther north than *Iceland!*"

"Dr. Ing, I assure you—"

"What would a charter flight cost, Toronto to Iqaluit?"

"Well, you'd need a turboprop or jet aircraft to cover the distance...it's about twenty-six hundred miles with no opportunity to refuel, so you aren't going in a Cessna 150. Then, the aircraft and flight crew would have to stand-by idle for five days while you and your colleagues conduct your business. Refuel in Iqaluit, where avgas is going to command an eighty-percent premium price...it would come to somewhere around" ...ticka-ticka-ticka... "thirty-four thousand six hundred eighty dollars."

"*Yeesh!*"

The ticketing agent made sympathetic and soothing sounds into the phone. "If I may suggest, Dr. Ing, why don't you and your team make your way to the airport here? I will do some intensive research and make a few telephone calls...perhaps there is a less expensive routing."

"What's the travel time, for the tickets you are showing?"

"Uhhh....sixty-eight hours and seventeen minutes."

"*Yikes!* Some long airport delays en route?"

"You leave Phoenix tonight at six-twenty p.m. Arrive Chicago eleven pm, Central Time. Seventeen-hour holdover in Chicago. You could see some sights...take in a Cubs game. Then a short hop to Toronto. Thirty-five hours holdover in Toronto, because there's only one flight every two days to Iqaluit. We ought to book you a nice hotel in Toronto so you can rest up. Then six-odd hours flight-time, Toronto to Iqaluit."

"*Ye gods!*"

"Well, as an option if you have eight or nine days to spare, couldn't you *drive*?"

"Nearest highway stops about sixteen hundred miles short of Iqaluit! Plus, Iqaluit is on Baffin Island...across from the extreme north end of the Ungava peninsula, across about two hundred miles of ice-cold North Atlantic Ocean! No ferries! Even if you *could* get there by car! Which you *can't!*" Dr. Ing tore at his sparse hair with his free hand. "Okay, listen. We've *got* to make this trip! But we were also planning on making a followup excursion from Hartford in three or four weeks. Considering the unbelievable airfare costs, I'm thinking we will reprioritize, and just accomplish everything in one go. Will it increase our air-travel costs significantly if we leave the return date open?"

"Mmmm...let's see...open booking, Iqaluit to Hartford" ...ticka-ticka-ticka... "Nope, not too bad. Only add a bit more than three hundred dollars to the airfare total."

"Okay...make those phone calls, if you'd be so kind. Then book the best arrangements you can, but see if you can save us some *money!* Leaving tonight. Book us an airport hotel in Chicago for tonight, hold for late arrival, of course. Two rooms, double or queen beds. Hold on a sec." Meebs clamped a hand over his cellphone and gave a questioning lift of eyebrows to his onlookers. Bertie nodded an enthusiastic uh-huh. Valeria gave him a big sexy smile. Just-Bree made a circle with her left thumb and forefinger, and erotically shoved her right forefinger through this orifice five or six times. Meebs put the cellphone back to his face. "Yeah...double or queen beds in Chicago. Another airport hotel accommodation in Toronto, same room arrangements. And book us into the Hotel Arctic on Mivvik Street in Iqaluit...again, two Queen-bed rooms, adjoining if possible. I'm seeing online it should be around one-seventy US dollars a night, per room. Three nights for certain, then an open booking for as much as ten more nights. I'll deal with the hotel management when we arrive." Dr. Ing broke the connection and collapsed in an exhausted heap.

No travel miracles manifested themselves. Nearly three full days and at least thirteen thousand dollars later, all told, the four of them dragged wearily off an aircraft in Iqaluit. Down an old-fashioned wheeled air-stair onto the tarmac…Iqaluit International was not equipped with enclosed jetways. In spite of its being an early afternoon in early July, the air temperature was a chilly fifty-one Fahrenheit. Just-Bree, thoroughly acclimatized to broiling Arizona temperatures, began almost at once to shiver spasmodically and chatter her teeth. The warmest garment she had in her clothes-gunnysack was a sleeveless Grateful Dead fleece vest. Dr. Ing loaned her his pinstriped wool suit-coat.

"We better get her a parka somewhere," he observed. "So…where's town? And how do we get there?"

Bertie took his nose out of his iPad. "That way!" he gestured. "About a quarter mile. Let's walk it…I could use a little exercise!"

Sure enough, Iqaluit was built smack up next to its airport. The city occupied an expanse of terrain scraped by enormous glaciers right on down to flat bedrock millennia in the past. Clearly, the privilege of becoming the capital of an enormous region had made the town prosper. Nice new administrative buildings rose three and four stories in some blocks, occasionally as tall as eight stories. There was evidence of what would pass for outrageous urban sprawl in many another usually-diminutive Arctic settlement. Commercial buildings had a pre-fab look about them. Homes and apartment blocks looked like conjoined rows and two-decker piles of modulars, as if much of the town had been rapidly stuck together out of Legos. Streets were crude affairs, most of them unpaved, but very few private vehicles were to be seen anyway. "We're on Mivvik Street!" Bertie sung out. "We just keep going down this way! We're looking for a cross-street called

148

Federal Road." What none of them knew was that at the intersection of Mivvik and Federal, Mivvik changed its name to Niaqunngusiarraq Street, far beyond the pronunciation capabilities of any of them. At the same intersection, Federal changed its name to Queen Elizabeth Boulevard, which thoroughfare curved south, then east, then north again to deceptively re-intersect Niaqunngusiarraq, née Mivvik, no more than eight hundred feet away from the actual intersection they were looking for. There was nothing resembling a 'grid' of streets anywhere in the spread-out expanse of Iqaluit. All this didn't matter, because almost none of the streets were identified by street-signs anyway. Fortunately, the Hotel Arctic turned out to be hard-to-miss, a handsome three-story white and red building with an adequate sign sporting an oversized set of caribou antlers right over the entry. They trudged up the stairs and in through the double set of glass doors.

A tiny young Inuit woman was staffing the check-in desk. "Are you Doctor Marcellus Ing's party?" she asked in an oddly musical intonation.

"I'm Dr. Ing!" Meebs responded. This is Bree Patroness, my companion. These are my colleagues, Dr. Bertram Koslosky and his close friend and associate Valeria…uh…Tam…Tamoritzkovitch."

"Tamoritskaya!" Valeria murmured.

"Right…Tamoritsky. …skaya. Sorry m'dear." To the check-in clerk: "She's Russian! Difficult names…such a bother! And…what is your name, Miss?"

"Sillattiavak Tuttusiuvvik Mialigaqtaliminiq." The girl pointed to a prop-up nameplate which read:

ᓯᓚᑦᑎᐊᕘᖅ ᑐᑦᑐᓯᐅᕝᕕᒃ ᒥᐊᓕᒐᖅᑕᓕᒥᓂᖅ

She smiled broadly and pointed to herself. "You can call me Miss Mialigaq. Or just Tiavak, for short! Or Katie...that's my Canadian name! Now, Doctor Koslosky, I've got you and *Gospozha* Tamoritskaya in Suite 266... *Prostite, G-zha Tamoritskaya , vasha otchestvo pishetsya 'Anjelika' , pozhaluysta?*[20] And Doctor Ing...or can I call you Amoeba? I must say, a most peculiar nickname! There must be a story! Perhaps you will join us for High Tea this afternoon at four...a bunch of the staff have been speculating about your nickname for a couple days now, and I'm sure they'd love to hear the story! Actually, it's more like Afternoon Tea...or Cream Tea...or maybe just a 'down-tools' Tea Break, with biscuits. Oh sorry! I'm always falling off my train of thought! Dr. Ing, I've got you and Dr. Patroness right next to Mr. Bertie and Miss Valeria, in 268. The stairs are just around there. Sorry...no elevator! Double-sorry...no bell-boy!"

"*DOCK*-ter Patroness!" Just-Bree murmured to herself, quietly amused.

Bertie had no idea what the distinction might be between various Anglophile tea rituals. The Amoeba had vague, alien notions, based on Taiwanese tea traditions recalled from his youth. Valeria was spawned from a culture that drank its tea from *glasses* and *samovars*, for Heaven's sake! Never in her life had tea in any form passed Just-Bree's lips.

Meebs had a question. "Ummm...do we get *keys*, Miss Tiavak?"

"Keys? Oh! You mean, to *lock the doors*? We've *never* done that here!" The girl tittered with fleeting delight. "We'll see you at tea-time, then?"

---

[20] **Pardon me, Ms. Tamoritskaya, is your middle name spelled 'Anjelika' please?**

TEA PARTY

Four-o'clock Tea was served in a nice roomy space in the Hotel Arctic's lobby. It was a serve-yourself affair. A two-burner hotplate held a couple of large glass tea-urns. Platters held arrangements of Oreos and frosted oatmeal cookies and shortbread wafers..."biscuits" in British and British-derived parlances. There was a neat three-tiered stack of handled cut-glass tea glasses, possibly a thoughtful touch for the out-of-town Russian guest. A stack of small plates. A fanned array of paper napkins. In attendance there was a smattering of hotel guests and local citizenry standing about, three or four chambermaids, Miss Mialigaq, and a couple of janitorial workers on-break.

Before coming back downstairs, the four Asteroid Associates had had a brief discussion on the advantageous necessity of attending Tea, and had concluded there was some prospect of payoff in the idea. That is, mostly Dr. Ing had done the concluding, probably because he was a confirmed tea-drinker from way back, and he'd arm-twisted the others into going along. The mission he and Bertie had taken on was to work the crowd for information that might lead them to an influential Iqaluitian with government connections. The mission for Valeria was to be sociable and lend an international flair to the group. Just-Bree's mission was to have a few cookies and a sip or two of tea, and to try to avoid any embarrassing gaffes. And maybe to find out where the guys could buy her some nice warm outerwear.

Bertie sidled into proximity with a trio of tea-sippers standing by a singularly ugly floor lamp. The three of them appeared to be Inuit, but dressed like businessmen from the same company or agency, one with a sufficiently strict dress-code as to border on a uniform. All three wore black shoes, dark-colored wool trousers, light-blue cotton button-up shirts, brightly-colored ties, and "Nunavut – Our Land, Our Strength" baseball caps further decorated with a nice embroidered red *inuksuk*. This is a picture of an *inuksuk*, borrowed from the Internet:

As anyone can plainly see, an *inuksuk* is a pile of rocks the size and shape of an average Inuit standing with outstretched arms, which rockpiles the Inuit, for the last fifty centuries, have erected and left scattered all over the Arctic countryside, particularly where vast numbers of caribou had to cram together in big bunched-up herds in order to ford rivers at the shallow places, so the caribou, which weren't very bright in the first place, would see nice quiet, perfectly harmless *inuksuk* and get used to figures of that size and shape, so that eventually an Inuit caribou-hunter could just stand patiently between a widely-spaced pair of *inuksuk* with a bow and a quiver of arrows, or, in more recent times, a loaded rifle over his shoulder, and pick off whatever caribou, unconcernedly walking past him at a range of twenty feet, looked especially tasty, while the rest of the stupid caribou would hardly flinch but just keep marching along. The word *inuksuk* has a rather subtle translation into English, something like 'acting in the capacity of a human'—sort of the *opposite* of a scarecrow. Kind of a dirty trick on the caribou, if you think about it...but the *inuksuk* was the beloved symbol of Nunavut Territory nonetheless. Anyway, the trio of guys enjoying a tea-break were hardly sporting what you'd call traditional high-Arctic garb. Government officials for certain!

"Afternoon, gentlemen," Bertie said by way of an opening. "I'm Dr. Bertram Koslosky. We just flew in this afternoon."

A round of handshakes and introductions ensued.

"Where do you call home, Dr. Koslosky?" one of the fellows asked.

"Connecticut...Hartford, Connecticut. My three colleagues and I are associates of the Northeastern Geophysical Society. Call me Bertie, fellows! Um...do I take it that you-all are connected with Territorial administration?"

"Iiii!" the biggest guy said, a massively rotund chap sporting a walrus moustache. This particular utterance is Inuktitut for 'Yes!,' which Bertie didn't know, but assumed from context in pretty short order. "Solomon Ikajuqtuq, Bertie!" the big guy said, by way of introduction. "Territorial Minister for Urban Wastewater Management, at your service."

"He drives the town honeybucket truck!" explained one of his colleagues in a stage whisper. "We refer to him as The TMUWM!" he added, pronouncing it 'Tum-Wum'.

"I see," Bert agreed. "And, are you in the Nunavut …ah…government as well?"

"Oh, iii! Territorial Vice-Minister for Urban Wastewater Management!"

"He's the guy that rides around with me on the honeywagon…he operates the sucker-hose!" This from The Tum-Wum. "Now, you wanna meet a *big-shot*, I present our friend and colleague Fitzgerald Ookpik! Take a bow, Fitz!"

The third chap grinned and bowed from the waist.

"Fitz has an important clerkship in the Department of Natural Resources! Annual caribou census, and issuance of special caribou-hunting permits for subsistence families and non-Canadian sport hunters. Just FYI, non-Canadian sport hunters are not permitted to use the *inuksuk* trick."

At this moment, Dr. Ing sidled up. Bertie performed introductions. "…and Fitz Ookpik here is involved with the Territory natural-resources administration," Bertie concluded, hoping The Amoeba would pick up the cue.

Meebs picked up, of course. "Oh? Natural Resources, eh? Would that be the agency which handles issues dealing with mineral rights, at all?"

Fitz shook his woolly head. "No, that's not us. You'd want the Mineral and Fossil Fuels Agency, under Indigenous and Northern Affairs. Nunavut handles its own exploration and operation licensing as granted by the Nunavut Land Claims Agreement Act of—"

"Er...would you happen to know anyone in that Agency?"

"Oh yes! Sure...Eddie Ulatuq's your man! He's a great fellow, a real ball of fire! You want his phone number?"

"I'd really appreciate it!" Meebs fumbled for a ballpoint and a scrap of paper while Fitz Ookpik dug out a pocket-sized planner and thumbed through its pages.

At this particular moment, Just-Bree, dressed fairly decently in an unlikely assortment of borrowed clothes, pushed her way into the little knot of guys. Dr. Ing was about to perform introductions, but Bree beat him to the draw. "Gimme the card, Meeber!" she insisted without preamble.

"Excuse me a jiffy, gentlemen," Dr. Ing mumbled. He groped for his wallet, thumbed through his motley stack of plastic and fumbled a worn MasterCard out of the pile. Without any explanation to the watchers, Bree snatched the credit card, pocketed it, whispered a few words in Meebs's ear, planted a big juicy kiss on his unsuspecting mouth, spun on her heel, and strode off toward the hotel's front door and freedom.

"My girlfriend," Meebs explained. "Oh...uh...my professional colleague, as well."

"What's she do?" Solomon The Tum-Wum asked.

"Bree? Well...she's an expert mineralogist," Meebs lied adroitly. "Yeah ...her focus is iron, nickel and cobalt."

"Looks like she's never dressed for cold weather before, Dr. Ing."

"Uh-huh. She hails from Arizona. Her suitcase turned out to be a little light on the bundle-up gear, and she's been shivery ever since we got off the airplane."

The three Inuit had a hearty laugh. Fitz, getting a grip on his mirth first, said, "You guys wait until Christmas! Today ain't cold at all! We'll get fifty below all December long. That's *Celsius*, fellows!"

"She's off to buy some warmer outerwear. I think she wants to go Traditional Inuit. Gonna shop someplace called NorthMart. Miss Molla-gwick over there...she recommended it."

"Iiii..." Fitz commented. "NorthMart's all right, not too pricey. They'll probably sell her touristy stuff, though...won't really do the job, but will look impressive on a hanger back there in Arizona. Oh lord, now I think of it, the timberwolves staffing that place will probably run your card up to its limit, and she'll come outta there with a bunch of glitzy, impractical clothes and boots to show for it. Look here, Dr. Ing...I'm gonna write down some items in Inuktitut, and—"

"Not those squiggly symbols, I hope?"

"Naw...I can't hardly read that ptarmigan-scratch myself! Okay, most important, she'll need a parka. Traditional Inuit parka in these parts is called *qulittaujaq*. Two layers. The outer layer's for show and for windproofing: heavy cloth, embroidered, or for fancy-dress, maybe caribou or sealskin with some decorative edging worked in, trimmed in fur around the hood and cuffs. That layer worn by itself is called *silapaaq*. Under that, there's a second cold-weather insulating layer of heavy felt, sort of a separate garment. In the old times, this inner layer was often made of felted qiviut...that's musk-ox wool, real soft and warm. At NorthMart they'll sell her a wool felt or a quilted goose-down one, probably run three or four hundred bucks, but she won't need it unless she's planning on staying until Christmas! She might be better off just wearing a *nuijagaq* under the *silapaaq*."

"A...what?"

"A sweater. Don't worry, I'm writing this all down. Traditional pants are called *qarliik*…some nice down-filled two-layer jobs that you stuff in your boot-tops are a good idea if you plan on going out into the tundra…probably too warm for July, but thick enough to frustrate the mosquitos. Then she'll want some boots. *Kamaaluuk* are best, this time of year…that's rubber boots, nice and waterproof but not particularly insulative. Think 'wellies'. But down at NorthMart they'll probably try to do her up in *kamiik*– traditional skin boots—walrus hide or sealskin with fur trimming and a dizzying price-tag. She ought to have *paaluuk* as well—mittens. The ladies always seem to want high-end mittens with embroidery on the backs, and big cuffs, fox-fur trimming. You won't be able to fight it, Dr. Ing, so just give in gracefully. Be sure her *paaluuk* have nice durable palms, though!"

"Why?"

Solomon and Fitz exchanged grins. "Because when you call Eddie Ulatuq, he's gonna tell you he won't meet with you tomorrow. It's a holiday! Friday before Nunavut Day…everything's shut down! Then, he's gonna invite you-all to go Arctic Char fishing with him, up on the Sylvia Grinnell River!"

"And how do you know all that?"

"Eddie and I have known each other since we were kids. He's as predictable as sunset. Wanna bet I'm right?"

"Not a chance!"

"Okay then! You better catch up with your girlfriend." Fitz gestured toward the sun-bright outdoors. "Ah, hell…I'm finished with tea and biscuits. Lemme grab my Pendleton and I'll go with you."

This left Bertie to be the one to phone up Eddie Ulatuq at the Mineral and Fossil Fuels Agency. By the time Bertie could gracefully break away from High Tea to make the call, the Agency was closed and deserted. So too was all the rest of Nunavut's governance. This was because it was 4:45pm, fifteen minutes after Quitting Time on Thursday the 7th of July, the day before Friday the 8th of July, a Territorial Holiday for all government workers (which was about 60% of the population of Iqaluit) celebrating the day before Nunavut Day, which wasn't actually until Saturday the 9th of July. Fortunately, the phone number Fitz Ookpik had written down was Eddie Ulatuq's personal cellphone, which he used for business purposes as well, instead of an office telephone, which he didn't have one of.

"Hello?" Eddie Ulatuq answered.

Bertie explained who he was, named off the other members of his party, and briefly blurted out what they were hoping Mr. Ulatuq could do for them in the way of fixing them up with a permit for collecting and legally removing an unspecified amount of meteoric metals from about forty-two thousand square miles of uninhabited Arctic barren-lands, for which they'd naturally pay the government of Nunavut a reasonable percentage of the per-kilogram spot market value as a royalty or acquisition fee.

"Whoa, hold up there, friend!" Eddie laughed. "I'm off work! Tomorrow's a holiday! Then it's the weekend! Can't talk business until Monday. Why don't you and your partners meet me in my office about, let's say...ten o'clock? Room 2388, Indigenous and Northern Affairs. Big brown building at the corner of Mivvik and Iglulik. Say, waitaminnit! What do you-all have on for tomorrow?"

"Uh...er...nothing, I guess."

"How about I collect the four of you and we go try our luck fishing for Arctic Char? Best-eating fish in the whole world! Tastes like trout mixed with salmon, only better. You'll be my guests for a thrilling day of coldwater fishing! There's a great big river just north of town, the Sylvia Grinnell River, named after a skinny white woman who never set foot in the Arctic, or in Canada at all, by a matter of three or four thousand miles, I'm pretty sure. The daughter of some rich British guy who bankrolled an American 'Arctic explorer' named Charles Hall in 1861—I guess he was taking a pass on the Civil War—who had to be led around by a bunch of Inuit so he wouldn't freeze his ass off or starve to death. Hall never thought to ask those Inuit guides whether the places they were showing him already *had* names…he just slapped white-man handles on those geological features in honor of folks back in America and in England! But hey! All us Indigenous Peoples are okay with all that! Since establishment of Nunavut in 1999, which is what Nunavut Day is celebrating, we've been changing names back into Inuktitut…just haven't gotten around to the Sylvia Grinnell yet. Inuit name is *Iqaluit Kuunga* which means *Iqaluit River*, and *Iqaluit* means 'Place of Many Fish', which means we're guaranteed to have real good luck! So… whaddaya say?"

"Fishing? Well, that sounds good, Eddie. We haven't got any gear, but—"

"No sweat! I got plenty gear! Pick you up early, okay? Where you staying?"

"Um…the Hotel Arctic. Early like *how* early?"

"Four o'clock! Bring snacks! Dress warm!" The phone clicked off. An instant later, the phone rang in Bertie's hand. "Bring bug repellent!" Eddie Ulatuq added. The phone clicked off.

DR. PATRONESS BUYS SOME CLOTHES

Speaking of dressing warm, when Dr. Ing and Fitz Ookpik got down the hill, a quarter-mile south on Queen Elizabeth Avenue to NorthMart, and located Bree in the Women's Indigenous Fashions department, no fewer than three salespeople were clustered around her. One lady had half a dozen Inuit outer-parkas over an arm, and was explaining the merits of a particular one suspended from a hanger in her free hand. It looked fancy enough that it might have been especially hand-made for Queen Elizabeth, who must have at one time or another visited Baffin Island, inasmuch as she had half of a prominent boulevard through the middle of Iqaluit named after her. Meebs said hello to the friendly sales-staff, smiled at his weird girlfriend, and slipped a look at the pricetag dangling from Queen Elizabeth's *silapaaq*. Even in Canadian dollars, the figure caused him to temporarily lose his ability to draw breath. The arms of the other two salesgirls were draped in garments and shopping-bags which doubtlessly amounted to the rest of the togs Bree had already selected for herself.

Fitz Ookpik drew the Parka Girl, who was obviously the Chief Sales Associate, a short distance to one side. There was an earnest, *sotto-voce* conference. The Parka Girl waved the other two Junior Assistant Salesgirls into the conference. Shopping bags were peered into. Garments which were presumably already selected were re-examined, discussed in heartfelt whispers, draped onto handy nearby racks. The two Jr. Asst. salesgirls scurried off in separate directions. Shortly, they came scurrying back, carrying other garments. The Parka Girl scribbled figures on a sales pad. Other figures were scratched out.

PG handed off Queen Elizabeth's parka to one of the two J.A. salesgirls, who scrambled away with it through a curtained doorway with a sign reading 'Sales Staff Only', and presently came scrambling back with a different Inuit outer-parka, almost as nice as Queen Elizabeth's, attractively trimmed in colorful, hand-done crewelwork and what appeared to be wolverine fur. More revisions were made on the sales pad. Finally, the three sales-staffers and Fitz Ookpik strolled back over to where Meebs and Just-Bree were cooling their heels.

PG, in her capacity as Chief Sales Associate, addressed Meebs, in his capacity as Clothing Transaction Moneybags. "Er...Mister—"

"*Doctor!*" Fitz corrected her.

"*Doctor* Ing...your friend Mr. Ookpik has made Miss Patroness's wishes—"

"*Doctor* Patroness!" Fitz corrected her.

"Er...*Doctor* Patroness's wishes clearer to us... traditional Inuit garb can be a bit confusing to those from Outside. I think you two will be happy with a few modifications to Miss— *Doctor* Patroness's selections!" The PG helped Bree into the more-affordable parka they had selected. "Oh...," the Parka Girl added, "also, since you are professional associates of Mr. Ookpik, NorthMart is pleased to extend you and Dr. Patroness its Local Citizen discount on these purchases." While Just-Bree PhD, inspected herself admiringly in a brace of mirrors, the PG gave Marcellus Ing PhD, a glance at the sales slip, on which the crucial part looked like this:

161

Total: ~~$2044.89~~

$796.00

FISHING FOR CHAR

Hordes of salmon were spawning in the Sylvia Grinnell River. How this worked was, the girl salmons fought their way up the swift-flowing river, over boulders and up rapids and over what very nearly amounted to brawling waterfalls as much as fifteen feet high. The boy salmons followed close behind, slavering over the sex pheromones being emitted by the girl salmons. Polar bears, anxious to store up reserves of fat for the coming winter, waded about, just above the rapids and waterfalls, swatting and snapping at both boy salmons and girl salmons, and whenever they connected with one, taking a big bite out of the bellies of the girl salmons where nutritious, fat-laden salmon eggs were to be found, and taking a big bite out of the bellies of boy salmons, whereupon, not tasting any eggs, the boy salmons were spat out and left to flop around in death agonies inasmuch as a big bear-bite had been taken out of their bellies. All this rather profligate one-bite bear action, painful and tragic as it was to the individual salmons involved, didn't matter much to the salmons as a species, since a sufficient number of both girl salmons and boy salmons made it unmolested past the bears, and since the unbitten bellies of any particular surviving girl salmon held thousands and thousands of eggs—plenty to compensate for her sisters lost to extravagant and inefficient bear predation. Bear predation mattered even less to the boy salmons, since any single one of the boy salmons had millions and millions of spermatozoa in his belly, and conceivably a solitary boy salmon surviving the voracious polar-bear gauntlet could fertilize every single egg laid by every single girl salmon in the entire summer run of salmons swimming up the Sylvia Grinnell River, if only the logistics of equitable distribution could have been worked out. Upon reaching a likely stretch of gravel river bottom, the girl salmons would immediately commence squirting their not-yet-fertilized eggs into the gravel. The boy salmons would go berserk, squirting their sperm into the gravel to fertilize the eggs. No actual sexual contact would be made between the girl salmons and the boy salmons, both genders of whom, after all this frenetic, exhausting sexual activity, would die pretty much immediately. What supernatural cosmic genius dreamed up this particular fun form of reproduction?

A large number of the eggs squirted into the gravel by the girl salmons would not wind up where they were squirted, but instead would be caught up in the swift current of the Sylvia Grinnell River. These lost eggs would roll and bumble downstream along the river's rock-strewn bottom. Great, vast numbers of fat, tasty Arctic Char would dash out from behind rocks and gobble up these salmon eggs. A diet of very little except salmon eggs would make these Arctic Char grow even fatter and tastier. The only gross aspect of this seamy little segment of the Great Circle of Life was that Arctic Char are pretty closely related to salmon...practically first cousins. It sort-of smacks of *cannibalism!* Oh well.

Guess what kind of bait any knowledgeable fisherman, such as Eddie Ulatuq for example, would choose to dangle in front of all those Arctic Char?

Meebs was first to get the call when Eddie Ulatuq arrived at the Hotel Arctic's front desk at a little before four in the morning. "Time to go *FISHINNNNGGGG!*" yelled Eddie into the Front Desk Night-Clerk's house phone.

"Unggg..." Meebs replied into his bedside telephone. But he pulled himself together, swung his legs off the bed, clicked on a lamp, and gently poked Just-Bree

164

awake. Just-Bree had chosen to come to bed the night before wearing nothing at all, except for her brand-new NorthMart-purchased Royal Canadian Mounted Police beaver-fur Winter Hat with its earflaps pulled down, their laces tied under her chin, because, on short acquaintance, she passionately loved her new RCMP cap.

The Amoeba padded barefoot across the room and pounded softly on the door which connected to Bertie and Valeria's hotel room. "Unggg..." came a muffled reply from Bertie through the door, then sounds of reluctant rise-and-shine movement and bathroom usage.

Ten minutes later, the four Asteroid Associates shambled into the Hotel Arctic's lobby, where Eddie Ulatuq, jazzed on a quart and a half of the hotel's complimentary coffee, was dancing from his left foot to his right foot in his anxiousness to get at the Sylvia Grinnell River's population of fat, tasty Arctic Char.

Eddie Ulatuq had driven a Territory of Nunavut motor-pool van down to the Hotel Arctic to pick up his guests, which was considerate insofar as his own private vehicle was a disreputable pickup truck, much banged-about and smelling of fish guts, cigarette smoke, and the stale, fermented effluvium of past caribou and seal carcasses, shot, slaughtered, and hauled home bleeding, shedding, and oozing residual foul fluids in the pickup's bed, where two or three of the Asteroid Associates would have had to ride, had Eddie not purloined a motor-pool van. Dr. Ing and his compatriots jumped in and buckled up. Eddie took off down Mivvik Avenue, then maneuvered northward past rows of two- and three-story apartments until turning onto Pingua Street, which abruptly became Qaqqahaq Street in the middle of a block, then a short distance later turned back into Pingua Street, then half a mile further on morphed into Qaqqamiut Street, then meandered off roughly northward into tundra and scabrock, whereupon it petered out at a dead end in the middle of nowhere. The Inuktitut word *qaqqaq*, visible in two of these street names, rather than representing the sound a duck makes as one might imagine, means 'mountain', but nothing resembling a mountain was to be seen along either Qaqqahaq Street or Qaqqamiut Street. Eddie Ulatuq had no clarification to offer.

"We're here!" he eventually announced as he yanked on the parking brake.

The Asteroid Associates bailed out. Immediately, a hundred million mosquitos winged up to them, making friendly overtures which plainly would *not* lead to any pleasant outcome. Bertie, having the day before gotten the word on bug repellent from Eddie Ulatuq, fetched a spray-can of Deep-Woods Off out of his parka pocket, uncapped it, took a shortstop spray for himself and then passed it around. "Where's the river?" he inquired, for nothing except a few stagnant, duck-frequented muskeg ponds were visible in any direction. The ducks were up early, paddling in circles and inscrutably crying "Mountain! Mountain!" to each other in Inuktitut.

"Thataway!" Eddie chirped, gesturing due-west. "About three-quarters of a mile! Stay right behind me and you won't sink out of sight into a quagmire! *Probably* won't!" He distributed miscellaneous bait-casting rods already rigged-up with leaders, weights and hooks, as well as tackle boxes, bait jars, and lunch supplies. They started walking toward the river.

Sure enough, fifteen minutes of hopping from one rock slab to another intermingled with short slogs through oozy bogs and there was the Sylvia Grinnell River! The watercourse was fast-flowing and went through a sharp zigzag, both the zig part and the zag part characterized by short stretches of particularly bouldery and tumultuous waterflow. Of the four Associates, only Bertie had much previous experience fishing in rivers. His eyes dwelt on the nice pools below each large boulder, and in his imagination he pictured the hungry Char lurking in these slack waters.

The river's environs seemed to teem with life! Both banks and the airs above them were liberally peppered with ravens, skuas, terns, jaegers and peregrine falcons, all hoping to breakfast on fish or fish-carcasses, or on one another's chicks. A family of snow-white arctic foxes prowled along the far bank, investigating washed-up salmon cadavers in search of just the one possessing a particular savor and succulence so as to meet foxy predilections. Half a mile upriver, an early-rising polar bear was wading around in the shallows, hunting for a nice girl salmon with a bellyful of salmon eggs to take a bite out of. The river water, presumably, was alive with salmon and Char, Northern Pike, Walleye, and a dozen other species of arctic game-fish. Close-in to each human face, a nimbus of insectile fauna zinged and buzzed and flitted, some of them hungry for mammalian blood, some of them just curious and persistent and bothersome.

Just-Bree had decided to wear her brand-new Inuit *silapaaq* and *paaluuq* and her beaver-fur RCMP cap. While the garments made her the most festively dressed of the seven, it may have been the least practical outerwear for an activity involving icky, bad smelling bait, riverbank mud, fish-blood and slime. The early dawn was rising cloudless and windless, promising a warm day, so Bree was likely to shed the parka and mittens sometime before lunch.

With a bit of instruction from Eddie, everyone unlimbered their gear, baited up, and spread out along a stretch of riverbank. Soon, salmon eggs on sharp hooks were being flipped out into promising spots in the Sylvia Grinnell River's flow.

"**что это**[21]!" Valeria yelled, yanking the tip of her rod about. Not thirty seconds after her bait hit the water,

---

[21] "chto eta?" = What's this?

the morning's first strike! She flailed about, quickly found herself jerked into the ice-cold water over her boot tops, the rod bent into an arc. Eddie, next upriver, swiftly retrieved his line, tossed his rod a safe distance up the bank, and went to assist. "Keep the rod up!" he yelled. "You've hooked a nice one! Reel that bad boy right in!"

Valeria had the fish within a couple yards of her feet. She hadn't given thought to exactly how she was going to retrieve, grab, land or net the fish, but that didn't matter very much, because at the last instant, the perfidious creature spit out the hook along with its skewered gob of salmon eggs, whereupon when the bent rod straightened up, the gooshy eggs flew clear of the water, zipped across the remaining distance and splatted into Valeria's shocked face. The freed fish hastily turned tail and ran for it, while Valeria gave vent to a string of corrosive vulgarities in unintelligible Russian.

This minor setback meant little, for within another thirty seconds, The Amoeba had a fish on. This one wound up flipping and flooping onshore when Meebs gave a mighty overarm yank on his pole. A nice three-pound Char. Within the first half hour, each of the fishers had experienced five or ten bites and landed one or two nice keepers.

…Except Bree. She was starting to feel as if maybe the Char population in the Sylvia Grinnell River just had something against her. Maybe they didn't approve of her smell. Or maybe they were put off by her colorful Inuit garb. Or maybe she was doing something wrong when it came to the baiting-up of her hook. On this latter suspicion, she retrieved her waterlogged lump of salmon eggs and had Eddie bait her up afresh. Ten fishless minutes later, she retrieved again, and found an eggless hook on the end of her line…the bait must have just come loose, because she sure as heck hadn't felt any bites. Disconsolate, she pulled off a mitten with her teeth, mashed a couple more bad-smelling eggs onto her hook and flung her tackle back out into the river. She was just finishing wiping her eggy fingers on the front of her parka when a massive tug bent her rod nearly double and tried to pull her off the bank into the seething rapids.

"*I got one! I got one!*" the usually laconic young woman bellowed. Fishline screamed off her reel. The rod tip thrashed. Bree danced and leapt into the air exuberantly, screeching, and at the far end of her line, so did the fish, albeit silently except for a lot of splashing noises. All Bree's compatriots simultaneously shrieked advice. She tried to crank the reel, got nowhere, gave up, and positioned both hands in a viselike grip on the whipping, jerking rod. Well and truly hooked, the fish eventually began to tire. Bree recovered a morsel of composure and tried cranking in some line. Gradually, her catch was retrieved. "Bring him up into the shallows!" Eddie yelled. A fin and a flashing tail broke water, and Eddie waded out to seize the exhausted critter by its gills and tail.

When Eddie hoisted Bree's fish out of the river, there was a collective intake of breath by the rest of the party. She had hooked a trophy Arctic Char, a fish just a few inches shy of three feet long, weighing a trifle over eighteen pounds. Eddie lugged the magnificent creature to the bank. Its jaw was mangled and bleeding copiously, having suffered a lot of damage from the hook in its fierce fight with Bree's tackle. Releasing the fish, which Eddie was usually inclined to do with spectacular trophy-sized Char, was a risk unlikely of a good outcome, although Bree pleaded for her fish's life to the point of tears until she too realized the animal would not survive its injury. Eddie dispatched the fish humanely after ensuring Bree that it would be admired, photographed, barbecued, and respectfully eaten, along with the rest of their day's catch, at the Mineral and Fossil Fuels Agency departmental

Nunavut Day picnic the following afternoon. She, Doctor Bree Patroness PhD, would be worshipped as a Nature Goddess of moderate importance for having been so clever as to hook and land such a behemoth, and she merely an inexperienced Southlander. This made Bree feel a little better as she remorsefully stroked her catch's glistening contours, the first fish of any species whatsoever she'd caught in her entire life.

The midsummer Arctic sun blazed down with surprising intensity. Before going back to fishing, Just-Bree retrieved the mitten she'd shed when she re-baited in order to catch her record fish. She pulled the other mitten off, and wiggled out of her parka as well. She draped the articles over a nearby rock, conveniently low, then got her hook baited and back into the river. Pretty soon she was absorbed in the challenge of hooking another finny monster. After a while, she'd reeled in two more Char, both of them around sixteen inches long and weighing more than a pound each. As she'd been instructed, Bree passed a cord through the fishes' gills and tied the stringer through a belt-loop on her pants, right next to the nice sheathed seven-inch fish knife Eddie had lent her. The fishes flopped against her brand-new bush trousers, painting them with slime and blood.

Some time later, a whuffling sound distracted Bree from her fishing. She turned to see a large, lanky polar bear sniffing her brand-new Inuit parka she'd left up the bank on a rock. The beast seemed unaware of Bree's presence. It turned its attention to one of Bree's beaded and embroidered, fur-trimmed mittens which she—or rather Meebs—had paid a hundred and thirty dollars Canadian for, just the previous afternoon. Finding the mitten's odor pleasing, the polar bear had taken it up and was mouthing it toothily as if in preparation for swallowing the thing whole.

"You great big furry *scumbag!*" Bree shrieked. "Put my mitten *down!*" Incensed, the diminutive woman charged up the bank, flailing and snapping her fishing pole like a buggy whip in the direction of the bear. Utterly surprised, the pathetic creature, only mortal flesh after all, dropped the mitten and bolted up-bank into the willow brush, seeking sanctuary. Thirty yards downstream, Eddie Ulatuq cried out *"Noooo!"* in panicked alarm as Bree vanished into the brush in rash pursuit of the bear. Eddie, Dr. Ing, and Bertie abandoned their rods and dashed after her, intending, it would seem, to rescue—empty-handed— their harebrained colleague from one of North America's fiercest apex predators.

Eddie broke through the thin band of willow scrub. He expected to find the polar bear standing over Dr. Patroness's steaming, dead, eviscerated corpse, the carnivore gulping mouthfuls of bloody entrails. Instead, what he saw was Dr. Patroness sitting on a rock cutting segments of Char with her razor-sharp fish knife and feeding them one-at-a-time to a docile and very hungry juvenile polar bear. As she thrust slices of fish at the creature's slavering jaws, Bree cooed placating words, repentant for having yelled so harshly and frighteningly at the poor creature. Imagine Eddie Ulatuq's incredulity.

Dr. Bree Patroness's status as an outlandish deity of moderate importance took a significant ratchet upward. Over the next few days, a north-country legend would take root and blossom, spreading by word of mouth through all of Iqaluit, and beyond.

Some while later, the fishers took a break for lunch. At least a billion mosquitos, blackflies and no-see-ums decided to join in, with the intention of lunching on the lunchers. Everyone applied another healthy dose of Off, the artificial floral scent of which failed to obscure the harsher odors of the repellent's active ingredients, and

171

added very little in the way of deliciousness to their baloney-on-Wonderbread sandwiches.

While they munched sandwiches and waved ineffectually at clouds of flying bugs, Meebs's cellphone emitted its lugubrious musical ring-tone, an excerpt of the Darth Vader theme, recognized the world over. The Amoeba picked up. It was Malcolm MacDooley!

"Hey, Malcolm! Where you calling from?"

"Jessie and I are back in Hartford! Mission accomplished! We rented a pickup and went to fetch the electronics trailer. We've got it stashed in a self-storage garage downtown. Meebs, you won't believe what we pulled off! Jessie was marvelous! Right here in my hand I got—"

"Mal, you better not talk about it on the phone! Why don't you and Jessica hop on a plane and fly up here?"

"Okay...."

"Listen...use your Associates credit card to pay the airfare. Don't sweat the overcharge for an immediate departure. And don't be shocked by what a pair of tickets is going to cost! There's nothing much you can do about it, so—"

"Excuse me," Eddie Ulatuq interrupted. He'd drawn certain conclusions from the half of the conversation he could eavesdrop on. "I can get your colleagues a pretty good deal on airfare."

"What kind of deal?"

"Oh, about four hundred bucks Canadian each, from Toronto. Actually...a little less if you connect through Ottawa."

"Yow! That's fabulous!"

"Lemme have the phone, Dr. Ing."

Meebs passed the cellphone over. Eddie introduced himself to Mal, made sure he had a pencil and paper handy, and reeled off the particulars and code numbers that would allow him and Jessica Moonflower to make the Toronto-to-Iqaluit leg at special, highly discounted Nunavut Government fares.

"Is that legitimate?" Meebs had to ask, after the phone conversation concluded.

"Oh, iiii!" Eddie assured him. "Totally legitimate for Iqaluit residents, property holders, Territorial officials, and all parties negotiating business with them. The $2800 airfare is special for tourists. Er…I assume that's what we're gonna be doing, Meebs…negotiating some kind of business?"

"A perfectly valid assumption! Well, for now, should we get back to the business of catching some more Char, or do you think we've got enough for tomorrow's barbecue?"

Eddie glanced at the row of fish cooling in the river shallows, strung through the gills on various cords. Bree's monster lumped large at the end of the lineup. "Should be enough! Are you folks ready to pack it in and head back to the van?"

As the van bumped over the rutted road entering the outskirts of Iqaluit, Eddie had a suggestion. "It's only two thirty, but you folks are probably going to want dinner sometime this evening, yeah?"

General murmurs of agreement.

"Well there's a restaurant called Big Racks Barbecue—"

The name put Dr. Ing, Valeria and Bertie in mind of Jessica Moonflower. Eddie received a subliminal twitch from the dreamy expressions on their faces.

"No, no! The name has to do with *antlers*! They got caribou and moose and elk heads and stuff like that on the walls! Walrus tusks! Narwhal horns! Jeez, you guys!"

173

"Okay, okay. Wait'll Malcolm gets here with his girlfriend...you'll understand then."

Eddie looked quizzical. "Anyway...I'll drop you-all at the Hotel so you can get cleaned up and change clothes. Then I'll get these fish prepped and put in cold storage for tomorrow. Then I'll come back for you about seven o'clock, say."

Big Racks Barbecue was not as casual a dinner spot as its name suggested. A nice table for five sported a 'reserved' placard and was set with nice tableware, candles and a spray of quite convincing artificial flowers in a vase. You couldn't get fresh flowers on Baffin Island or anywhere else within a thousand miles. Oddly, the establishment did not offer wine, beer or drinks. But the menu listed a nice selection of steaks and chops and fish and mollusks and crustaceans and pasta dishes. The waitstaff took orders and then directed the diners to a peculiarly-stocked salad bar, with plenty of canned vegetables, relishes, nuts, chips, bread, rolls, dressings and the like, but the skimpiest imaginable bowls of actual salad greens and fresh sliced items...a limitation imposed by being located two thousand miles north of the nearest fresh-produce farm.

A plump, shy waitress who could not possibly have been more than sixteen years of age worked her way around the table. When Bertie asked her for a recommendation, the best she could manage was to point at the section of the menu listing grilled steaks, using the eraser end of her pencil. Bertie opted for the pan-grilled tenderloin of caribou. Eventually the waitress worked her way around to Bree, the last diner around the table.

"You got chips 'n salsa?" Bree asked.

The shy waitress only nodded, but in fact she wasn't certain, since it wasn't listed on the menu and since she didn't know what 'chipsensalsa' was, exactly.

"Real hot?"

The waitress nodded again. What else could she do?

Eddie, occupying the place next to Bree, took in this exchange. "Siksik," he murmured to the waitress, "Doctor Patroness is from Arizona, so she likes her salsa *real* hot. See if Cookie's got a jar of *Fuego de Sonora* Pico de Gallo back there in the kitchen, the kind with serrano chilies, habaneros, and chipotle…it'll be marked *PELIGRO! Muy picante y caliente diabólica!* Lemme have that notepad and I'll write it out for you. And bring her *nacho* chips, the thick corn kind for dipping…when Arizonans ask for chips, they don't mean *potato* chips, honey. And bring her a big glass of milk, just in case she needs to put out the fire."

Siksik the shy waitress nodded, blushing. Done with taking orders, she scuttled off toward the kitchen.

Eddie turned to Bree and asked "That sound about right to you, Doctor Patroness?"

Just-Bree smiled her agreement. "I *like* chips 'n salsa," she explained.

"So! Dr. Bree! I understand your gentleman told The Tum-Wum that you are the team's specialist in meteoric metals and metal ores?"

"Ulp!" Bree swallowed. She had about as much knowledge of this particular technical topic as she had about brain surgery or rocket science. "Mmm…yeah! Metals!" she fibbed.

"I would've thought that metallic meteorites were pretty scarce don't we usually get mostly just stony chondrites, instead of iron bolides?"

"Nope…th' iron kind."

"Oh. Okay. Didn't know that. And…other metals, too?"

Just-Bree racked her brain for what other metals she'd heard the others discussing. Something useful popped into her memory. "Well...there's *nickels*!"

"Oh yeah! Nickel! And a small percentage of cobalt too, isn't that so?"

"Yep. 'N also, there's *gold*!"

This last crucial word only half-registered on Eddie Ulatuq, because at that precise instant an enormous peal of laughter erupted from The Amoeba, Valeria Tamoritskaya, and Bertie. Eddie naturally turned his head to see what was up.

"Hey Eddie, check this out! Meebs and I just got a text message from Malcolm and Jessica...they're on their way, should be here about noon tomorrow. Mal tacked on a nice pic of the two of them. It's mostly a nice glam shot of Jessie!" Bertie brandished his iPad and passed it down the table.

Rather than a selfie, some accommodating stranger must have snapped the shot of the two of them in the airport departure lounge, because Jessica Moonflower had one arm wrapped around Malcolm's neck and the other waving a bouquet of two dozen bon-voyage roses which were certain to make a big hit in flowerless Iqaluit. Her mouth was agape in an enormous laugh of triumph, while Malcolm, also smiling toothily, had the entire Jessica Moonflower wholly supported in his arms, left arm under her bare thighs with her skirt hiked dangerously far above the knees, right arm under her wriggling torso. The pair of anatomical features which most specifically typified Jessica Moonflower were displayed at their spectacular best, the top three buttons of her satiny blouse unfastened and a lace-trimmed blue rayon brassiere accentuating her breathtaking cleavage.

Eddie, only a mere male mortal after all, gasped and goggled. Any feeble recollection of Dr. Bree Patroness uttering the word 'gold' got brutally shoved back into a

176

dim, distant recess in Eddie's brain.   But...*not entirely
obliterated.*

25

STONE SOUP

Jessica Moonflower and Malcolm MacDooley had been routed from Hartford, Connecticut to Philadelphia on a Regional commuter airline. The flight departed several hours before the sun came up. Philadelphia was at least two hundred miles in the wrong direction, but that's the way air travel works these days. From Philly, they were going to be herded onto a flight to Toronto. From Toronto they were to connect to a flight direct nonstop to Iqaluit. This is a good thing, since between Toronto and Iqaluit there *was no place* to stop, barring as a pile of smoking, twisted metal on the featureless tundra somewhere extraordinarily remote.

Except for two and a half hours in the early morning languishing in Philadelphia, the connection times were pretty good. Jessica used their Philly time to good advantage, leaving Malcolm parked with a stack of magazines in the departure lounge while she took care of some shopping.

"What'd you get?" Mal asked. Jessica had come back trundling a big cardboard box on a SmarteCart, not five minutes before their flight was due to board. She handed the box off to the gate agents to stow in the baggage compartment.

"Oh…just a little something for Valeria!"

"What? What?" Dooley pleaded.

"You'll see!"

Meebs was there to greet them as they deplaned in the July sunshine at Iqaluit International. "Where are the others?" Malcolm asked.

"There's a big potluck lunch! We're all invited and they are there already. Today's Nunavut Day. Let's grab your bags quick, because I gotta stop at the market and get some stuff!"

Shortly they stood on the sidewalk in front of the terminal, wheeling another SmarteCart with their luggage piled on it. The suitcases were topped with Jessica's big boxed purchase from Philadelphia. "Where's the cabs?" Malcolm asked.

"No cabs! Town's only about two hundred yards thataway. But! I borrowed Eddie's panel-van because the potluck is out at the picnic grounds by the soccer field, and that's 'way out on the far edge of town!"

"Okay. Uh…Eddie the guy who lined up the fabulous airfare?"

"Yep. Eddie Ulatuq. Natural Resources employee. We gotta handle him right, 'cause if *anybody's* gonna, he's the guy that's going to issue us our permit to take the…uh…*material* from Sarpedon-E!"

"Okay. So, what do you gotta get at the market?"

"Well, it's a potluck, see? So everyone's supposed to bring something. Yesterday, the four of us went out with Eddie and caught about a hundred pounds of fish to barbecue. So there's fish. People start showing up, and the first eleven people all brought the same thing: cans of Pringles potato chips. NorthMart had a giveaway promo on cans of Pringles, is why. Then the next three brought condiments: ketchup, salt & pepper, peanut butter, mustard, pickled jalapenos, jars of olives. Then a few folks showed up with nothing at all. Then a guy comes in with a six-pack of club soda! Woo-hoo! One couple brought a styro freezer-chest stuffed with about fifty pounds of muktuk! We're staying at a hotel, so we didn't have anything foodwise to bring at all, so we brought a big pile of paper napkins and some plastic forks we got from the kitchen. But there's no paper plates! People try not to drink much

179

up here because a lot of Inuits have a pretty bad case of the standard native-American metabolic intolerance problem with alcohol…so, there's nothing to drink! No one thought to bring milk or pop or anything. Eight or ten people brought stuff in cans, but it's like canned peas or creamed corn or canned green beans or pickled beets or carrots or chili con carne, for Heaven's sake…random stuff like that! And nobody's got a can opener! So I gotta stop at the market and get some *real* picnic food, or the best we're going to be able to do is make fish soup out of the Arctic Char we caught along with all that miscellaneous stuff…except we don't have a sixty-gallon stewpot and we only got barbecue grills to cook on anyway. I'm thinking maybe I'll buy some sandwich bread and cold cuts, and a few gallons of ice cream."

"So for now everyone's out at the picnic grounds hungry?"

"Well…they've got hors-d'oeuvres."

"What've they got?"

"Muktuk and potato chips."

"Er…what's muktuk, again?"

"Whale blubber. Actually…whale *skin*."

"How is it cooked?"

"It isn't…you eat it raw. Whaleskin sushi."

"Sort of makes you yearn for one of Fin Fin's six-course Midday Refections, doesn't it?"

Meebs grinned. "Not all that much!"

Jessica chimed in. "Well don't you fret, Dr. Ing…I got just the thing in that nice big box there…I bet Valeria will be happy to share!"

"What's in there?" Meebs asked.

"Five dozen individually foil-wrapped, extra-large Philly Cheese Steak Hoagies, all packed in freezer-pacs! Bought 'em in the Philadelphia airport! Toss 'em on the grill for about two minutes to hot 'em up and re-melt the cheese, they'll be ready to go!"

Jessica's hoagies saved the day. When Valeria tore into her gift box and saw what Jessie had brought for her, her delight and enthusiasm was so irrepressible—even though expressed in fulsome Russian—that the Iqaluit partygoers could not help but become infected with her avid spirits. In addition to five dozen Philly hoagies, one late-arriving guest had brought seven nice big seal-flipper pies, a peculiar northeastern Canadian delicacy which none of the Asteroid Associates had ever heard of or imagined the existence of, not to mention tasted. Meebs had scored a big jar of triple-hot salsa imported from Texas and a couple bags of corn nachos at the market, even though the price-tags for these delectable rarities had been outrageous. So Dr. Just-Bree, who was the object of hushed veneration because of those fishing-trip incidents being whispered around, was well taken care of. For a while she amused herself persuading innocent Inuits to try a gob of fiery salsa on a nacho and noting their blazing-tongue responses, although mercifully she toted a two-liter bottle of sugarless lemonade so as to offer her dupes some on-the-spot flaming-mouth relief. This mischievous diversion usually persuaded her victims to turn their attentions to Cheese Steaks rather than take a second dip of salsa. As with hot-hot salsa, many Iqaluitans had also never munched a Philly Cheese Steak before either, but by the end of the day, every last hoagie had been gobbled. And most of the grilled Arctic Char, indeed the tastiest fish on the planet. And all the available Pringles, and all the strawberry ice cream that Meebs had hauled back from his market run. There wasn't even very much muktuk left.

Eddie Ulatuq asked Dr Bree her opinion of muktuk. "It's real chewy! Like fish-flavored bubble gum!" Just-Bree observed. "I *like* it!"

Jessica Moonflower, naturally, was marveled at by all Iqaluitans of the male persuasion, for the usual reasons, she being a certifiable bombshell. But also, when it became apparent that Jessica, conversing in breezy fashion with Valeria, was effortlessly fluent in Russian, a further layer of awestruck marvel was laid upon her. To the Inuit ear, Russian seemed to be as tricky a tongue as Inuktitut. And Malcolm MacDooley inspired transcendent reverence for the simple reason that Jessica Moonflower clung adoringly to his arm and conferred periodic smooches on his face. The lucky sod!

26

A SUNDAY AFTERNOON IN IQALUIT MUSEUMS

A s usual, Valeria was the early riser on Sunday, if almost nine-thirty in the midmorning could be still called early. She dressed, then gave Bertie an encouraging wakeup kiss. This failed to move him to anything more than a half-conscious, raspy exhalation and a sheet-thrashing rollover, so she slipped into her clothes and quietly exited their room.

The far-North day was not too cold. She strolled northeast a few blocks, just breathing in the ethereal midsummer air, then rounded the block and wandered back to the Hotel Arctic's lobby to browse tourist brochures for a while. The afternoon before, nobody had put forward any plans for the day, so Valeria surmised she might just as well consider that task being up to her. Fifteen minutes of sorting through the brochure rack and she had an agenda all planned out. She drifted over to the table bearing the hotel's complimentary coffee and bagels and helped herself. Half an hour later, Bertie ambled downstairs. Within another half-hour, the other Associates made their appearances, one at a time.

"Valeria has the day all planned out!" Bertie announced when everyone had a few restorative slurps of coffee in them. "Tell them what we're gonna do, Sweetie!" he encouraged her.

"*Da, pravilnye*! Feerst, we walk to Iqaluit Veezeetir Ceentriya!" Valeria waved vaguely southward. "Afteer, we go one hoondreed *metriy* to...to Nunatta Sunakkutaangit Moozeeooom!"

Everyone thought Valeria was just butchering the actual name of this museum as usual, since in the short time she'd been on the North American continent, her ditzy pronunciation of English had not improved very much. But no, that was the Inuktitut name of a small, tasteful art museum just down the block from the Unikkaarvik Visitor's Center, both destinations just a nice downhill walk southward along Queen Elizabeth Street, then a short distance east on Sinaa Avenue.

"We gonna have some *breakfast* first?" asked Jessica. After all, it was nearly eleven o'clock, and there hadn't been an abundance of regular feedings en route since she and Dooley had started out in Hartford about thirty-eight hours earlier.

"Nyet! *Lyubimyy*[22] Jesseeka, at peek-neek you gobble **two** *bol'shoi* Pfeelee Tcheeznya Steckskis...*tozhe, mnogo*[23] muktuks! *Potomu, nykto* breekfists![24] We itt...*vtoroy zavtrak?*—loonch?—at Restooran *My Hero!!* afteer we look at airt in Nunatta Moozeeoom! You itt joost now nize beagle weeth coofee, thet's all you geet!"

Bertie scrolled through his iPad map of Iqaluit, trying to keep pace with his ostensible Russian girlfriend's itinerary. There wasn't any restaurant *My Hero!!* anywhere at all in Iqaluit.

The Unikkaarvik Visitor Center proved to be quite informative and diverting. The Center sprawled over eight or ten thousand square feet of one-time commercial space. Perhaps it had been a grocery supermarket or a warehouse, but now the building was tastefully converted into snowy displays, icy dioramas, a well-stocked gift shop, and a bank of informative help-yourself brochure dispenser-racks. The six of them slowly drifted apart into couples, which seems to be the accepted method for roaming about in museums the world over. One thing about wandering from display to

---

[22] dearest
[23] Also, a lot of
[24] Therefore, no breakfast!

display in a museum with one's Significant Other: there is no more effective way to discover whether the two of you are particularly well-suited. Are your museum tempos compatible? If not, do you make those little sacrifices to accommodate yourselves to each other's pace? Do you sop up miscellaneous facts at the same rate? Do the two of you read the little cards under each artifact at much the same speed? Or read the pertinent parts out loud, to each other? Or forego reading them altogether? Do you delightfully point out often-overlooked minor curiosities to each other? Can you perceive when your partner is reaching the saturation point and is ready to call it quits? Is your tolerance for browsing the gift shop and your resistance to the lure of its overpriced *tchotchkes* about the same? If you can honestly answer all these questions in the affirmative, there's some hope for the long-term survival of your relationship. Amazingly, all three pairs of Asteroid Associates, whom an impartial observer might have reasoned were three of the most unlikely, ill-matched couples on the planet, took delight and contentment from each other's company as museumgoers.

"Someone went a little crazy with the fake plastic ice dioramas!" Dooley opined at about one-third of the way through. At the moment they stood bathed in pearly luminescence of filtered fake sunlight, under a simulated ice floe as if immersed in a simulated arctic sea full of plastic narwhals, codfish, and assorted frolicking pinnipeds immobilized in mid-frolic. Mac's observation about the fake ice tickled the quirky humor synapses in Jessica Moonflower's brain and fueled a running sequence of gags and giggles and *bon mots* between the two of them all the rest of the way through, whenever they encountered another mass of plastic ice. No one else tuned into the weirdness of chunky plastic ice-blobs assembled as if from ice-shaped Legos when the two of them tried to pass along their amusement, later on.

185

Just-Bree, chronically lacking in formal education and somewhat permanently brain-fried due to past methamphetamine overconsumption, nonetheless had a running conversation with Dr. Marcellus Ing PhD concerning the amazing adaptive abilities of pre-Contact Inuit cultures to survive the planet's harshest environment while equipped with a profound paucity of tools, resources and technologies. Bree's end of these conversational exchanges were her usual condensed sentence fragments and monosyllables...but Meebs got her gist, honored her viewpoint, and gallantly suppressed his natural tendency to natter-on pedantically.

And, somehow, the yawning linguistic gulf that lay between Bertie and Valeria failed to diminish their shared delight as they drifted from one display space to the next, holding hands and rubbing shoulders the whole time.

"Well, that was certainly edifying!" Bertie gushed when they all six rendezvoused in the lobby.

"Whatcha got there?" asked Meebs, indicating Valeria's Unikkaarvik Visitor Center gift-shop bag.

Valeria blushed and declined to reveal her acquisition. The bag concealed a tiny diorama: on a simulated plastic slab of fake ice stood a white plastic igloo, a colorful plastic Inuit with a harpoon, and a furry plastic sled-dog...all inside a clear, fluid-filled plastic dome. When you shook it, little plastic snowflakes eddied about. A snowglobe! The archetypal useless tourist trinket the world over! But when, roaming through the gift shop, she'd encountered a shelf displaying several dozen various snowglobes all lined up. This particular knick-knack had caught and held her eye, and she'd been unable to stop herself giving it a good shake to make the tiny encapsulated snowstorm swirl, then watching rapt and rapturous as the sparkling, dancing flakes settled out...an action she repeated over and over again. Bertie had bought the snowglobe for her with neither editorializing nor judgment.

"C'n we go have lunch *now*?" Jessica Moonflower whined. "I'm starvin' like a scrawny orphan wolf-pup with a five-pound *tapeworm*!"

Valeria, blanching at Jessie's vivid imagery, was insistent. "*Nyet*! We go neext Airt Moozeeoom! *Afteer*, we hev loonch! Thees ees zee *proogrem*!" But she thrashed around in her bag and slipped Jessie a nice Kit Kat bar she'd bought for her in the gift shop, just in case her friend might be hungry.

Out into the sunlight they went two-by-two, and down the sidewalk no more than two hundred feet to the Nunatta Sunakkutaangit Museum, which was virtually next-door to the Visitor Center. When in the gift shop buying the schlocky snowglobe, Bertie had picked up a compact, abbreviated Inuktitut/English glossary, which he thumbed through the whole three minutes it took them to stroll from the Visitor Center to the Art Museum. He decided without feeling very much confidence that *Nunatta* might mean **The Land** or **The Community**, or perhaps **The North**, but reserved drawing any conclusions until he found out what *Sunakkutaangit* meant. He guessed it might be one of those long, concatenated word-strings that you find in the German language, like for example *bewundernswertezurückhaltung*. But he was unable to find a glossary entry for *suna* or *sunak* or *akkut* or *taangit* or *angit* or *git*, and that's all he had time for before they arrived at the glass-doored entry to the Museum, overlooked by a genuine *inuksuk* reproduction on a stonework pedestal, in case any caribou should wander by. So he stuffed his glossary back in his coat pocket and gave up.

The Museum was partially devoted to Baffin Island history and cultures, and pre-Contact Inuit artifacts. Tables

187

spread with loose-leaf albums showed that the Museum served as a repository for Iqaluik's historic photographs, some dating back to the late 1800's. But the institution was mostly devoted to Inuit art, and there were shelves and cases and walls and glass-topped display tables crammed with artwork. The galleries housed a multiplicity of media: embroidered tableaux on cloth, oil or acrylic paintings on canvas, welded and cast metal sculpture, bas-relief carvings or scrimshaw-like etchings on caribou antler or bone or walrus-tusk ivory. Hundreds and hundreds of sculptures in soapstone or other mineral materials, featuring birds, sea creatures, dogs, polar bears, pipes, wands, combs, pins, wristlets, pendants, buckles, masks, seal-oil lamps, ritual tools and appurtenances, spirit faces, caribou, whales, walruses, foxes, ravens, Snowy Owls, ptarmigan…and many, many parka-clad Inuits in a thousand poses and performing a thousand tasks of toil, survival, craftsmanship, ritual, child-nurturing, procreation, relaxation, and daily life.

Bree wandered from case to case, transfixed by what she was taking in of the unique stone artistry of North American Arctic cultures. In one room, the left-hand wall hosted a glass-fronted case of older, 'traditional' Inuit stonecarvings, items created by anonymous winterbound seal hunters or fur trappers, laboriously scraped out of soapstone or argillite with little more than a flint burin or a discarded nail mounted in a caribou-antler handle. Any particular artifact had likely been traded for a sack of biscuit flour, or half-a-dozen rifle cartridges, or a bolt of printed cotton cloth. The right-hand wall's matching case held more-contemporary stone sculptures of identical motifs, but these ones had been executed by young, modern-day Inuit artists who had studied at universities in Montreal or Winnipeg or New York City…studio art that tried to meld traditional motifs with contemporary art-gallery appeal. Bree bounced back and forth between these contrasting styles for twenty minutes, detached from Meebs and lost in befuddlement.

"What's up, Bree?" her boyfriend finally asked.

"Same...but *different*!" she answered.

"Well...*yeah*!" Meebs was unsure what else to say. "Which do you like better?"

Just-Bree unhesitatingly jerked a thumb toward the simple, powerful traditional artistry on the left-hand wall

They all reconnoitered outside, under the inuksuk. Jessica Moonflower noticed that Bree was looking a little glum. "What's Bree down about?" she surreptitiously asked The Amoeba.

"She's bummed by the impact of contemporary artistic commercialist trends overwhelming aboriginal naturalistic simplicity, in relation to traditional Inuit Art."

"Oh. Ya don't say? Yeah...I guess," Jessie responded vaguely. She wandered away from Meebs, to where Bree was moodily staring upward at the inuksuk as if expecting that silent stone eminence to explain it all to her. Jessie took Bree's arm in solace and guided her toward where the others were clustered, waiting. "Hey, Honeylamb," she whispered. "You'n me both'll feel a lot better, we go get a little *lunch* inside of us!"

Once again, the six of them stood bunched up on the sidewalk in the Arctic sun. Bert had the Google map of Iqaluit up on his iPad. "Okay, Val...so where's this *My Hero!!* restaurant of yours?" he asked. "I can't find any eatery like that anywhere in town!"

Valeria contemplated the map. "Heer iss! Neext to aeroportsky!" She pointed at a spot on the map maybe a quarter-mile away from where they were standing, on Mivvik Street just a short way from Iqaluit International Air Terminal.

Meebs craned to have a look at the map. "Hey!" he exclaimed. "I remember that place! Long skinny brown building with a green roof! We walked right past it. Seems to me it's a *Lebanese* restaurant! Valeria, could it be called *My **Gyro***?" He, like most Americans and acculturated Taiwanese immigrants, pronounced the word to start with a *soft* 'G', like in the name *George*, and to more-or-less rhyme with *Cairo* (the capital of Egypt) or *Biro* (the European ballpoint pen) or *pyro* (the lunatic arsonist), rather than rhyming with *zero* (nothing, nada, zip, or the WWII Japanese fighter-plane) or *Hero* (the handsome, brave young fellow with super-powers) or *Nero* (the horrid Roman Emperor).

"*Nyet*! Ees *My **Gyro**!!*" Valeria insisted, pronouncing the word like most Russians and ancient Greeks would, more-or-less like the word *Hero* except with a little more guttural intonation on the *hard* 'G', or maybe the 'G' being somewhere in between a 'G' and an 'H' and a 'Y', and the 'y' being more like an 'e', only lengthened a bit until it's almost like 'ee'. The confused pronunciation arose, naturally, from the fact that the particular comestible in question was prepared by impaling a whole bunch of spiced, marinated meat slabs on a spit, piled up into a big cylindrical blob, then setting the spit vertically in front of a fire or an electric element or a vertical gas burner, to slowly rotate by means of an electric motor or a hand-crank for hours and hours—to *gyrate*, don't you see?—while the meat slowly roasts and oozes out its juices and smells pretty darned good, then the meat is shaved off vertically in thin slices which are piled into a folded pita-bread or onto a hoagie roll along with sautéed onions and peppers and sour cream and hummus and tahini sauce and pickles and yogurt and tzatziki and marinated turnip slices and even stranger condiments than these, and served to the hungry diner as a Hero Sandwich or a Gyro or a Shawarma or a Souvlaki or a Hecatomb (if you happen to be Odysseus and are

190

attempting to appease the gods with a measly, half-burnt tidbit of braised meat so they'll eventually stop jerking you around and let you get home to Ithaca and your gorgeous wife as you attempt to return from the damned, blasted, nine-year-long Trojan War! Check your *Odyssey*…every single chapter starts with the 'hecatomb' bit!). Yikes!

Bertie looked up from his iPad with a big smile. "Well *okay* then! *My Gyro!!* Here it is…right near the airport!" He stabbed a finger at the exact same spot on the Google map that his seriously aggravated Russian girlfriend had already pointed out only a minute ago. Valeria stamped her foot and glared at her dimwit genius boyfriend. Everyone else rolled their eyes heavenward and just started walking.

My Gyro!! was not very far away at all. The noon rush had tapered off, since it was 2:45 p.m. when they climbed up the weatherbeaten wooden steps and pushed in through the glass doors. Plenty of unoccupied tables. Jessica took the initiative and grabbed the nearest six-place table available. Evidently she was famished to the point of hypoglycemic hallucinations, hungry enough to imagine the whole restaurant and all the food in it would vanish like a shimmery desert mirage if she didn't take rapid, definitive action. She had a menu out and open before the others managed to snag themselves a seat.

"Woo-HOO! Look at these plate-lunches!" she cried. "I'm havin' one of *ever'thing!*" She didn't really mean it, but her eyes quickly fixed on the picture of a Large Mixed Shawarma Combo, served with a side of potatos, rice or Lebanese salad. Jessica didn't know what a Lebanese salad was, exactly, but it sounded pretty good to her. So when the waitress drifted over with a pencil poised above her order pad, the Large Mixed Combo was what Jessie ordered.

"Can I have the potatos AND the Lebanese salad?" Jessica asked.

The rotund waitress eyed Jessica Moonflower's alluringly slim, leggy albeit busty figure, cornflower-blue eyes, golden tresses, and high-cheekboned, pixie-cute face with ill-concealed envy. "Sure, honey...anything you like! What ya want to drink?" With the eraser end of her pencil, the waitress indicated Jessie should have another glance at the menu.

Mixed in with the fine print discussing side orders was the phrase 'comes with one (1) can pop'...there weren't any other drink options offered, although Jessie wouldn't have turned down a Margarita if one were offered. Or a whole pitcher of Margarita. "Coke, I guess," she decided. Canned pop, she mused...pretty classy restaurant.

Sitting next to Jessica, Meebs was running his eye down the right-hand column where the prices were listed. Jessie's Shawarma Combo came in at $39.50. Admittedly this price was in *Canadian* dollars, which were currently trading at $1.43 to the US dollar. But it did NOT include the additional VAT and GMT taxes, whatever those unfamiliar initials might mean. Taxes on purchased items can be startlingly complicated in Canada—running as high as 14% in some provinces—but this add-on only amounts to 5% in Nunavut. Still, Meebs had to wonder whether *My Gyro!!* restaurant, which was basically serving casual fast-food fare in an unprepossessing environment rather than *haute cuisine* in a chic candlelit café, was surreptitiously in league with the $2800 airplane-ticket people.

The final tab may have come to quite a bundle for the six of them, but the food turned out to be pretty good, and plenty of it. The whole bunch of them were stuffed and satisfied with a Sunday well frittered-away when they finally settled their bill and wandered on back to the Hotel Arctic. Tomorrow was the Big Day...time to negotiate with Eddie Ulatuq and the authorities of Nunavut about mineral rights to their inward-bound Earth Crosser.

27

NEGOTIATIONS PROCEED

Ten o'clock promptly! The six members of the Asteroid Gang stood outside Room 2388 in the Indigenous & Northern Affairs offices waiting for Eddie Ulatuq. At ten-fifteen, Eddie strolled in, his arms full of documents and file-folders. He was accompanied by two other Nunavut government officials: a man and a woman. The man most of them recognized; it was Solomon Ikajuqtuq, The Tum-Wum. The woman was someone new.

"Good morning everybody!" Eddie effused as he fumbled to open the office door, which was, like every other door in Iqaluit, not locked. "You already know Solomon, our Tum-Wum, and this is Lizzie Maatsi. She's the requisite *Maligaliuqti* for our little panel this morning...that means she's a member of the Legislative Assembly.

Each of the Gang smiled and shook hands with Ms. Maatsi, and shared a few cordial words of greeting. Privately, Dr. Ing gave thanks that 'Maatsi'—which is Inuktitut for 'May', the month—was pretty easy to pronounce, and lacking in any instances of the letter 'q' which seemed indispensible to Inuit names and subject to half a dozen alternate pronunciations. Unbenownst, Ms. Maatsi's actual name was 'Naggajjaupaimaatsi'—which is Inuktitut for 'Monday the Fifth of May', Lizzie Maatsi's birthday.

The bunch of them filed into a comfortable conference room. Its walls were adorned with photos of dignitaries, celebrities and common folk shaking hands with a particularly good-looking, smiling Inuit fellow. A striking oil portrait of the same fellow occupied a central place, framed ornately.   Certificates and honors and testimonial letters from important people worldwide, framed behind glass, hung to one side.   "Paul Okalik!" Eddie announced, indicating the portrait with a reverent gesture.   "These were his chambers when he was first Premier of Nunavut.   Two terms!   From 1999 to 2008…quite a guy!   Still serves in government and comes around pretty often.   Maybe you'll meet him!"

Malcolm had read a bit about Okalik.   First Inuit law-school graduate called to the Bar in Nunavut.   As Premier, he'd done much to set the course for Nunavut. His administration had pursued ambitious priorities for the Territory: education, health care, housing, electrification, free Internet connectivity, economic self-sufficiency.   Mal scribbled a few notes on his scratch-pad and passed it down the line as a tipoff for the others.   Paul Okalik had been a tireless advocate for the education of the youth of Nunavut, for improving housing, nutrition, hospitals, public services and work opportunities for all its citizens, and for moving the Territory away from its overwhelming ninety-percent reliance on Canadian governmental fiscal support, and in the direction of economic self-sufficiency.

"Well!   Let's get comfortable!   There will be an Assembly page along in a little while with some coffee. Now, Dr. Ing, I'm guessing you will want to have the floor, and tell us what your interest here in the Far North amounts to!   Before we get too far along, let me make it clear that we ought to keep things nice and informal.   Also, if there's to be a decision on your request, the three of us will discuss until we arrive at consensus…like a unanimous resolution through conversation rather than strictly a vote.   That's the traditional deliberative process in Nunavut."

Dr. Ing sat up straight and began.   "Eddie, as you know, we're interested in metallic minerals obtained from meteorites.   The expansive uninhabited areas of Nunavut, excluding its parks and game preserves of course, offer

195

thousands of square miles in which to locate what we seek, without a lot of timber or brush, or high-relief mountain ranges or—"

"Yeah, but we've got almost no roads!" interrupted Solomon. "Travel's a lot harder than you might imagine! Nunavut doesn't have particularly more meteoric material than any of the rest of the world, does it?"

Meebs shuffled through a bunch of photographs. "Actually, yes. There have been some notable events. Here's some pics of nearby meteoric impact craters. This one's Lake Wiyashakimi in northern Quebec...the crater's twelve miles across. And this one's the Île René-Levasseur, an impact feature that's *fifty* miles in diameter."

"Een Yeer Twentiye-Theertin...ees Chelyabinsk metyooreet!" Valeria inserted. "*Tozhe*, een yeer Nineteen-Eeght, heppins Toongooska Eveent! **Blooee**! *Bol'shoye* eexsploozhin in sky! *Nye* Canada, but preety fair noorth een Rooshyan *Tseebiryeh, da?*"

"*Da*, pretty far north!" Meebs agreed. "Well, and here's a shot of Chubb Crater...its modern Inuit name is *Pingaluit*. It's in the very northern extreme of the Ungava Peninsula. Two-plus miles across, thirteen hundred feet deep. Then there's this one: the Haughton Impact Crater on Devon Island, just north of Baffin Island. Fourteen miles across. And have a look at the southeastern bight of Hudson Bay. It's almost perfectly circular along a circumference of about a hundred-sixty degrees...if it's part of an impact feature, it would be *three hundred miles in diameter!*"

Here's a map of Hudson Bay, showing the circular feature in question:

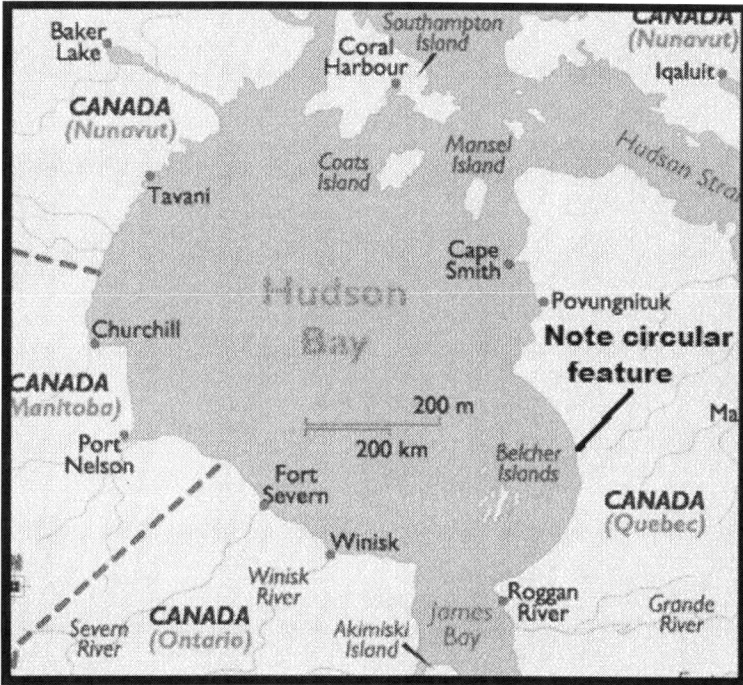

"But what about the Belcher Islands?" Ms. Maatsi asked.

"Ummm...you're right. Geologists disagree wildly on the Southeastern Bight crater hypothesis, specifically because of the Belcher Islands."

The Belcher Islands are one of the weirdest geological features in the world. They stick up out of the icy waters of Hudson Bay as if they are a swirl of maple syrup dripped from a giant pitcher. But no, they are made of rock. Not just rock, but rock that's almost two *billion* years old. And they are smack in the center of that nearly perfect circular feature described by the southeast shore of Hudson Bay. Islands like this have no legitimate business being in the middle of an impact crater, so it's pretty unlikely that it is an impact crater after all. Here's an aerial

197

view of the Belcher Islands, borrowed from the Internet. *You* decide!

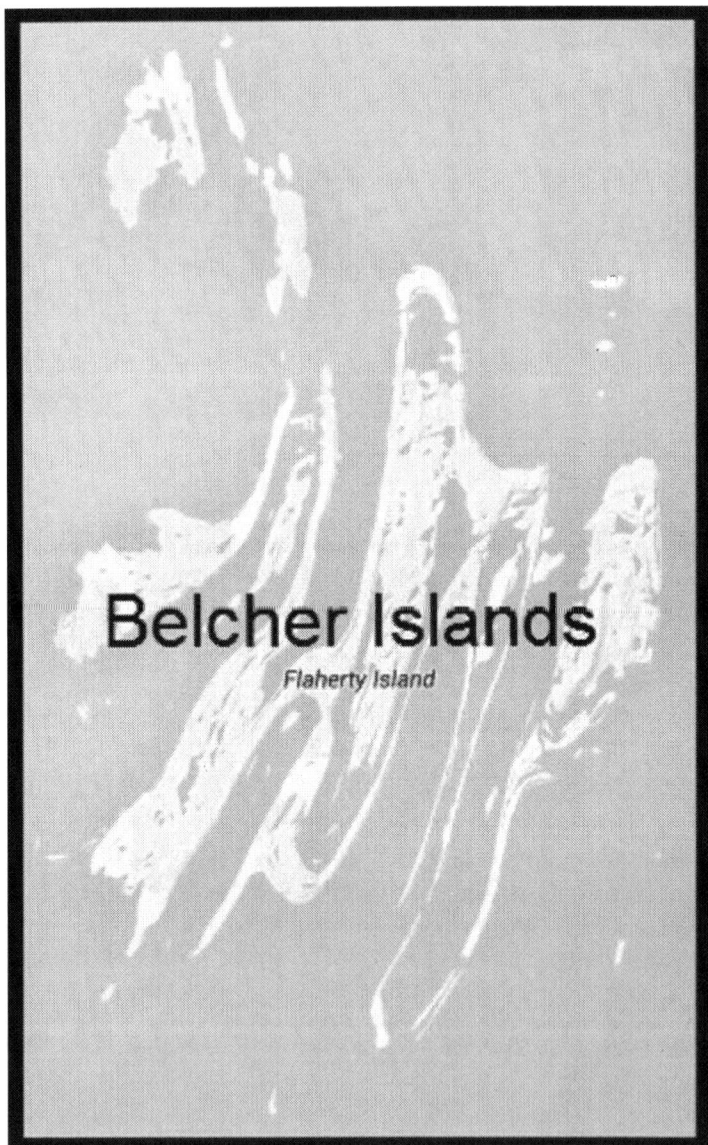

"Wait just a minute, Dr. Ing," Lizzie Maatsi protested. "You are not showing us mere meteor impacts! These are *huge* impacts…like *asteroids*!"

"Ummm…yes, you'd have to say asteroids. The guess, for example, is that the Île René-Levasseur impact, in the middle of Lake Manicouagan, was an asteroid five kilometers in diameter. It's believed to be the fourth largest visible, dry-land meteoric impact feature on Earth."

"So why hasn't anyone mined *that* crater for metals?"

"Well, Ms. Maatsi, it was almost certainly a stony asteroid, not a metallic one. And it impacted at very high velocity. Probably about seventeen kilometers a second. It shattered into a gazillion flinders!"

"Into a gazillion…*WHAT*?"

"Flinders. …Smithereens, if you prefer."

"Which one, flinders or smithereens?" Lizzie asked dubiously.

"Yeah, and how many smithereens are there in one flinder?" This from Solomon Ikajuqtuq.

"Maybe you should stick to *siuraq* or *tuapak*, Meebs," Eddie contributed.

"Huh?"

"Grains of sand…bits of gravel."

Dr. Ing shrugged and grinned. "Okay…point is, even those great big stony asteroids shatter to tiny pieces when they impact at high velocity. We're hoping for a much denser *metallic* bolide, impacting at much lower speed."

"Don't you mean '*looking for?*'…you said '*hoping for*' just now!" There was an expression of intense skepticism on Lizzie Maatsi's face.

Busted! Dr. Ing thought quick. His conclusion was that beating around the bush wasn't going to work with these shrewd individuals. He exchanged glances with Bertie, Malcolm and Jessica. All of them gave him infinitesimal nods, the International body-language sign for "you better tell 'em!"

"The fact is…well, the simple fact is, we are expecting the probable impact of a particular metallic meteor in which we have great interest."

"Where?" Eddie demanded.

"When?" Lizzie Maatsi queried.

"How big?" Solomon the Tum-Wum inquired.

"We don't know exactly where, but most likely impact will be in sierra or tango timezone, about the latitude of Baker Lake or a little north, but probably somewhere a good deal west of there, and trending east-southeast. If the asteroid breaks up in the atmosphere, the impacting fragments could spread over hundreds of miles. The asteroid's about a hundred meters in diameter. It will impact on the nineteenth of March next year. When exactly, Bertie?" he asked.

"One twenty-six a.m., tango timezone, give-or-take twenty-five seconds. 'Tango' is known as 'Mountain Standard Timezone' in the U.S. but I'm not sure what it's called in Canada."

Eddie's face wore a suspicious expression. "Wait a second! You talk like this asteroid's *your property*! And how can you be so certain of that impact time?"

"First off, we've got what amounts to a deed of ownership indicating we purchased it fair-and-square from the US General Services Administration, who inherited it from NASA and the Pentagon, who originally occupied it, robotically, and thereby laid claim to this particular asteroid, you might say, in 2003. If we can get your permission to salvage its metal content from Nunavut Territory we'll be happy to furnish you with certified copies of this bill of sale. In answer to your second question, we *have* got the ability to control its trajectory, using hardware whose ownership we also legally purchased from GSA. At the moment, the asteroid's about ninety-four days away from a…a midcourse flight-path correction. We'd all be better off not talking about exactly *how* we can accomplish this, or in the case of you guys, not even *knowing*, actually. Let's all presume that the thing is just on its own personal, random collision trajectory. But if it turns out you-all cannot accept having a smallish asteroid brought to earth in the unpopulated wilds of Nunavut, we'll have to redirect to a backup impact zone somewhere else." Bertie hated to be resorting to veiled caveats, but the implication was right there, out on the table: you snooze, you lose.

Eddie twiddled his fingers on the tabletop. "So… how can you guarantee this asteroid of yours won't just smash into a zillion unrecoverable pieces of *siuraq*?"

Bertie was so glad someone asked! He and Valeria had worked all this out together. "Well you see, the energy of impact is calculated by the asteroid's mass times the *square* of its impact velocity! We can't do anything about its mass, but if we can contrive to make its impact *velocity* less, we'll *greatly* decrease its impact *energy*! First of all, this asteroid is an Earth Crosser with an orbit almost identical to Earth's orbit…so it isn't travelling very much faster than the Earth, in terms of its orbital velocity around the Sun. Then, we're gonna have it enter the upper atmosphere at a very low angle of incidence on the Earth's dark side, 'way out over the western Pacific, at a late, late local time when the Earth's surface at the impact site is rotating *away* from the asteroid's direction of approach! Due to its revolution, the Earth's surface is moving west-to-east at somewhere near a thousand miles an hour, so it's almost exactly like an aircraft carrier traveling at flank speed, and a jet coming up aft of it for landing on a *moving deck*! The net landing speed is the jet's airspeed minus the carrier's forward speed! We figure the asteroid's impact energy will be less than one-fiftieth what it would be if it

201

just randomly plowed in from outer space, like most meteors do!"

Of the three Territorial officials, both Eddie and Lizzie had enough college-level physics to get the gist of all that. Sol had served six years in the Canadian Navy, which didn't have any aircraft carriers, but frequently participated in maneuvers with U.S. naval task-forces, which had *plenty* of aircraft carriers, so he got the gist of Bertie's description from a pragmatic point-of-view.

"Can you draw us a sketch of how it's going to come in?" Eddie asked.

Bert ripped a blank sheet of paper out of Malcolm's notebook. He drew a big rectangle representing a map of the Earth, as viewed from space directly above the Pacific Ocean, with the continents roughed-in. "You gotta imagine this in 3-D. It'll come in below the Equator at an altitude of about two thousand miles, over South Africa. No one in Africa is likely to scramble fighter-aircraft or fire any missiles at it or anything. It's pretty-much grabbed by Earth's gravity, 'cause it won't be moving a lot faster than the Earth, with respect to its orbital velocity around the Sun. It'll begin descending at a shallow angle, eastward across the Indian Ocean...sort-of spiraling in, do you see? It'll cross the equator moving northeastward, zoom across western Australia, then across New Guinea. We don't expect any interceptor missiles from New Guinea either. Then it'll head across the Pacific. This big S-shaped path is actually a more-or-less circular orbit, but tilted with respect to the Equator. It will have entered the upper atmosphere over the mid-Pacific, and will start being slowed by atmospheric friction. It won't blaze like usual meteors do, because it'll be moving a lot slower...more like the Space Shuttle's re-entry velocity. That's, like, somewhere around one and a quarter kilometers per second, versus twenty to seventy kilometers per second for normal meteors. So it'll get darned hot, but won't ablate too much...its surface won't melt away into vapor. It reaches maximum North latitude over northern Alaska and curves over into a slightly southerly-sloping trajectory. It ought to strike down right about here...two hundred miles east of Port Radium on Great Bear Lake." Bert's pencil, which had been tracing an orbital path as he talked, sketched a crude outline of Great Bear Lake, and a dotted line representing the boundary between the Northwest Territory and Nunavut. "That is, if it doesn't break up into a million smithereens," he added.

Here's a map sort-of like Bertie's sketch, but a lot better, because it's been borrowed from the Internet. You gotta love the Internet!

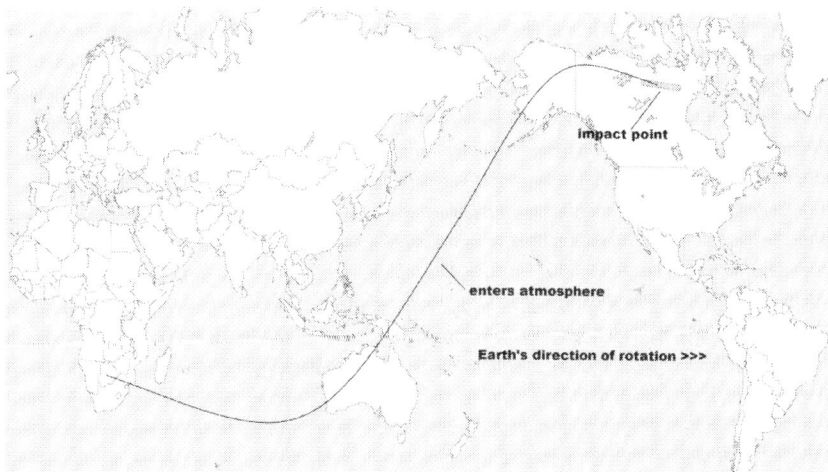

"Is there any prior history of a large metallic meteor surviving Earth impact in one big piece?" Eddie asked.

Just-Bree—or Doctor Patroness as she was coming to be known—had been briefed on this one so she could have something substantive to contribute. "Uh-huh!" she chimed in. "The Chinguetti Meteorite in Mauritania. Back in 1916, this British guy doin' some geologic surveying 'r somethin' in Africa got taken to see a big chunk of iron-nickel-cobalt, an' it hadda be a meteorite just like ours! Looked like a big mountain a hunnert 'n twenny meters long an' sixty meters high! It was down in a depression that could have been a seriously-weathered crater, 'cause it prob'ly happened fifty billion years ago. The African guide who took him there insisted the guy travel blindfolded, 'cause th' iron mountain was a big-deal local secret. The guy managed to bring back a ten-kilogram chunk of meteorite: iron-nickel-cobalt. It's in the British Museum. No one else has been able to find the damn meteorite-mountain again, so ever'one thinks it's a scam! But *our* asteroid ain't no scam, an' it's comin', an' no one's gonna stop it!"

"What do you call this asteroid of yours?" Lizzie Maatsi wanted to know.

Bertie answered that one. "Sarpedon-E. It's a Trojan asteroid from the Fifth Lagrange Point. An Earth-Crosser."

"Okay...an Earth-Crasher named 'Sharp Donny' from the Fifth Lounge Point." Lizzie imagined she might have just been told the asteroid was a flying saucer from the Fifth Dimension. She halfway suspected she and her two Nunavushian colleagues were having their legs pulled. "Okay, assuming this...this Trojan Asteroid actually exists, and a bunch of Greek warriors aren't gonna climb out of it an' cut our throats with bronze swords...what kind of metals are we talking about here?" Lizzie asked.

"Just like Bree said. Iron, mostly. Eighty percent by mass."

"And don't forget nickel!" Jessica Moonflower contributed.

"*Da, pravilnye!*[25] Neekeel!" Valeria seconded.

---

[25] Yes, certainly!

"Yeah...about ten percent nickel. A little cobalt as well." Dr. Ing waved his hands airily, trying to avoid having to make any further elaboration on these figures.

Eddie Ulatuq sat up a bit straighter. "Anything else?" he asked.

"Uhhh...anything, like what?"

"*Precious* metals? Like maybe...*gold*?"

Dr. Ing just stared. Double-busted! he thought.

"You better tell them!" Bertie encouraged him. Jessica nodded her acquiescence, and so did Mal. "*Da!* Tell!" murmured Valeria. Bree, blushing crimson because of having spilled the beans to Eddie a couple days before, examined her thumbnail with intense scrupulosity and didn't say anything.

"Four percent, we think."

"Four percent...*gold*?" Eddie asked, goggling.

"Uh-huh."

"Four percent of an iron meteor three hundred feet around?"

"Three hundred feet *in diameter*. Closer to three hundred and *thirty* feet. That's about eighteen and a half million cubic feet. Should have a mass of about ten billion pounds. Four-and-a-half billion kilograms, more-or-less."

"I can't even imagine how to calculate how much that's worth!" mumbled a stunned Eddie Ulatuq.

"Seven trillion dollars. Approximately."

"*Whaaaa?*" Eddie said. He was not the first to react to this incredible figure with this particular expletive. "Where...what...*HOW* do you figure?"

Bert took him through the numbers. "Four percent of four-point-five billion kilograms divided by thirty-two-point-two grams per troy ounce. That's five-point-six billion troy ounces, at $1266 per troy ounce...current price for gold. Seven trillion bucks. That's just the gold. The other metals add nine or ten billion more."

"Seven…! *Seven trillion dollars Canadian?*"

"Nope," Meebs answered. "Seven trillion dollars *U.S.* In Canadian dollars, that's— Help me out here, Bertie!"

"Ten point zero-one trillion Canadian."

The three Nunavushian officials exchanged stunned gazes. Solomon was the first to regain the power of speech. "And…what's our cut?" he asked.

Meebs coughed self-consciously before replying. "We were thinking fifteen percent as a royalty…or maybe call it a 'landing fee' or 'port duties.' Another five percent set aside for paid services over the next twenty or thirty years from citizens of Nunavut…like security, recovery efforts, legal fees…stuff like that? Ought to be administered through a Nunavut civil authority of some kind, eh?" Momentarily, he felt very Canadian, uttering that last syllable.

The three Nunavushian officials performed some very rapid mental arithmetic.

"Er…that comes to 525 times the current national GNP of Nunavut," Bertie offered. "No…wait a minute! That's working in US dollars. In Canadian dollars, it comes to 750 times the current national GNP of Nunavut. That's fifty million Canadian for every man, woman and child in Nunavut. No…wait! That's just the fifteen percent! If we include the other five percent assistance wages, we're talking…" He stopped to tap some numbers into his iPad, for the moment too flustered to do the relatively-simple mental math. "…We're talking a *thousand* times the current national GNP of Nunavut. *Sixty-seven* million apiece for everyone…on average. More-or-less."

"Fiscal self-sufficiency and jobs! Virtually *forever!*" Eddie mused aloud.

"Schools! Housing! Hospitals! Roads!" Lizzie Maatsi murmured. Whatever thoughts she might have had about flummery and deception evaporated in a wave of benevolent materialism.

"Wastewater treatment!" Solomon whispered in reverent tones. "Sewers!"

The three of them stuck their heads together for about thirty-five seconds of intense conferencing.

"We're *IN*!" Eddie Ulatuq yelled, his face contorted in a fantastic grin.

"Wonderful!" Meebs exclaimed.

"Fabulous!" Malcolm MacDooley added.

"Terrific!" contributed Bert. "Oh…one other thing I was gonna ask. D'you guys have some Nunavut Territorial official who could maybe handle getting Valeria and me married? Y'know, license and paperwork and ceremony, all that stuff? So it'd be legal back in the US?

His buddy Mal was dumbstruck! "Bertie!" he yelled. "When did *this* come about!"

"Well, three things. One: the Canadian Customs guy in Toronto on our way up here said Val was probably going to get a lot of gas from US Customs when we fly back home, considering her passport and tourist visa are Russian, so we figure if we're legitimately married, she'll be okay. Then number Two: don't you remember we agreed one of us had to marry her so she wouldn't blab to the KGB? And so she could stay in the US instead of having to go back to Chelyabinsk and freeze her ass off pardon my French? So it might as well be me. And then there's number Three."

"Yeah? Number Three?"

"Well…I *love* her! And we both think maybe there's a darn fine chance she could be *pregnant* by now. You know…considering." Bertie smiled beatifically.

Valeria had no trouble comprehending a couple of words in Bertie's Thing Number Three summation: 'love' and 'pregnant.' So she also smiled beatifically.

28

SARPEDON-E PRANGS IN

So over the next few months as the icebox of another Northern Canadian winter descended on Nunavut, here's how the Asteroid Associates and their Canadian Territorial co-conspirators divided up the duties:

Jessica Moonflower and Malcolm stayed in Iqaluit, taking the Far-North posting. Eddie Ulatuq requisitioned a nice little apartment for the use of any Asteroid Associates visiting Iqaluit, and Mal and Jessie took up residence. Their plan was to reposition to Baker Lake a short while before the big day.

Everyone came to refer to the big day, or rather, the big moment—One Twenty-Six a.m. tango on Nineteen March, give-or-take twenty-five seconds—as 'Impact.' In the months remaining before Impact, Mal and Jessie coordinated Associate activities with Eddie Ulatuq and his selectively-recruited 'special activity' staff, all of whom were solemnly sworn to secrecy.

First priority was to make certain that no citizen of Nunavut would be anywhere within a strip of tundra seventy miles wide and six hundred miles long on Impact Day. There were no permanent human habitations within this entire area, but there *were* a small number of hardy traditional Inuit hunters and fur-trappers who ventured into these Arctic wilds at any season of the year, including in the dead of midwinter. No problem...these hard-nosed individuals were well known, and Eddie's staffers simply contacted these guys and their families and offered them irresistible bribes to agree to be elsewhere on Nineteen March. Elsewhere, like Calgary, or Montreal...or on a

Royal Caribbean cruise-ship in the Bahamas. All expenses paid, courtesy of a special Territorial Treasury fund.

Next was to be certain that the possible harm done to highly-valued Arctic wildlife would be minimized. Caribou were not much of a problem, for in spite of being not very smart, they were at least clever enough to migrate south and spend the winter munching twigs and spruce-needles in the scrubby forests of Manitoba, five hundred miles away from the zone of Impact. Musk-ox, however, were another matter. The mainland Canadian population of these hardy, stubborn, wool-covered critters was down to perhaps ten thousand, distributed in small herds across the immeasurable vastness of the Eastern Canadian Arctic. Fortunately, the location and movements of each individual herd were pretty well known, thanks to telemetry tags which over the years had been placed on one or two members of each group. Most herds occupied territories farther east and north than the Impact strip, but a few were to be found along the upper Thelon River inside the zone of greatest risk. The plan was to send crews out on ski-planes and snowmobiles, weather permitting, a week before Impact. They would attempt to haze the at-risk herds out of the zone. Unfortunately, Musk-ox are as skittish as alley-cats and don't haze worth a damn. Also, Musk-ox don't tend to voluntarily stay very long where they are hazed to. All other wildlife—beasts, birds, rodents and insects—were just going to have to take their chances.

Another activity involved what might be called measures of deception. If word got out into the world at-large that there would soon be seven trillion dollars worth of gold slammed across forty thousand square miles of Nunavut's Arctic wilderness, nothing would hold back a gigantic gold-rush. The Associates and their Canadian compatriots figured that, sooner or later, some satellite or radar installation or astronomic observatory would detect the approach of Sarpedon-E, calculate its trajectory, and freak out. The word would leak. But Summer turned to Autumn, then to Winter…and the world press uttered not a squeak about an incoming Giant Perilous Collision-Bound Asteroid, intent on obliterating all terrestrial humankind. Everyone involved in the scheme kept their fingers crossed and counted off the days.

In a more proactive sense, Eddie Ulatuq came up with a nifty plan to thwart the world's seismographs from accurately detecting the moment and position of Impact. Here's the gist of Eddie's cunning deception: About sixty miles north of the town of Baker Lake on the Thelon River, there is a big open-pit operation called the Meadowbank Anico Eagle Gold Mine. The ore is pretty low-grade, and mining operations in that difficult country are arduous and expensive. Consequently, gold recovered from the ground cost them about $1150 an ounce to dig, chemically concentrate, smelt, mold into ingots, and transport…and is worth $1266 an ounce, more or less, in international trade. The mining operation is therefore pretty marginal. Eddie Ulatuq arranged with the Mine's management to surreptitiously borrow about fifty tons of high explosives from the mine's on-site stocks, along with the services of several experienced blasting technicians from the Meadowbank operation. These people, assisted by willing and well-compensated Inuit roustabouts, prepared a huge detonation a long way west of the mine pit. It was electronically timed to go off half a minute before Impact. Several smaller caches of explosives here and there were rigged to go off very near the exact moment of Impact. Meadowbank personnel would issue a press release speaking of an enormous accidental string of explosions of a number of the mine's closely-spaced dynamite storage shacks…fortunately, the world would be told, there were no fatalities. The attempt was to mislead the seismographs of the world as to the nature and location of Sarpedon's Impact.

Another thing Eddie dreamed up was a cleverly-orchestrated failure of all Nunavut's microwave satellite communication links with the outside world. No telephones, no e-mail, no media links, no nothing. Failures of this system weren't uncommon, since its tower-mounted uplink/downlink antennas were frequently buffeted by winds up to a hundred forty miles per hour, and its coaxial cable links were subjected to massive icicle loads as well as temperatures of minus-sixty degrees Celsius. A bogus outage, just prior to Impact and lasting eight or ten hours, would not surprise anyone and would prevent wagging tongues from blabbing to anyone on the Outside about a huge fireball followed by a couple of big *ka-boom*s in the Canadian Arctic night.

Jessica Moonflower abruptly sat up in bed in the middle of the night some time in late September and poked Malcolm awake. Something had been gnawing at her for a while, and a nebulous concept had just coalesced into resolution. "Hey, Dooley!" she begged him. "I gotta good idea!"

"Mrrnnggg…" Mal responded, nowhere near complete consciousness.

"No…hey…wake up! Ya gotta hear this!"

"Mmmmokay. Whattaya got?"

"Well listen, Sweetie-pie…Y'know how ever so often, one or th' other you guys says sompthin' about what if our great big seven-trillion-dollar pile a gold makes th' worl'-wide market price a gold take a nosedive?"

"Mmmmokay. Could happen."

"Well you *bet* it could happen! Like, what if some fool at th' Prada shoe-factory came up with a…a machine or sompthin' could just real eas'ly stamp out fifty million pairs a high-end ladies *foot*ware ever' day? What'd happen to th' price a *shoes*? Price'd drop like a dead rat offa cliff! 'N who'd wanna buy Pradas, if there were fifty million of 'em, costin' seven bucks a pair 'nstead a nine hundred damn dollars?"

Mal pried his eyes open in order to feign interest. "Mmm...so Honey, you got an idea?" By this point in their relationship, Mal could tell when Jessica was totally jazzed about something, because her English diction, which was usually pretty adequate except for the occasional rather colorful colloquialism, underwent a temporary degeneration back to her pre-Charm-School days.

"'N idea? I sh'd *think so*! Here it is...we haven't really decided how we're gonna *deal with* th' gold, 'r th' nickel 'n iron 'n stuff. Gosh, Sweetie...we gonna gather it up ourselves, you'n me? Build a smelter fact'ry an' refine it? Haul it ta...ta wherever they haul bars a' gold ta? Like, *Fort Knox*?"

"No...I don't suppose we—"

"Well sh— Well heck no! So, let's just put out contracts f'r a buncha big ol' mining comp'nies ta bid on payin' us a flat rate f'r a share of th' metals! A *great big ol'* flat rate, up front! Like, sixty-five p'cent of th' *current market value* f'r th' whole damn est'mated sixty zillion troy ounces a th' stuff! Leaves thirty-five p'cent f'r them! Maybe closer ta *thirty* p'cent, after th'r extrack'shn costs. Should work...th' damn stuff's not gonna r'quire any blastin' outta th' ground, 'r leachin' with nasty-ass chemicals, like they gotta do up there at Meadowbank. N' shoot!...*they're* gettin' by right now on profits of 'bout *nine* p'cent a th' value! Let somebody like *them* take the risk, not us! We figure out some way ta be sure th' Territorial Gov'ment gets its share...we c'n have Eddie get one'a his boys ta, like, *oversee* ever' licensed comp'ny's fiscal op'rations? Like, make sure they ain't sneakin' more gold 'n stuff th'n they's *allowed*? 'N if total gold production runs under seven trillion (by *today's* value!) time it's all gone, we reimburse 'em for th' shortfall. Runs *over* seven trillion, that's th' point we by-gosh renegotiate! Shoot,

212

Dooley...any big minin' comp'ny worth its salt'll have ways ta manage th' international gold-price thing, 'n *they* ain't gonna want th' per-troy-ounce value ta go inta free-fall any more'n *we* are, p'tick'ly if they's payin' us *up-front!* Shoot, controllin' market price been workin' f'r *di'monds* f'r better part 'f a cent'ry...jus' ask th' folks at th' de Beers comp'ny! 'N us Associates c'n stick our money in th' bank an' just get on with our lives! Jus' a matter a workin' out th' details! What d'ya think?"

"Sweetie," Malcolm said, taking his enthused girlfriend in his arms, "I think working out the details is right up your alley! Just don't let the cat out of the bag until she's *in* the bag!"

In late February, during one of those idyllic breaks in the winter weather that made for a couple hours of clear, twilit skies, with the Arctic's midnight-sun peeking low over the horizon, the air crisp and crystalline, Malcolm and Jessica packed up their bags, bundled themselves in polar garb, and were flown by ski-plane to the little snow-dusted town of Baker Lake, on the heavily frozen-over Thelon River. There they took up residence in snug quarters to wait out the three and a half weeks until Impact.

Something about life in a small Arctic town appealed to Jessica, and she flourished in the challenging environment of the ice-cold isolated village. Within a month, every single Baker Lake resident adored her, and was at least tolerantly polite toward Malcolm. Of course, vague rumors of impending wealth and notoriety, somehow connected to the two of them, contributed heaps to Mal and Jessie's popularity. The two of them kept in touch with Meebs and Bree and Bertie and Mrs. Bertie a.k.a. Valeria via satphone, on a daily basis.

Okay, that takes care of Malcolm and Jessica. When they got back to Hartford, The Amoeba and Bertie put their heads together and decided one of them should hitch a rental SUV to the GSA-acquired communications trailer and haul it somewhere remote and private, in order to monitor and communicate with the command module welded onto their fast-approaching golden asteroid.

"Where's a good, private place to set up monitoring?" Bertie pondered.

"The **Death to Serpents** compound, of course!" yelled Meebs. "They'll take us in, won't say anything, might come in handy somehow or another…like, maybe Aidan taking care of some legal details. And! They're right across the desert from the Goldstone Deep-Space Communications Center, so if anybody triangulates on our commo trailer, maybe they'll think they are seeing transmissions from Goldstone!"

"Okay! Which one of us goes?"

"I'll do it!" volunteered The Amoeba.

When his ditzoid girlfriend heard the specifics of his plan, she immediately degenerated into high-Freakout mode: fetal-position heebie-jeebies with banshee whimpers and a couple of *petit-mal* episodes.

"I don't think Bree wants to go back to **Death to Serpents**," Meebs observed, stating the obvious.

"Well…okay. Valeria and I will take the Arizona end." So Bertie took Valeria—who was now known as 'Mrs. Koslosky' and was indeed six weeks pregnant by this juncture—and the two of them took a leisurely six-day cross-country drive to Arizona in a rented Honda CR-V towing the communications trailer with its eight-foot microwave dish strapped to the roof, stopping every so often for a bit of sightseeing as they drove. Before departing Hartford, however, they stuffed the empty spaces of the trailer with cartons and shopping-bags of non-spoilable food in boxes, bottles, jars, airtight foil packets, and cans, so as not to be in the position of relying on Fin Fin and his grotesque multi-course midday refections of desert provender. Included in the supplies was a nice compact air-conditioner and a five-thousand-watt portable propane-powered generator.

This left Dr. Ing and Miss Just-Bree Patroness in Hartford. Meebs had concocted a plan to temporarily take control of NASA's 'Geostationary Operational Environmental Satellite' (GOES) system...temporarily, like for about five seconds at exactly the crucial moment. There are a number of GOES satellites keeping permanent station over the Northern Hemisphere. GOES-10 has a terrific bird's-eye view of almost all of North America. You don't have to be a CIA or NSA employee to enjoy a look at this view, or for that matter a government employee of *any* kind...anyone with a laptop and a connection to the Internet is welcome to do it! Google-up the NOAA GOES website and take a look at the GOES-10 Northern Hemisphere Composite Infrared Loop (NOAA, by the way, is the National Oceanic and Atmospheric Administration). You'll see an infra-red picture of the entirety of North America as a slightly-jerky moving picture, one frame snapped every thirty minutes, for the last seven-and-a-half hours...in fantastic full-spectrum false-colors! Wow, pretty cool imagery! Better than any TV weather report! Check out all the hurricanes and weather fronts! Watch dawn come up like thunder and bring warmth to the deserty Western states! See the Jet Stream haul-ass in from the Gulf of Alaska! Availability and cost to anyone with a personal computer? *FREE*!

Well, this was the imagery Meebs was afraid of. At One Twenty-Six a.m. tango on Nineteen March, give-or-take twenty-five seconds, Sarpedon-E was going to come tearing into that infra-red imagery hot and hasty, blazing across Northern Canada while throwing off a temperature signature of about fifteen hundred degrees Celsius. Tracking their gold asteroid as a whole, or as any fragments it may have split into, would be child's-play for anyone with access to the GOES-10 imagery…and that could theoretically include *everyone*! Well of course there are other satellites obtaining all kinds of imagery of Earth in many electromagnetic wavelengths, but nearly all the rest of them are NSA or CIA hardware, which are (1) not necessarily interested in meteors, and (2) so intensely secret that whatever they pick up, they're not likely to share with the general public anyway, and (3) probably a good deal beyond Meebs's ability to hack, and (4) liable to land Meebs in Leavenworth Prison, if not outright *dead by clandestine assassination*, along with all his associates, were he so lucky as to be able to successfully mess with those satellites' imagery, even a little bit. So what Meebs had set as his primary task was to hack into NOAA's real-time imagery receiving system in Silver Springs, Maryland, and set up a one-time-only disappearing virus to randomly scramble a couple dozen scan-lines of satellite imagery in the Nineteen March, One-Forty-Five a.m. tango-timezone image frame. Except of course, he'd want the virus to capture and send back to one of his own personal secret locations in the 'Cloud,' wherever the 'Cloud' was, the *non-scrambled* frame for the Asteroid Association's own particular edification. This would be the frame most likely to show the heat signature and precise locations of Sarpedon's trajectory and impact site…or *sites*, if it broke into multiple fragments. His objective in scrambling the frame, of course, was to prevent the spread of useful knowledge about Sarpedon-E's impact to any casual observers. And all he had to do was scramble a couple dozen lines of image pixels east-to-west across the Canadian Arctic. It would look like transmission garble. No one would suspect a thing, even the folks at NOAA, who would probably say "Oops! Sunspots or something!" Momentary image-transmission dropouts happened all the time.

216

Speaking of dropouts, Meebs decided it would be a good thing if his barely-functional girlfriend made productive use of the months up until Impact on the nineteenth of March and their return to Nunavut sometime after, when the springtime weather permitted. He urged her to enroll in one of Hartford's many colleges to spend her time in a manner that might improve her connection with reality. He and Bree searched around and found Capella College, an institution with lots of flexibility, online programs, self-study resources, and not so much structured intercranial poking and prodding, as more traditional universities are inclined to do. She chose classes in a nursing specialty for no particular reason except perhaps due to a lot of prior contact with the medical profession, in the capacity of blitzed-out overdose patient. Oh, and maybe a desire to actually *merit* that sobriquet 'Doctor' they had erroneously given her up in Iqaluit. She spent a lot of her time in Capella's Virtual Library, reading everything she could get her hands on about the Canadian Arctic.

One morning in March, about two days before Impact, Bertie down in Arizona was checking on Sarpedon-E's progress. He was using the GSA-purchased downlink system to get some precise three-dimensional location coordinates from the asteroid's still-functioning Command Module, which was close enough to have linked itself into the Earth-orbiting 'Global Positioning System' satellite network by this time. He penciled the coordinates onto a scratchpad.

Valeria, eight months along and bulging with child, looked over his shoulder. The eight months since her anabasis to the United States had occasioned a remarkable improvement in her English, except for intermittent errors in syntax and a lovely remnant of her Voronezh-Chelyabinsk accent. It was almost *easy* for any native

American English speaker to understand her, more-or-less. "Bertie..." she asked. "You are sure, *da?*, about those coordinateses?"

"I'll just check them again..." In the thirty seconds since his last readout, Sarpedon-E had hurtled several thousand meters through space. But the new position was consistent with what he'd already written down."

Valeria backed up and assumed an awkward pregnant-ballerina imitation of First Position. Think pink hippopotami in *Fantasia*. Going *en pointe* was out of the question. "Here is midcourse retrofire..." She pirouetted and pointed into the sky. "Here is...is current locatzyon...*da?*" Her pointing finger swung a wide arc and stopped, her imaginary finger-laser spearing Sarpedon dead-center. "And...here is Sarpedon-E when he Impact!" Again, another finger-point. "Oh-oh...Bertsie! Not good! Was supposed to be latitude 66.78085 North, longitude 115.78188 West, isn't this right? But...he's going to go a little *long!*"

Bertie knew better than to doubt Valeria's instinctive sense of cosmic positions. "*How much* long?"

"From where we hoped for, two hundred kilometers farther east? Maybe two-and-*fifty?* Or *three* hundreds, is poosseeble?"

Bertie's mathematics had been based on an aiming point no more than thirty miles inside the western edge of the target rectangle...but there were myriad unpredictable factors which would doubtlessly affect the precision of the asteroid's re-entry trajectory. "Mmmm...that's not so good. It puts the impact site a lot closer to Baker Lake! We got about two thousand Nunavushians in Baker Lake!"

"Beertie, we got also the Dooley and the Jessie in Baker's Lake!"

"What should we do?"

"We'll call them up and tell them to get their asses *out* of there *ochen' bystro*...um, very queekly!" Her voice had an edge of panic to it.

But they could not get a call through. Malcolm's satphone was on the blink, and terrible weather had temporarily taken down Baker Lake's cellphone microwave link with the Outside. The Nunavut weather made all forms of travel impossible anyway. Valeria and Bertie could do nothing but track the precise coordinates of the incoming asteroid, and wring their hands, fretting. They ticked off the hours and minutes until Impact, and in Hartford, Connecticut, the Drs. Ing and Patroness did the same.

Far away, in Baker Lake on the night of Impact, Jessica Moonflower peered through an ice-rimed thermalpane window into a snowy, windy night. Skies had been choked with clouds for a week, with neither star nor sliver of moon to be seen. There was little likelihood of them seeing the asteroid either, although Jessie had images of watching their golden Earth Crosser streak brightly overhead anyway.

Malcolm cradled his digital clock and watched the seconds tick away. "How long?" Jessica asked, chewing her bottom lip in anxiety.

"Six minutes."

"How long now, Sweetie?" she asked, a very short while later.

"Two minutes...one minute fifty...one minute forty..." Malcolm counted the last moments off. With precisely thirty seconds to go, there was a faint, distant rumble."

"*Was that it?*" Jessica cried out.

"Eddie's dynamite! Shhhh now...seventeen seconds...sixteen...fifteen..."

At Impact Minus Three, an abrupt, massive *crack* shook their little house, followed a jiffy later by a sound like nearby thunder. Sheets of ice rime jittered off the windowpane. "That's gotta be it!" Jessie screamed. But it wasn't.

Mal kept counting. "Zero...plus five...plus ten..." When his counting got to plus sixty-five—a bit more than a minute after that big abrupt crack—a slow *rumble* was felt to pass through the foundations of the world, seeming to lift their house a few inches and then gently put it down again.

"Now THAT was it!" Malcolm told Jessica, smiling broadly.

"Why is it *late*?" she demanded.

"Because it impacted...let's see..." He tapped some numbers into his iPad. "It impacted maybe two hundred fifty miles from here! That was the P-wave! At plus two minutes eight seconds, we'll feel—" Mal's words were interrupted by a second slow rumble, right on time, almost as sharp as the first. Jessica was nearly shaken off her feet. "—We'll feel the S-wave, I was gonna say!" Malcolm yelled triumphantly. "Honey, those are seismic waves that travel through the ground...'Primary' and 'Secondary' waves! That's our baby, yelling its great big solid-gold head off, right through the Earth's crust!"

Jessie glanced dubiously out into the dark. "Will there be any more?"

"Sure! At about Impact plus eighteen minutes, we ought to *hear* the sound of the crash...like, normal sound-waves through the air, travelling much slower than the P and S waves!"

Jessica poured them both a steaming cup of coffee and they settled down at the kitchen table to wait. After a few minutes of twitching and sipping, she had a thought. "Mal, sweetie...what was that first big noise? The one just a few seconds *before* Impact?"

Mal looked up from his clock. "Mmmm...I think it was a fragment. It sure couldn't have been a very big fragment...that *ka-bam* was not any one-point-one megatons! But it wasn't very far away distance-wise, I bet! You'll see...when we go out scouting, I think we'll find a nice chunk of Sarpedon just a few miles from here!"

"Why was it so early?"

"Well, it wasn't really early at all! Just a lot closer! It probably hit ground at the exact same time as the greater mass...likely no more that a second or two sooner. But the seismic energy got here 'way sooner! And the sound too, almost simultaneously, so it couldn't be more than four or five miles out! A piece must have broken away just when Sarpedon entered the atmosphere."

"We ought to phone Valeria! Okay...maybe Meebs first." They fiddled with the cellphones for a while but there was no reception. Nor with the satphone.

Eighteen minutes and forty-six seconds after Impact, the windowpanes started shaking as a low-pitched thunder began, like a bunch of heavily-loaded trucks with knobby tires rolling past on a nearby Interstate, or as once the Concorde had thundered, taking off. The sound built in intensity. It seemed to go on and on for a minute or more, then slowly faded into the silence of an Arctic late winter night.

"That was it?" Jessica asked.

"That was it!" confirmed Mal. "Our baby's on the ground!"

THE SEARCH FOR SARPEDON

There! There it is!" yelled Malcolm. Jumping about in his excitement he would have tumbled right out the wide-open frame where the midships door had been detached, had he not been firmly belted into his seat. And since the open doorframe was next to the port-side midships passenger seat just behind the pilot position of a Bell 206L4 helicopter, currently doing about a hundred fifteen knots at an altitude of four hundred feet above an unforgiving terrain, the tumble would have done Malcolm a good deal of harm.

They had leased this helicopter, along with the services of an excellent pilot, for a week. Meebs was up front, riding co-pilot...except he had been strictly warned not to touch anything whatsoever or the 'copter would come out of the sky like a brick pitched out a fortieth-floor window, horribly killing everyone aboard. He'd taken this warning deeply to heart, more than he ought to have, so he was sitting on his hands for fear that otherwise one of them might involuntarily sneak out and in a spirit of insane contrariness push a random bright-red dashboard button labeled something like **CRSH HELO NOW** and that would be then end of them all. Sitting on his hands made it awkward for Meebs to deal with the clipboard on his lap which held the terrain map they were supposed to be following, at *his* direction, which was the sole copilot duty he'd been entrusted with, so Mal's intemperate yell came as a relief, more-or-less, since it was apt to lead to a landing and bring a temporary halt to this terrifying flight.

It was mid-June. The ice was out of the Thelon River. The snow was gone from the vast reaches of tundra, except for an occasional drift on the lee side of the low ridges which were probably ancient glacial eskers. The snow had been replaced by miles and miles of early-summer flowers, pink, purple and yellow, and whole rafts of waterfowl on every bog or pond, and clouds of nasty, bloodsucking, flesh-biting insects intent on doing malevolent harm to any warm-blooded vertebrate they might encounter...*anything*, from meadow-mouse up. The Asteroid Associates were of course utilizing this Bell 206L4 to do the initial search for pieces of Sarpedon-E. To Mal's right, Eddie Ulatuq was also strapped down tight next to an open doorframe, searching the starboard-side ground as it sped by. Taking both midships cabin doors off had meant a lot of windswirl and rotor noise in the cabin, but it improved the view outward and down, which was essential for the searchers. In the back row of passenger seats, Jessica Moonflower and Bertie Koslosky rode along, huddled in parkas, watching as well as possible through their respective Perspex windows. The noise and wind was an intense bother, but neither of them had ever ridden in a helicopter before and they weren't going to miss this for anything, not even for seven trillion dollars in gold!

"Where?" demanded Edward Behr, their devilishly handsome blond helicopter pilot, whom Jessica tried desperately *not* to accidentally call 'Pooh.' She couldn't imagine what his parents Mr. & Mrs. Behr were *thinking* when they named him Edward. Everyone else seemed content to temporarily nickname him 'Grizzly' instead of 'Eddie', which prevented confusing him with Eddie Ulatuq. "Where is it?" Griz repeated, yelling to make himself heard.

"Passed almost over the top of it! Come around back over that last pond...there's a clearly-visible trench in the reindeer lichen, goes west-to-east in a straight line fifty feet or so!" Mal had to lean forward into his restraints and yell in the pilot's ear. Griz put the craft into a gut-wrenching one-eighty, descended precipitously to a hundred feet above the boggy terrain, and reduced speed by tipping the craft up sharply and rotor-braking.

There it was! A long strip of torn-up soil that had probably been frozen as hard as iron at the time of Impact. That explained the skid-trench, in lieu of a crater. At the trench's far end, a big chunk of meteorite! The helo settled onto a nearby mound of mossy dirt interspersed with angular glacial rock fragments. Pilot Behr flipped a row of caged switches and the turbine noise started to wind down as the rotors gradually slowed to a stop.

When they could all hear again, everyone yanked buckles and shrugged out of harnesses. There was a pile-up at both door-holes as all the passengers tried to exit simultaneously in order to dash for the meteor. Grizzly just flipped open the pilot's hatch, slipped to the ground, stepped a safe distance away from his craft and casually lit up a Winston. No sense him getting excited…he wasn't in for a share.

Mal's sighting was the first fragment found. But then, they hadn't been searching for more than forty-five minutes yet. By Dr. Ing's map, they were only about four miles out of Baker Lake, from whose compact airport this morning's flight had originated.

"Wow! Sarpedon!" murmured an awestruck Meebs.

"See any *gold*?" Jessica asked avidly.

"Well, it's metallic for sure. Maybe those flecks are gold. Probably not though…it's likely to be alloyed with the iron and nickel. Interspersed at the crystalline level. Don't worry, Jessie…it's gotta be in there, and we'll get a field assay done as soon as we take samples back to Baker Lake."

Malcolm ran his hand lovingly over the slightly-pitted surface. "This has to be the chunk Jessie and me heard smacking down at Impact Minus Three!" he enthused. "How big is it?"

Bertie dipped a tape measure out of his pocket. The meteorite was like a very irregular circle in its planar outline, sort-of shaped like a dome, or a jellyfish, or a flattened gumdrop. Perched on its flat side, wider than it was high. Bert took a couple of rough measurements across its diameter in various directions, mentally adding the dimensions, then calculating an average. "One meter forty-three centimeters," he reported. Maybe...um... eighty-seven centimeters in height, at the middle...we'll take two-thirds of that as the average vertical dimension. That makes it, I'd guess...thirty-three cubic feet. Times five hundred twenty-four pounds a cubic foot for Iron-Nickel-Cobalt in the usual proportions...that's seventeen thousand two hundred and ninety-two pounds. So...how we going to get this piece of metal back to Baker Lake? Eddie, you got any ideas?"

Eddie scratched his scalp, pondering. "It's a hell of a load, but we're only about four miles from town...right, Meebs? Get it on a timber sledge with hand-jacks, get a D-6 out here, and we *might* be able to drag it back to town, if we don't get bogged in a muskeg. Be better if we just jack it onto a sledge and wait until Freeze-up. Drag it back over ice 'n snow a whole lot easier!"

"Couldn't we bust it up into manageable pieces, and take them out on one of those Baker Lake tracklaying tundra vehicles?"

Jessica was kneeling by the big beautiful chunk of meteorite, running her hand over its exotic contours. "Well you guys, it seems a damn shame busting up this lovely thing. We just *gotta* get it to civilization in *one piece!*" She rose, backed off, and began snapping pictures of the meteorite with her cellphone camera.

Ed Behr came ambling over, his dangling cigarette now mostly ash dripping down the front of his flightsuit. "How big you say it was?" he asked.

"Call it eighteen thousand pounds." Bertie offered. "That might be a little conservative."

"Well shee-UT! Sling-load it out by helicopter!"

All eyes except Griz's swiveled to look at the Bell 206. There was grave doubt on every face.

"Cripes, not *that* little teapot!" Griz laughed. "Meadowbank Anico's got a *Skycrane* under contract! They're phasing out of the gold business and moving into oil and gas exploration. They're using that big mother to fly great big heavy drill-rig parts a couple hundred miles out into the tundra!"

"A *Skycrane*?" asked Meebs dubiously. "What's that?"

"Skycrane...shit yeah! Sikorsky S-64! Biggest damn helicopter they make! Twenty thousand four hundred pounds slingload, for short hauls. Get max payload, you gotta go light on the fuel 'n take the doors off to save some weight. Don't hire no lard-ass pilot and don't take no copilot at all! Cost you about eight thousand bucks per flight-hour 'n two thousand bucks per ground hour to lease that puppy!"

Eight thousand dollars an hour seemed like an awful lot of money to Meebs. And to Mal and Jessie. Valeria was back in Baker Lake with three-month-old Violet Koslosky, who she would no more take on a highly-dangerous helicopter ride than take her SCUBA-diving, naked, in sharky seas. Bree Patroness was also back in Baker Lake, terrified to the point of hysterics of the very notion of riding in helicopters, and certain that her Dr. Ing, for whom she had built up a mammoth psychological dependence as well as quite a pathological fondness, was going to perish in a fiery crash out in the tundra somewhere. Both of them would likely have felt that eight thousand dollars an hour was an awful lot of money too.

Eight thousand dollars an hour seemed like an awful lot of money to Bertie as well, until he did a little arithmetic. Four percent of 17,292 pounds was 691.7...that's how may pounds of gold were probably in that irony chunk over there. Divide by 2.2 to get kilograms...multiply by 1000 to get grams...divide by 32.2 to get troy ounces. That comes to 9,764 troy ounces. Times $1266 per troy ounce gives.... "Hey guys!" Bertie exclaimed. "There's twelve million, three hundred sixty-one thousand, two hundred twenty-four dollar's worth of gold in that meteorite! Considering that, I think we ought to be able to afford a Skycrane to get it down to the riverside in Baker Lake!"

Four days later, the entire citizenry of Baker Lake turned out to watch the Sikorsky S-64 Skycrane Heavylift Helicopter, on short-term sublease from the Meadowbank Anico Eagle Gold Mine, come swooping into town, looking like a gigantic green dragonfly with a big pair of wheels dangling down under its belly and a pretty big metallic rock suspended in a heavy webwork sling at the end of a fifty-foot-long payload hoist cable. The machine hovered above the empty cargo yard at the Baker Lake commercial boat landing. The electromagnetic hook at the bottom end of the long cable opened up, probably when the pilot pushed a button or something, and '*ploof!*' the meteorite and its sling fell about six feet into the dusty yard, raising a small cloud of greyish dust. Everybody cheered and clapped!

When the field assay came in, it turned out this particular chunk of Sarpedon-E had a gold content of *five-point-two* percent, rather than only four! That made its value more like sixteen-point-oh-seven million dollars. The fifteen-percent share for Nunavut came to about two-point-four million, US, or three-point-four-four-seven million, Canadian. Which was about a hundred and fifteen dollars for every man, woman and child in Nunavut Territory. Which doesn't seem like very much...until it is noted that Fragment One only comprised about one five-hundred-and-sixty-thousandth of the entire mass of Sarpedon-E, the rest of which was out there in the Impact Zone somewhere! With numbers, that figure is:

$$1 / 560,000$$

which makes the likely total share, once the *entire* meteorite was recovered, something more like sixty-four-point-four *million* bucks Canadian for every citizen of Nunavut. Providing they were able to find the entire rest of Sarpedon-E, and not very much of it had vaporized on re-entry.

"Can't wait to see the pile of gold ingots that comes outa that chunk!" Meebs enthused. "Just wait 'til we get it barged down to Churchill and onto a railcar. Ship it to the metals smelter in Detroit, and—"

"And *nothing*! Jus' you-all waitaminnit, you guys!" Jessica Moonflower interrupted. Her friend Valeria had just ambled up to the crowd surrounding Fragment One, with baby Violet in a cute Inuit-beaded moosehide baby-cuddler up against Val's quite nicely pregnancy-enlarged breasts. She groped in the cuddler and retrieved a wrinkled piece of paper from somewhere behind Violet's bottom. What Val handed Jessie was a printout hot off of Bertie's printer up at the house. "Fellas," Jessie smirked, "I got here in my hand confirmation of *purchase* for this here little bitty meteorite!"

"Wait...*what*?" her boyfriend goggled.

Jessica just smirked the more. "Boys, four days ago I put our adorable little gold-nugget out for sale on Craigslist, just to see what the interest might be. Started getting bids right away. Ended up watchin' a big three-way bidding war develop...the Smithsonian Insitute, the British Museum, and some dang super-rich anonymous Japanese collector who's jus' wild about meteorites! High bidder was the British Museum!"

"How much! How much!" Meebs hollered intemperately.

"*Forty-eight-point-six million dollars!*" Jessica announced. "An' that *ain't* no **Canadian** dollars!"

Seven days later and two hundred miles west-north-west, completely unaware of the exciting meteoric doings near Baker Lake, a wiry sixty-six-year-old Inuit fur trapper was laboring on foot across a stretch of squishy tundra. That morning, he'd abandoned his winter camp and was attempting to hike cross-country to the Thelon River, twenty-six miles further south. He had abandoned the raggedy canvas tent insulated with caribou-moss and willow branches that had been his winter abode while he serviced his eighteen-mile-long loop of traps. He had abandoned his meager cooking gear and his lamps, his teakettle, his blanket roll, and his depleted stores of lamp oil, sugar, biscuit-flour, and tinned spam. He'd even abandoned his cache of costly steel leg-hold fox traps. What he had *not* abandoned, and what now comprised the eighty pounds of backpack he struggled under, was his winter's take of dried, stretched, baled-up prime Arctic Fox pelts, a hundred and thirty-six of them, each of which would fetch him $40 cash at the Hudson's Bay in Baker Lake. Easily sufficient income to live on all summer, and then re-equip him for another winter's trapping.

There was a long, low ridge up ahead he'd have to climb over. The ridge was only about thirty feet high. It was a glacial esker, which is a remnant of a stream that flowed on top of, through, or beneath the thick continental ice sheet covering North America as far south as Tennessee during the Wisconsin Glaciation, which didn't turn loose of the continent until about twelve thousand years ago. These glacial streams, like their overland counterparts, carried lots of gravelly, sandy sediments and built them up in their icy streambeds. Ice melted, streams vanished, streambed sediments remained...in the form of a long, winding ridge—an *esker*!

The old trapper struggled up the steep slope, his pack's straps biting into his shoulders. Up and over the top. What met his eyes on the far side was enough to make him freeze in his tracks. He shrugged out of his pack and sat down on the damp ground to stare a while.

A raw bowl-shaped depression five hundred feet across had been blasted into the level tundra just to the esker's south. A shallow pool of groundwater had seeped into the middle of this depression, but in its center there stood an enormous blackish rock unlike anything the old fellow had ever seen in a lifetime of roaming around the Canadian Arctic! The rock was a major fragment of Sarpedon-E. It would turn out to be eighteen hundred times as massive as Fragment One, which was now snugly crated and on its way by river barge, Hudson Bay steamer, railroad, highway and trans-oceanic cargo vessel to its eager purchaser in London, England—the British Museum.

The old fur-trapper struggled downhill into the crater. Gradually he made his way around the impressive chunk of iron, pitted with the fierce heat of atmospheric re-entry. The thing loomed twelve or fifteen feet above his head. Halfway around, there was a cluster of four flat disk-shaped pads arranged in a square. The pads appeared to be welded to the rock's surface, and a short stub of very stout titanium pipe protruded from each pad's center. The free ends of these stubs looked as if they had been melted off, which is precisely what they had been. What the old guy was seeing turned out to be the landing-structure remains of Positioning/Observation/Steering Module Number Five, the particular POS that had returned a value of 26.4% for the element gold. Which was the next feature that fell under the old fur-trapper's eye: a vein of gold nearly four inches wide, snaking its way up the slope of the meteorite's side.

"*Guulu!*" the old fellow murmured in awe. Two guesses what that Inuktitut word means!

There were a few loose metallic fragments which had spalled off the meteorite, lying half-immersed in the shallow, scummy water . The trapper sorted through these until he found a nice five-pound chunk with a generous, visible amount of gold in it. He shoved the chunk into his pack among the fox pelts. He hoisted the heavy pack onto his shoulders and set off southward toward the river.

"You gotta come see this!" Eddie Ulatuk enthused. Malcolm, Bertie and Meebs sat around the kitchen table sipping at steaming cups of coffee in the Baker Lake house. "Come with me down to the Bay!"

In any Far-North community, 'the Bay' means the local Hudson's Bay Company store, which can be anything from a hole-in-the-wall store selling bare necessities and acting as a village meeting-place and fur-purchasing station, on up to a glitzy supermarket rivaling any WalMart anywhere in the world. Baker Lake's version of 'the Bay' fell somewhere midrange. When the four of them got there, it was to encounter a wizened Inuit fur-trapper seated at a spindly-legged wooden table sipping his own steaming cup of coffee and reeking of eight unwashed months' hard work, out on the winter tundra. A detailed map of western Nunavut lay spread-out to one side on the table, and a few magazines, newspapers and dirty dishes littered its surface. "Show them what you got, *Ataatatsiaq!*"[26] Eddie said.

The old guy reached under the table and produced his five-pound chunk of meteorite out of a bulging canvas backpack. Streaks and flakes of pure gold shone in the iron

---

[26] Grandfather

231

matrix. "Wow!" Meebs enthused. "Another piece of Sarpedon?"

"Bet your ass!" Eddie assured him. "Big one!" Eddie recounted the possible dimensions of the old guy's find. "It's the richest fragment yet!"

"Will he tell us where it is?"

The old trapper was shrewd enough not to have told *anybody* yet. Eddie patiently explained that the mineral rights to the meteorite—including the gold—were vested in the Asteroid Associates, with a generous portion of the value going to the Territory of Nunavut, and that, consequently, the old guy's *finding* the piece of meteorite did not legally permit him *keeping* it. He further explained that a finder's fee of one-tenth of one percent of the Territory's cut of the meteorite fragment's total value would be paid, out of the Nunavut share, to him, *Ataatatsiaq* Fox-trapper, personally. And although one tenth of one percent didn't sound like much, it would amount to something like twenty-eight-and-a-half million dollars, Canadian.

"How many foxee-pelt, dat?" the old fellow asked.

Bertie rapidly scribbled the division problem on the margins of a two-week-old newspaper, using a vacant space next to the half-completed crossword puzzle. "Seven hundred and twelve thousand eight hundred prime pelts, figuring forty dollars a pelt." Bertie replied.

The trapper's eyes widened. He reached over and gently took the newspaper from Bertie. The old fellow might not have been particularly literate, but he had no trouble with figures. His eyes ran over that quotient several times: **712,800 fox pelts**. He handed the newspaper back to Bertie and gesticulated toward the filthy backpack containing his winter's take. "One winter trapping...one hunned threety-seex foxee-pelt. How many winter, dat?" he asked...meaning, that gigantic number of pelts Bertie had just calculated.

Bertie did the long-division. "Uhhh…comes to five thousand two hundred and forty-one winter's fox trapping. I don't imagine there are that many foxes in the entire Canadian Arctic anyway!"

The wily old trapper had already reached that conclusion. He hoisted the chunk of iron laced with gold that he'd lugged back from the crater. "I keep?" he asked.

His four interrogators exchanged amazed, quizzical looks. "Sure!" they all said in unison.

The trapper pulled the map of Arctic Canada toward himself. His finger glided across the map, traced the course of theThelon upriver from Baker Lake, then slid northward out into the trackless tundra. "Here!" he said, tapping a spot on the map.

HAPPILY EVER AFTER

All six of them remained in Nunavut for the next twelve months, more-or-less, participating in the ongoing search for bits of their meteorite. Eddie Ulatuq took personal delight in spearheading the hunt, and had hired-on and trained a number of search-crews outfitted with helicopters and tundra-crawlers and float-planes whose movements he orchestrated. In the end, there were only six major fragments like the one the fox-trapper had found, and eleven smaller pieces on the order of Fragment One...but none so large and splendid as that first one discovered. These finds accounted for four-point-nine billion kilograms of metallic meteorite, illustrating that their original estimate of Sarpedon-E's mass was a little low. Also a little low was their estimate of Sarpedon-E's gold content. Laboratory assays of samples, along with early smelter yields, demonstrated gold content at 7.8%, not 4%. This was because the 26.4% 'vein' gold content indicated by POS No. 5 turned out to be a lot more extensive in Sarpedon-E's interior than the other eleven POS's shallow surface readings had indicated. The asteroid's gold value was probably going to top-out at something like thirteen-point-six trillion dollars US. Everybody was very pleased about that little development, expecially the Nunavushians.

Jessica, with Bertie along as her computational mastermind, and also Valeria—Violet too!—as her protégé and companion, took numerous trips Outside to conduct Asteroid Associates business. She succeeded in selling several of the smaller pieces to museums and outer-space aficionados for four or five times the value of their metals content, until the worldwide demand for big, fat,

Iron/Nickel/Gold specimen-meteorites started to taper off. Therupon, she turned her market savvy to the delightful task of negotiating mineral exploitation rights to dozens of companies worldwide, at least fifty of whom were slavering to get their hands on all that gold. These international companies, and the corporate and national powers behind them, were largely US, Russian, Chinese, Brazilian and miscellaneous European concerns, all of whom were ravenously greedy for gold—specie or bullion. Jessica and Bertie soon found that nobody had any particular designs on the iron, nickel, cobalt or trace elements. They negotiated contracts which stipulated the separation and ingot-casting of these materials, and their retention in the ownership of Asteroid Associates. Over time, several tens of billions of dollars worth of 'by-product' materials would pass into their hands and into world markets. Excepting, of course, the nickel…which Valeria and Jessica caused to be warehoused in Hartford, Connecticut for no better reason than they'd negotiated their personal ownership of the nickel at the outset of their earth-crosser adventure, and they both enjoyed watching big bars of the stuff pile up in their very own warehouse where once in a while they could visit and run their hands covetously over the neatly stacked chunks of their nickel hoard.

Advance payments from all those fabulously-wealthy corporations also started piling up, but in the Asteroid Associates offshore bank accounts. Jessica Moonflower had shrewdly seen fit to establish financial relations in the tax haven and corporate sanctuary of the British Virgin Islands. She and Malcolm took a trip to the BVI, ostensibly to firm-up certain business arrangements there, but additionally to have a nice Caribbean getaway. In secret they had one other objective: they got married.

"Dooleykins...I gotta idea!" Jessie whispered in Malcolm's blissed-out ear one tropical honeymoon midnight.

"Mmmm?" he replied. Jessica's ideas were almost always spectacular.

"Well let's arrange a nice getaway vacation for ever'body else! Bring 'em down here for a coupla weeks! Shoot, let's get Eddie Ulatuq down here too! I gotta nice ebony-skin Island Girl he'd flip over, 'n he needs a girlfriend something awful!"

There was no arguing with that idea. The two of them made calls and vetted hotels and set up restaurants, bars, beach clubs, sailing charters, florists, liquor providers, and spas for the event. They booked a nice antique limousine for shuttling between the airport and the interisland boat harbor on Charlotte Amalie, and reserved a fleet of day-glo green mopeds for scooting around on the nine-and-a-half miles of roads on the small, remote island that was their secret destination. Jessica Moonflower spent a long, Margarita-fueled lunch accustoming Miss Cecilie Karınne-Jones, their hotel's diminutive, midnight-black, dropdead-gorgeous concierge, to the idea of an arranged introduction to a single male friend in desperate need of a week's worth of sophisticated female companionship, a friend who was a nice-looking, bright, personable, charming, courteous, handsome hunkoid—not to mention on the road to becoming very wealthy—an Inuit confederate of the Asteroid Associates, as well as a highly-placed official in Canadian Arctic Wildlife Management circles.

Just about the time that Jessica and Malcolm succeeded in spiriting-off their colleagues to a fabulous BVI getaway on the intimate island of Jost Van Dyke, the US Department of Justice decided to open hearings on the whole Sarpedon-E affair. DOJ had directed the FBI, CIA, NSA and Connecticut and Arizona State law enforcement

236

agencies to collect information on the goings-on of the Asteroid Associates, as to exactly what sort of criminal malfeasance had precipitated the acquisition of such monumental wealth by this gang of nobodies. What DOJ was really after was some angle by which the federal government could chisel in on the preposterous windfall from Sarpedon-E. Six weeks of hearings resulted in the inescapeable finding that the Asteroid Associates had not actually committed any legal wrongdoing at all...not a thing that anybody could prove, or even coherently imply. Every step in their convoluted plot to obtain themselves a gold-laden asteroid had been more-or-less aboveboard, if not exactly pre-advertised in the world's media. Moreover, in the Miami Herald, a renowned columnist, widely admired for insightful commentary on social, political, business, financial, economic and environmental matters, noted that the Asteroid Associates had created a colossal amount of wealth without exploiting masses of laborers in Third-World nations, without battening on government giveaways or tax loopholes, without defrauding or misleading hordes of stockholders, and without despoiling any of the planet's hard-pressed natural resources. Their source of astonishing wealth was not going to pollute any streams or aquifers, nor smog up any air. Their enterprise did not emit any carbon dioxide, nor any other greenhouse gases. Harvesting their wealth consumed no petro-chemicals in its manufacture, beyond the smelting of metals so pure as to produce almost no useless byproducts. Only modest and incidental amounts of petrochemicals were expended in their products' transportation. All the world's age-long love affair with gold would ultimately be enhanced by their lassoing of Sarpedon-E. The meteoric impact had been accomplished without harming a single human being, moose, musk ox, caribou or polar bear, while generously enriching the populace of a wholly innocuous, poorly-favored, economically stressed little territory at the forgotten end of the Earth. All the while, the Associates' charm and audacity earned the astonished admiration of nearly the entire world's population in the accomplishing of their astounding feat. And! The Associates possessed a legitimate Bill of Sale for Sarpedon-E together with all attached hardware from the US General Services Agency! The columnist concluded by suggesting that the Department of Justice pull in their antlers, get the *Hell* off the Asteroid Associates' backs, and let them enjoy their triumph of creative endeavor.   The Herald's editorial opinion circulated widely in world media for weeks and weeks. Even the US President made humorous comments in her State-of-the-Union message, suggesting that NASA might do well to mount an expedition to go in search of another windfall asteroid she might be able to use to reduce the nation's burden of debt.   Seeing the public-relations handwriting on the wall, the DOJ dropped the issue. In Canada, similar inquiries never made it past establishing the ironclad veracity of the Nunavut mineral-access license.

The Associates had such a wonderful two weeks on Jost van Dyke Island that they decided to buy one-half square mile of the idyllic place. Since JVD is only about eight square miles, they wound up owning about 6% of what is perhaps the best-kept island secret in the Caribbean, since 'Jost', as its island citizens affectionately call the place, is blessed with beautiful terrain, tropical verdure, salubrious climate, azure ocean waters, dive sites profuse with reef life, a contented population of only about three hundred souls, and miles of sparkling, barely-populated white sand beaches. Along with their three hundred twenty acres of paradise, the Asteroid Associates became the caring guardians of a three-quarter-mile stretch of stunning Jost beachfront. In time, the six of them were granted BVI citizenship, and little Violet as well.

A magnificent villa suitable for harmonious community dwelling, yet designed with a number of separate suites in a variety of tastes, took shape on an upland site overlooking spectacular ocean cliffs. The Associates moved in, decorated their respective suites to their own desires, and tried to live in respect of the Caribbean lifestyle simplicity that was traditional on JVD Island. One suite was held in perpetuity for the exclusive use of Eddie Ulatuq and Miss Cecilie, his ravishing new Island girlfriend. Notwithstanding the British Virgin Islands being a bountiful tax haven, they agreed to devote the greater part of their monstrous windfall to charitable pursuits, both locally and globally. On the local level, Meebs and Bertie joined forces with several prestigious longtime Jost residents to form a commission whose purpose was to plan for longterm abatement of issues consequential to the gradual rise of sea level, due to the effects of global climate-change. Jost is a high island, but beachfront developments were likely to become inundated sooner or later. Building codes were revamped with respect to new foundation elevations above current sea level. Long-term plans were laid for relocating small-craft harbor facilities, breakwaters, oceanside roads, and public buildings. Asteroid Association matching funds were committed to this effort. In addition, every last Jost resident or business that had a seaside structure which might be threatened in time by sea-level rise, had an upland site purchased for them outright out of Association funds, with further money set aside for future moving or reconstruction costs. The commission's motto became

JOST IS NOT GOING UNDER!

In time, the Associates used some of their pooled wealth to have a splendid octet of six-unit beachside guest houses built, each of them graciously and separately staffed and serviced by teams of generously-compensated employees from within the small island community. They operated this laid-back facility semi-charitably, such that one-third of the suites were perpetually made available for an all-expenses-paid week at no cost to certain selected clientele who might apply for the privilege. This included couples celebrating twenty-fifth or fiftieth wedding anniversaries, newlyweds of all stripes, people of limited means suffering from poignant disabilities or dire terminal conditions, all citizens of Nunavut, and all confirmed members of **Death to Serpents!**...subject to the dual provisos that (1) they kept their murdering hands off the entire interesting and diverse serpent fauna of Jost van Dyke Island, and (2) they did not request from Room Service or in any of the Island's eateries, nor bring along in their luggage, any ghastly Arizona Desert comestibles such as their sect's erstwhile chef Fin Fin had laid before them at those memorable Midday Refections a long time back. Demand for this charitable courtesy far outstripped the available accommodations, so a drawing was conducted weekly, which nonselected individuals were perfectly welcome to re-enter the next week. The drawing's conduct and results were kept scrupulously aboveboard, and eventually were followed in the world's news media with as much delight as any National Sweepstakes might have been. Each guest—whether paying or charitable—was sent home with a nice commemorative medal struck from pure asteroidal nickel. Valeria and Jessica figured they had enough nickel warehoused to sustain this little *lagniappe* for six thousand four hundred and eighty years, more-or-less. It should be mentioned that the single Asteroid Associate who took the greatest delight in managing the guest-house giveaway operation was...*Dr. Bree Patroness*!

As the years passed, there were babies born, adventures and travels undertaken, joys and disappointments experienced, temporary and minor

240

fallings-out along with their eventual mendings, and many, many Margarita-energized reminiscences of the complexities and wonderments involved in the salvaging of an abandoned intergalactic combat vessel, which, arguably, was some sort of description for Sarpedon-E. There were no more undertakings so convoluted and unusual falling to them in their collective futures, but nonetheless...they all lived happily ever after. More-or-less.

OTHER NOVELS BY LEWIS MACLEOD:

MISS MAI

MISS MAI is a romantic memoir set in the final years of the Vietnam War. The chronicler's progress as a naive draftee through the rigors of military training as an intelligence analyst inexorably lead him to the exotic streets of wartime Saigon. He meets Tuoi Mai under accidental circumstances and his life is altered forever after.

TWENTY-ONE FORTY-SEVEN
—Book One in "THE SOLAE' series

In the year 2147, humankind has begun to exceed the critical planetary ecological tipping-point in many frightening ways. Global population exceeds nine billion souls. Unspoiled areas on every continent are shrunken, their wildlife depleted. Poverty is rife in every nation. Petroleum reserves worldwide are nearly exhausted. Sources of water for domestic and agricultural use are severely overtaxed. Air quality has never been so compromised. Still, there is hope. Technology has led to stunning advances, and man's ventures into space have proceeded spectacularly. A new faith—that of the Solae—has arisen from the urban slums of South America, promising a new and vital view on human interactions. Perhaps humanity's future is not so grim after all.

On 15 September, in the year Twenty-One Forty-Seven, all that changes

THE SOLAE
—Book Two in 'THE SOLAE' series

It is nearly a thousand years beyond the present day. The globe and the human race are slowly recovering from the horrors of a devastating war and plague that occurred in the year 2147. Humanity lives simply, without the technologies of today, for the net of industry, medicine, and science was shattered beyond recovery by the tribulations of that war. Small villages of farmers and herdsmen cluster against the flank of the mountains once known as the Rockies. On the High Plains, a few fiercely protective bands of nomads make their seasonal migrations, practicing their arts and trades with whatever peaceable folk they encounter. Deep in a mountain fastness dwells a secretive sect, whose avowed purpose is to collect and safeguard scraps of scientific knowledge that survived the Laser War...safeguard this knowledge until the Deserving One their faith prophesies will come forward to receive this store of wisdom. And always, bringing terror and death as their ally, the bands of pitiless, thieving murderers wander this cold and terrible world, marauders known by all men as ULTS.

...But a change is about to come upon this savage world.

SOLAE INHERITOR
—Book Three in 'The Solae' series

The Union of Eriss has grown and consolidated for more than a hundred years since its founding in the famine-depleted High Plains of the continent. To the east, an implacable enemy stirs: the Atlan Empire, warlike, aggressive, greedy for land, for power and for slaves. The Union is vigorous and vital, but not without its difficulties: one-third of its population are Ults, restless descendants of a conquered race of one-time wildland brigands and marauders on whom the veneer of Erissard civilization lies thin and uneasy. It is the special task of the House of Eriss, descendants of Old Salin lineage, to defend the Union. But the family's elder, the Domin Therisam, is aged, weak and vacillating. It is good fortune that his eldest son and proxy Jericharek is a man of fierce determination, although his character is flawed by the hateful evil of bigotry directed toward the Ultish populace. Jeri's younger brother Mairhos, although not born into leadership, has a gentler spirit and a keen sense of duty and honor. He heeds the call to serve his nation in less-celebrated ways. But another call also rises in his heart: the impassioned love of a girl from the poorer classes of Pikemond City. Karil Feros is innocent, beautiful, skilled, fearless, and kind of heart, but, may the Sacred Solae pity Mairhos, Karil is one thing more.

Karil is Ult.

SOLAE REDEEMER
—Book Four in 'THE SOLAE' series

In the months following the defeat of the Atlan Empire, many citizens of the Erissard Union and its allies remain scattered by the dislocations of war. Karil Feros, Ultish paramour of the High Domin of Eriss himself, waits for her lover in the wilderness reaches of the Sulfur Basin, along with the wives, children and oldsters of her Brisach Ult forbears. The Basin is an ancient volcanic caldera, known in earlier times as the Yellowstone.

There is a cataclysmic eruption, as geologists have been predicting since the nineteenth century a.d. By a miracle, Karil and her cousin Rechalas are temporarily absent on a diplomatic mission westward. Their survival is chancy and unlikely, and Mairhos has scant effort to spare in their rescue. But with help and great good fortune, he manages.

...Only, it takes him eight years to find Karil.

CÚC — a short novelette

This novelette explores the tenuous connection between an American GI who spent a year of service in Saigon VN and a two-year-old orphan child who came to believe the man was her father. Central to the narrative is the child's-eye experiencing of a horrific occurence, historically accurate, which took place a short time before the Fall of Saigon in April 1975...an event which should never be forgotten worldwide, in the annals of that doleful chapter called the Viet Nam War.

THE BRAWLER

Hans Raufer, the novel's title character, has led a turbulent life! Discovering Raufer's chaotic past is our narrator, a Boston-based engineering specialist who, on a flight returning from a grueling field trip in the Canadian Far-North, comes plummeting out of the icy Arctic sky when his aircraft experiences a sudden engine failure. The plane makes an emergency landing in Churchill Manitoba on Hudson Bay, the Polar Bear Capital of the World. Business associates arrange for our narrator to stay in Hans Raufer's spare bedroom for the several days it takes to get the engine repaired. In spite of worlds of differences, our narrator and Hans become friends. Gradually, Hans tells the tale of his tortuous past, revealing an unbelievable chain of conflicts, near misses, and catastrophes which range from a rough adolescence in the Hitler youth, the invasions of Austria, Czechoslovakia, Poland and the USSR, a stint with Erwin Rommel and the Afrikakorps, the theft of a submarine, Dien Bien Phu, and a hitch as a mercenary in the Belgian Congo. In the end, Hans Raufer, the Brawler, turns out to be something other than one would have suspected. Our narrator returns to his placid life in Boston chastened and uplifted both by what he has learned...and in happy possession of an unexpected gift.

Made in the USA
San Bernardino, CA
27 June 2018